THE HOUSE & GARDEN
Cookbook

THE HOUSE & GARDEN
Cookbook

COMPILED BY VICKY JONES

CHATTO & WINDUS
LONDON

Acknowledgements

At the end of each recipe, the author's initials are given. Their names are as follows.
CB Christophe Buey, chef at L'Ecole de Cuisine Française, Litlington, East Sussex; NC Nicola Cox; SCP Shona Crawford Poole; SD Silvija Davidson; RD Roz Denny; JD Jim Dodge, pastry chef at the Stanford Court Hotel, San Francisco; HDM Hugo Dunn Meynell; KD Kate Dyson; PF Paola Fletcher; BGM Beryl Gould Marks; JH Jacqui Hurst; MJ Meg Jansch; VJ Vicky Jones; EL Elisabeth Luard; PM Paul Mitchell, chef at The Hunting Lodge restaurant, near Auckland, New Zealand; SM Sallie Morris; AN Ann Norris; MN Mary Norwak; SO Sri Owen; CP Charles Plumex, chef at Le Prieuré restaurant, Thonon-les-Bains, France; JR Jennie Reekie; ER Elisabeth Riely; RS Rena Salaman; MJS Maria José Sevilla; HW Hilary Walden; SJW Sue Jane Warren; SW Stephen Wheeler; AW Anne Williams; AWS Alice Wooledge Salmon.

Photographs: Howard Allman: pages 57, 84, 90, 169. Jan Baldwin: pages 147, 148, 157, 159, 163, 173. Eric Carter: pages 13, 14, 17, 23, 30, 31, 43, 45, 46, 58, 66, 75, 78, 88, 91, 104, 107, 110, 117, 121, 155, 158, 160, 162, 170. Michael Cook: page 109. Alex Dufort: pages 10, 28, 35, 55, 60, 92, 100. Paul Forster: pages 21, 64. Nicky Gibbs: page 176. Tim Hill: pages 27, 63, 77, 87, 124, 143, 181. John Hollingshead: pages 6, 12, 19, 40, 48, 137, 140, 141, 144, 152, 177. Jacqui Hurst: pages 22, 39, 123, 132, 135. Tim Imrie: pages 53, 69, 70, 72, 113, 127, 128. Graham Kirk: front cover, pages 9, 83, 95, 96, 99, 103, 112, 165, 171, 174, 183, 185. Scott Morrison: pages 115, 118, 120. James Mortimer: pages 37, 51. James Murphy: back cover, pages 131, 133, 139, 151, 167, 179, 187. Jasper Partington: pages 54, 106. Fritz von der Schulenberg: pages 18, 32. Chris Thornton: page 149. Simon Wheeler: page 25.

Designed by John Bridges and Jenny Newton

Published in 1990 by
Chatto & Windus Ltd
Vauxhall Bridge Road
London SW1V 2SA

© The Conde Nast Publications Ltd

A CIP catalogue record for this book is available
from the British Library

ISBN 0 7011 3647 2

Photoset by Rowland Phototypesetting Ltd
Bury St Edmunds, Suffolk
Printed and bound in Great Britain by
Butler and Tanner Ltd, Frome, Somerset

CONTENTS

INTRODUCTION

The *Wine & Food* section of *House & Garden* magazine has featured literally thousands of imaginative, practical recipes by an impressive group of contributors. This *Cookbook* is a collection of some personal favourites.

Our contributors include professional chefs, cookery writers with a background in home economics, authors who have come to writing about food from other disciplines, and people who are simply accomplished home cooks, providing for family and friends. All have two things in common – a genuine love of good food, and a generosity that is essential to successful entertaining.

Each author has his or her own style of cooking and writing, and no attempt has been made in compiling this book to disguise their individuality. The variety is a vital part of the collection.

Roz Denny, who has contributed a large number of the recipes, has combined her creative flair with her training in home economics to devise a splendid variety of original recipes, as well as to adapt traditional ones to the demands of today's busy cooks. Alice Wooledge Salmon, author of *House & Garden Cooking with Style* (Octopus, 1987), has an inventive and literary style, deriving inspiration from her extensive travels, and drawing from her own eclectic repertoire of culinary ideas. Silvija Davidson's Latvian parentage has given rise to her delight in Baltic cookery, while her self-taught expertise in the techniques of classic French cuisine is applied to all manner of ingredients. Elisabeth Riely's writing has that special freshness and individuality which reflects the best of current American gastronomy, while other cooks draw on the rich fund of European culinary traditions. Elisabeth Luard, for example, lived in Spain for many years, and wrote *European Peasant Cookery* (Bantam Press, 1986); Maria José Sevilla is another Spanish specialist; Rena Salaman is not only an expert in the cookery of her native Greece, but also the creator of many original recipes. Nicola Cox, Anne Williams and Jennie Reekie all live in the English countryside, and tend to write about the customs and recipes of a more British-based cuisine.

Right *Rice with salt cod, garlic and spinach (recipe on page 48); sopa morellana (recipe on page 33); and scrambled eggs with truffles.*

FIRST IMPRESSIONS

Crisp filo pastry parcels; pâtés and mousses; fresh and smoked fish; colourful salads and stuffed vegetables – these tempting first course dishes will stimulate the palate without dulling the appetite

SMOKED SALMON AND PLAICE ROULADE WITH TARRAGON CREAM

Soaking fish in fresh lime or lemon juice is a way of preserving it that has been used for centuries in the Caribbean, South America and the Pacific. Even so, it is obviously essential that if you are going to eat uncooked fish, it must be very fresh to start with. Ideally, buy it from a reputable fishmonger or supermarket wet fish department and tell them that you are planning to eat it raw or, failing that, buy good quality frozen fish fillets which should have been frozen within hours of being caught. Allow them to defrost and then use as soon as they have completely thawed out.

> 4 fillets of plaice weighing about 6–8 oz
>   (175–250 g) each
> Salt and freshly milled black pepper
> 1½ teaspoons dried tarragon
> 4 oz (125 g) sliced smoked salmon
> Juice of 4 limes
> ¼ pint (300 ml) double cream

> TO GARNISH
> 1 ripe avocado

Skin the plaice fillets and remove any bones and dark pieces of flesh from around the stomach. Lay the fillets out and sprinkle each one with a little salt and pepper and a very little tarragon. Put the slices of smoked salmon on top, then roll up the fish fillets, starting at the tail end. Cut each one into 4 rolls and place them in a shallow dish, fairly close together, but not so that they touch. Sprinkle with a little more tarragon (you want to be left with about half a teaspoon) and pour over the lime juice. Leave to marinate for about 8 hours, turning them over several times and liberally basting them with the lime juice.

Remove the rolls of fish from the lime juice and arrange on a serving dish. Add the remaining tarragon to the cream in a basin. Add about half the lime juice, season with salt and pepper, then taste and add a little more of the lime juice if wished. Pour over the fish fillets in the serving dish.

Halve the avocado, peel, remove the stone and cut into slices. Dip these into the remaining lime juice, then use to garnish the edge of the plate. Chill until ready to serve.

Serves 4.   JR

SPICED HERRINGS WITH CUCUMBER SAUCE

Spiced herring fillets (sometimes also slightly inaccurately called matjes herrings) are pickled in a sweet/sour mixture, usually with onions, and can be bought either in packets from supermarkets or

Right *Smoked salmon and plaice roulade with tarragon cream and (below) spiced herrings with cucumber sauce*

loose from fishmongers. They can be served in a variety of ways, but are especially good as a light starter, with sour cream and cucumber sauce.

4 spiced herring fillets, about 8 oz (250 g)
¼ pint (150 ml) soured cream
4 oz (125 g) bulb fennel
½ cucumber
Freshly-milled black pepper

Remove the herring fillets from the preserving liquor and arrange on a serving dish. Strain the liquor and reserve any pieces of onion. Blend with the soured cream. Finely chop the fennel, reserving any pieces of green frond, and cut the cucumber into ¼ inch (5 mm) dice. Add to the soured cream with plenty of freshly-milled black pepper, then pour over the herring fillets. Garnish with the pieces of reserved green frond.
 Serves 4.   JR

Glazed salmon tartlets

GLAZED SALMON TARTLETS

Crisp cream cheese pastry tartlets, baked blind and left to cool, are filled with pressed salmon on a lime mayonnaise and yoghurt base and topped with lime aspic. They are perfect for dinner parties, as the glaze allows you to prepare this dish ahead without the tartlets getting tired. Decorative strips of cucumber peel and sprigs of fresh herbs add the finishing touch.

PRESSED SALMON
12 oz (350 g) middle cut of salmon
1 tablespoon sea salt
1 teaspoon white sugar
Grated rind ½ lime
Pepper

FILLING
5 fl oz (150 g) mayonnaise
5 fl oz (150 g) natural thick yoghurt
Lime juice to taste
Salt and pepper

CREAM CHEESE PASTRY
6 oz (175 g) plain flour
4 oz (125 g) soft butter
4 oz (125 g) cream cheese
¼ teaspoon salt

LIME GLAZE
½ pint good aspic, such as Haco
Lime juice to taste

DECORATION
Strips cucumber skin
Sprigs dill, parsley or chervil

PRESSED SALMON
Fillet and skin the salmon. Mix the salt and sugar with a little grated lime rind. Sprinkle some on a plate, lay one piece of salmon on this and sprinkle over some more salt and sugar: lay the second piece of salmon on top and sprinkle with the remaining salt and sugar mixture. Cover and press lightly and leave for 12–48 hours in the fridge. Remove, pat dry and slice very thinly.

CREAM CHEESE PASTRY
Cream the butter until really soft, work in the cream cheese then sift and add the flour and salt; work lightly together and form into 4–6 flattened

discs. Chill, wrapped for 1–2 hours in the fridge. Roll thinly and line 4–6 individual tartlet tins of about 4–5″ (10–13 cm) diameter. Prick the bases, line with tinfoil, fill with baking beans and cook in a hot oven (400°F, 200°C, gas mark 6) for about 8–10 minutes until set.

Remove the beans and tinfoil, turn down the oven to moderately hot (375°F, 110°C, gas mark 5) and continue to cook until light golden brown and completely cooked. Cool on a rack.

LIME GLAZE

Prepare the aspic according to the instructions on the packet and flavour generously with lime juice. Cool until syrupy.

FILLING

Fold the yoghurt into the mayonnaise, adjust seasoning and add lime juice to taste.

DECORATION

Blanch and refresh some strips of cucumber skin. Cut in thin strips.

TO ASSEMBLE

Spread a little mayonnaise filling in the base of the tartlets, arrange thin slices of pressed salmon over this, decorate with cucumber strips and sprigs of herb and cover with a very thin layer of lime glaze. Chill until the glaze sets and the decoration is stuck down then run over another thin layer of glaze and leave to set. Serve on individual plates with a sprig of herb and a slice of lime.

Serves 4–6.   NC

SQUID WITH LITTLE GEM AND SESAME DRESSING

Squid, once a rarity, is now widely available from fishmongers and the wet fish counter of most supermarkets, where it can often be bought ready cleaned. If this is not the case, do not despair as cleaning is a fairly easy process.

Inexpensive and versatile, it can be fried, stuffed, braised, or used in a salad.

1 lb (500 g) squid, cleaned (see below)
2 pints (1.2 litres) boiling water
Juice of ½ lemon
¼ cucumber
4 spring onions
2 teaspoons sesame seeds
2 Little Gem lettuces

DRESSING
2 tablespoons cider vinegar
3 tablespoons sunflower oil
1 tablespoon sesame oil
1 teaspoon Dijon mustard
Salt and pepper to taste

To prepare the squid, cut tentacles from the head just above the eyes, then squeeze to remove the little bone in the centre. Wash and reserve tentacles. Using fingers, pull the quill and innards from the body cavity and discard. Rub away the fine mottled skin from the outside of each squid. Wash and pull off wing pieces and reserve. Turn each squid inside out and wash thoroughly to complete cleaning.

Cut each squid down one side and lay on work-top inside uppermost. Using a sharp knife, lightly mark a fine lattice all over the surface of each squid, taking care not to cut through. Then cut into three strips from tip to base.

Drop the squid into the pan of boiling water to which the lemon juice has been added. Cook gently for about 5 minutes, when the squid will have formed curls and will be quite tender when tested with a skewer. Lift out and drain.

Cut the cucumber into matchsticks. Slice the green tops from two spring onions into 2″ (5 cm) lengths, and slit each end several times with a sharp knife leaving the centre intact: place in ice-cold water and they will form attractive curls. Shred the remainder finely. Dry fry the sesame seeds till just golden and set aside. Place all the dressing ingredients in a screw-top jar and shake well together when required.

Arrange lettuce on serving plates. Pour dressing over squid, add cucumber and shredded spring onion. Spoon onto lettuce, sprinkle over sesame seeds and garnish with spring onion curls.

Serves 4.   SM

EGG AND SPINACH MOUSSES

These mousses, topped with green spinach, make very pretty individual starters.

12 oz (350 g) fresh spinach, with a few leaves of sorrel if available
7 fl oz (200 ml) milk
1 small onion stuck with 4 cloves
1 bay leaf
1 small carrot, halved
1 oz (25 g) butter
1 shallot, chopped
1 oz (25 g) flour
4 size 3 hens' eggs, hard-boiled and chopped
1 dessertspoon dry sherry
1 teaspoon gelatine crystals
3 tablespoons whipping cream, lightly whipped
1 egg white
3 quails' eggs, hard-boiled, peeled and halved, or 2 very small hens' eggs, sliced
Salt and black pepper

Blanch the spinach and sorrel, if using, then squeeze dry. Divide between the bases of 6 lightly greased ramekin dishes. Cool.

Meanwhile, scald the milk with the onion, bay leaf and carrot and allow to cool for 15 minutes. Strain, reserving the milk only.

Melt the butter in a saucepan and sauté the shallot lightly for 2 minutes. Stir in the flour and cook for about a minute until grainy. Gradually stir in the milk, mixing until smooth. Bring to the boil and simmer for a minute or two until the milk has thickened. Stir in the chopped eggs, sherry and seasoning. Sprinkle the gelatine onto 2 tablespoons of boiling water and stir briskly until dissolved, then mix into the sauce. Cover and cool, stirring occasionally to prevent a skin forming.

Fold in the whipped cream, then whisk the egg white and fold that in. Spoon the mixture on top of the spinach and allow to set.

To serve, run a knife round the edges of the ramekins, turn out onto individual plates and garnish with the quails' or small hens' eggs.

Serves 6. RD

A PATE OF SARDINES AND LEMON

Simple yet delicious, this pâté is both inexpensive and easy to assemble.

8 oz (250 g) can of sardines in olive oil, with oil drained off and backbones removed
10 oz (300 g) unsalted butter, softened
Juice of 2 lemons
½ teaspoon cayenne pepper
Freshly ground black pepper to taste
Twist of lemon peel and salad leaves to decorate

Put sardines into a bowl and mash well with a fork. Add butter, and start to blend with a wooden spoon. Add lemon juice and continue blending. (Blending must be slow, or the mixture will overheat and the butter will separate.) Add a little salt, cayenne, and lots of black pepper.

Refrigerate for 24 hours. Take out 1 hour before the meal and serve with crackers, toast or wheat wafers.

Serves 6. HDM

A pâté of sardines and lemon

CELERIAC REMOULADE WITH SMOKED MEAT

This classic salad can be made up to a week ahead: it strengthens and mellows in character with time. Garnish at the last minute with pickled capers, anchovies, gherkins, or olives. Just be sure the mayonnaise coats the celeriac to keep it from darkening. Try the recipe with various mustards: wholegrain mustard gives this light mayonnaise plenty of texture.

1 egg
3 tablespoons lemon juice
2 tablespoons Dijon or wholegrain mustard
½ pint (300 ml) vegetable oil
½ teaspoon salt
Pepper to taste
1 large celeriac bulb, about 1 lb (500 g) in
*   weight*
Red leaf lettuce to line plates
Thinly sliced smoked chicken, ham, or duck,
*   2 slices for each serving*
Cornichons, olives and capers for garnish

First make the mayonnaise. Put the egg in a food processor or blender with the lemon juice and mustard. Turn on the motor briefly to combine them, then in a slow, steady stream add the oil. As the mayonnaise thickens and forms an emulsion, add the remaining oil faster. Sharpen the seasoning with salt, pepper and more mustard or lemon juice if you like. Scrape the mayonnaise into a medium-size bowl and set aside.

Peel the celeriac, cutting off the rough exterior and any spongy interior flesh. Cut the bulb into thin slices, then cut the stacked slices across into matchstick juliennes. As soon as the celeriac is cut, fold it into the mayonnaise, stirring to coat every piece. Cover and chill.

To serve, line 6 serving plates with lettuce. Pile the celeriac on the lettuce, dividing it among the plates. Curl or ruffle the slices of meat and place them attractively around the celeriac. Garnish with cornichons, capers and olives. Serve at once as a first course or salad.

Serves 6–8.   ER

Spiced meat pouches

SPICED MEAT POUCHES

Tasty little canapés that can be prepared and baked in advance. If liked, the same filling can be made into Turkish *borek* by cutting and folding the filo into triangles.

4 sheets filo pastry
2 oz (50 g) butter, melted

FILLING
1 tablespoon olive oil
1 small onion, finely chopped
1 clove garlic, crushed
8 oz (250 g) lean minced beef or lamb
1 teaspoon ground cumin or coriander
1 egg, beaten
2 tablespoons fresh chopped parsley
A little chopped fresh mint or dill, optional
2 oz (50 g) flaked almonds, toasted and lightly
*   crushed*
Salt and ground black pepper

First, make the filling. Fry the onion and garlic in the oil for 5 minutes. Add the minced beef or lamb and fry for another 5 minutes. Sprinkle in the spice and season well. Cook for a further minute, then remove and cool slightly.

Beat in the egg, herbs and nuts. Ideally, if you have time, allow to cool completely, as this makes it easier to fill the pouches.

Cut the pastry sheets into 4, brush each quarter well with butter and fold in half. Divide the mixture between the 16 sheets of dough and pull up the edges around the filling like a purse. Press hard to seal, and place on lightly greased baking sheets. Brush the outsides of the pouches with butter.

Bake at 350°F (180°C, gas mark 4) for about 20 minutes until crisp and golden. Allow to cool slightly before removing to a wire tray.

Makes 16.   RD

GINGER AND CORIANDER CHICKEN IN FILO FLOWERS

These make wonderful, quick supper-party dishes because they look so pretty and taste good too. Lay them out on elegant white plates with any accompaniments served separately. The cases can be made beforehand and reheated before serving.

Ginger and coriander chicken in filo flowers

4 sheets filo pastry
1½ oz (40 g) butter, melted, or 4 tablespoons olive oil

FILLING
2 tablespoons olive oil
1" (2.5 cm) cube root ginger, peeled and chopped
2 cloves garlic, crushed
2 shallots or 1 small onion, chopped
1 lb (500 g) boned and skinned chicken breasts, sliced thinly in strips
2 teaspoons ground coriander
1 medium courgette, sliced thinly
8 oz (250 g) carton Greek yoghurt thinned with 3 tablespoons milk
Salt and ground black pepper
Freshly chopped coriander or flat leaf parsley, to garnish

Brush the insides of four 4" (10 cm) flan dishes or Yorkshire pudding bun tins with a little melted butter or oil.

Cut each filo sheet into four and layer into the tins, brushing liberally in between with butter, and arranging the sheets so that the corners alternate, forming a flower shape.

Bake at 375°F (190°C, gas mark 5) for about 7 to 10 minutes until golden and crisp, checking to see that the edges don't burn. Cool in the tins, then remove. If making them in advance, store in a large airtight container.

To make the filling, heat the oil and fry the ginger, garlic and shallot or onion until softened – about 5 minutes. Add the chicken pieces and fry for a further 5 minutes until firm and cooked. Sprinkle in the coriander and stir again.

Add the courgette slices, then cover and cook gently for about 3 minutes until they have just softened. Season well. Stir in the thinned yoghurt and reheat without boiling.

Reheat the filo cases if necessary, then spoon in the filling and scatter over the chopped coriander or parsley. Serve hot.

Serves 4.

NOTE This is also good with a small, sliced green pepper instead of the courgette, but cook pepper at the same time as the onion.   RD

SALMON FILO KOULIBIACS

These little 'turnovers' make particularly good starters or picnic food. Based on the Russian fish and rice pastry called koulibiac, these are not only light and crisp, they are also easier to make.

> 8 oz (250 g) filleted fresh salmon, e.g. from the tail
> 1 large shallot, chopped (save the skin)
> 1 bay leaf
> 4 oz (125 g) basmati rice, rinsed
> 1 tablespoon chopped fresh dill
> 2 tablespoons chopped fresh chives, or 1 spring onion, finely sliced
> 6 tablespoons double or soured cream
> 1 egg, hard-boiled and chopped
> 4 sheets filo pastry
> Salt and ground black pepper
> About 2 oz (50 g) butter, melted, or 3 tablespoons olive oil

Poach the salmon in ½ pint (300 ml) water with the shallot skins, bay leaf and some seasoning, for about 7 minutes, or until firm. Remove the fish, take off the skin and flake. Scoop out the shallot skin and bay leaf.

Return the water to the boil and add the rice and shallot. Bring to the boil, cover and simmer gently for about 12 minutes until cooked and the stock is absorbed. Cool and stir in the herbs, cream, egg and fish.

Cut the sheets of filo in half lengthwise. Brush well with butter or oil and place about an eighth of the mixture at one end of one half-sheet in a mound slightly to one side. Fold over at right-angles to make a triangle, making sure the edges are straight and meet. Then fold over again, on itself, to make another triangle. Continue like this until you have a turnover shape. Remove to a greased baking sheet.

Repeat with the other pastry sheets and filling. Brush the tops well with any remaining butter or oil and bake at 375°F (190°C, gas mark 5) for about 15 minutes or until golden and crisp. Serve warm or cold, with a salad garnish.

Serves 4–6.   RD

PARMESAN CHEESE TARTLETS WITH QUAILS' EGGS AND HOLLANDAISE

Although slightly fiddly to make, these tartlets can be prepared in stages beforehand. Eggs, cheese and smoked salmon make an excellent combination.

> PASTRY
> 4 oz (125 g) butter
> 8 oz (250 g) plain flour
> 2 tablespoons freshly grated Parmesan cheese
> Good pinch cayenne pepper
> 2 egg yolks

> SAUCE
> 3 tablespoons wine vinegar
> 1 bay leaf
> A few peppercorns
> 1 blade mace
> 2 egg yolks
> Pinch each salt, ground white pepper and mustard powder
> 4 oz (125 g) unsalted butter, softened

> FILLING
> 16 quails' eggs
> 3–4 oz (75–125 g) smoked salmon
> Sprigs of parsley to garnish

Rub the butter into the flour, cheese and cayenne. Mix to a firm dough with the egg yolks, adding a little cold water if necessary. Wrap in cling film, and refrigerate for half an hour, then roll out and use to line about sixteen 2″ (5 cm) tartlet tins.

Prick the bases and bake blind for 10–15 minutes at 400°F (200°C, gas mark 6). Cool and remove the baking beans.

To make the sauce, reduce the vinegar by boiling down, with the bay leaf, peppercorns and mace, to 1 tablespoon. Strain and reserve.

In a small, heatproof bowl over a pan of gently simmering water, mix the egg yolks with the pinch of salt, pepper and mustard and a knob of butter, until thickened. Gradually mix in the rest of the butter in pieces, taking care not to let the mixture overheat or it will curdle. If it does curdle, splash in some cold water and beat until smooth again. When all the butter is incorporated, remove from heat, and add vinegar.

Poach the quails' eggs for just a minute or two until firm, then remove with a slotted spoon and drain on kitchen paper.

Cut the salmon into 16 strips and form into rolls. Arrange an egg and salmon roll in each tartlet and coat with sauce. Garnish with a sprig of parsley and serve as soon as possible, allowing 2 tarts per serving.

Serves 8.   RD

MUSHROOMS WITH PORCINI AND MOZZARELLA

Large flat mushrooms are always popular – even more so when stuffed or, rather, topped. For an extra rich mushroom flavour, add some soaked Italian *porcini* mushrooms and enclose them in a melting blanket of mozzarella.

½ oz (15 g) dried porcini mushrooms
4 large flat mushrooms
A little olive oil
1 small onion, chopped finely
2 cloves garlic, crushed
2 sticks celery, chopped
2 oz (50 g) green bacon, chopped
1 tomato, skinned and chopped
1 oz (25 g) butter
Salt and ground black pepper
2 tablespoons cream
4 oz (125 g) mozzarella cheese

TO SERVE
Sprigs of fresh marjoram
Triangles of toast

Soak the porcini in a little boiling water for 20 minutes. Drain and chop. (The liquid can be used in stocks so don't discard it.)

Brush the mushrooms lightly on both sides with olive oil. Grill for about 5 minutes on each side, depending on the size.

Meanwhile, sauté the onion, garlic, celery, bacon and tomato in the butter until softened. Season well and stir in the cream.

Pile on top of the mushrooms. Slice the mozzarella thinly and arrange on the filling, then return to the grill until just melted and bubbling. Serve immediately, garnished with marjoram and accompanied by toast.

Serves 4.   RD

TOMATOES STUFFED WITH CUCUMBER AND FROMAGE FRAIS

A light, pretty starter using a low fat filling flavoured with chopped fresh herbs.

6 large, round, firm tomatoes (not beef ones), skinned
¼ cucumber, peeled and grated
8 oz (250 g) fromage frais
4 oz (125 g) curd or low fat soft cheese
1 tablespoon fresh chopped mint
2 tablespoons fresh chopped chives
2 tablespoons fresh chopped parsley
1–2 teaspoons fresh chopped dill
Salt and ground black pepper

TO SERVE
Mixed cress and endive salad, tossed in vinaigrette dressing

Cut the tomatoes in half and scoop out the seeds. Sprinkle the shells with salt and leave to drain upside down for half an hour.

Sprinkle the cucumber lightly with salt and leave to drain also, in a colander, for the same time. Squeeze dry and mix with the two cheeses, herbs and extra seasoning if needed. Pile into the tomato shells and chill before serving surrounded by the salad. These tomatoes can be prepared a few hours ahead, but some liquid may ooze out, which can simply be poured away.

Serves 6.   RD

Mushrooms with porcini and mozzarella, and (in background) tomatoes stuffed with cucumber and fromage frais

SCALLOPS WITH GINGER AND LIME

Ideal for a dinner party, these ingredients can be prepared before the meal and the dish cooked as people sit down. Ask the fishmonger to detach the scallops from their shells, but to return 6 deep shells to you for serving the dish.

18 scallops
12 spring onions
1½" (3.75 cm) piece fresh ginger
1½ limes
2 oz (50 g) butter
Seasoning

Wash the scallops well and slice each in 3 horizontally. Leave to dry on kitchen paper. Trim the spring onions and cut into 1" (2.5 cm) pieces, including some of the green stalks. Peel and finely chop the fresh ginger. Pare the rind from the limes, shred this and put into a sieve, then pour boiling water through it to soften the rind. Squeeze the juice from the limes and reserve.

Sauté the spring onions with the ginger in the butter for a minute, add the scallops and cook very briefly till just opaque. Pour on the lime juice, season and serve in clean, warm scallop shells, sprinkled with the lime rind and surrounded by dressed salad.

Serves 6.   AW

Smoked salmon with smoked trout mousse

SMOKED SALMON WITH SMOKED TROUT MOUSSE

Creamy smoked trout mousse enclosed in a wrapping of smoked salmon.

> *8 oz (250 g) smoked salmon*
> *3 smoked trout*
> *2 tablespoons double cream*
> *1 tablespoon single cream*
> *Worcestershire sauce and lemon juice to taste*
> *Seasoning to taste*

Line a pie dish about 9″ (23 cm) in diameter with the smoked salmon, leaving some of the slices hanging over the side of the dish, to cover the mousse later.

Skin and clean the smoked trout, removing any bones, and put in the food processor. Process to a mousse, adding the cream while the machine is running. Add Worcestershire sauce and lemon juice to taste and blend thoroughly.

Pour the trout mousse into the pie dish, making sure that it is well packed, and cover with the overlapping slices of smoked salmon. Cover with plastic film, and refrigerate until ready to use. Turn out on to a serving plate, and decorate if liked.

Serves 6. PF

ARTICHOKE AND ANCHOVY TARTS

Ideal as a starter or, if served with salads, a light supper course. Make up the cases beforehand, then fill just before serving.

> *6 oz (175 g) plain flour*
> *3 oz (75 g) each butter and vegetable shortening*
> *2–3 tablespoons fresh grated Parmesan cheese*
> *Ice-cold water*

> FILLING
> *2 large globe artichokes*
> *½ Spanish onion, sliced thinly*
> *1 clove garlic, crushed*
> *2 tablespoons olive oil*
> *1 × 14 oz (400 g) can chopped or peeled tomatoes*
> *3 tablespoons dry white wine*
> *1 tablespoon fresh chopped marjoram, or 1 teaspoon dried*
> *1 × 60 g can anchovy fillets, drained and chopped*
> *Ground black pepper*

> TO GARNISH
> *Stoned black olives and fresh marjoram sprigs*

Rub the flour and fats together until like fine breadcrumbs, then mix in the cheese and just enough water to make a firm dough. Knead gently, then divide into 4 and roll each piece out to fit four 4″ (10 cm) flan cases, or use to make one 8″ (20 cm) flan case if preferred. Prick bases lightly. Chill. Bake blind at 400°F (200°C, gas mark 6) for about 20 minutes until crisp. Cool and store in an airtight container until required.

Pull the leaves off the artichokes, cut out the hairy chokes and peel off any other tough parts. Cut into chunks and boil immediately in salted water with a squeeze or two of lemon juice for about 5 minutes.

Meanwhile, sweat the onion and garlic in the oil until softened. Add the tomatoes, wine, marjoram and pepper. Cook uncovered, on a medium heat, for about 10 to 15 minutes until thick and little liquid remains. Stir in the artichokes and anchovies. Cool.

Spoon into the cases to serve, and garnish with the olives and marjoram. The tarts are best eaten at room temperature.

Serves 4.   RD

DUCK BREAST AND ROCKET SALAD WITH ORANGE DRESSING

Roast duck breast fillets, thinly sliced, combine wonderfully well with slices of fresh orange, crunchy water chestnuts and orange dressing.

> *2 duck breast fillets*
> *2 oranges*
> *8 water chestnuts from a can*
> *Handful rocket or other leaves if preferred*

DRESSING
4 tablespoons orange juice
1 tablespoon lemon juice
1 teaspoon Dijon mustard
4–6 tablespoons sunflower oil
Seasoning to taste

Cook the duck breasts according to directions on the packaging. Allow to cool. Finely pare the skin from one orange and cut into shreds. Place these in a small pan with boiling water and simmer for 4 minutes. Drain, rinse and drain again. Reserve shreds of orange peel for garnish.

Peel both oranges, making sure there is no pith, and slice finely. Slice drained water chestnuts. Wash and dry leaves. Prepare dressing by shaking all the ingredients together.

Cut the duck breasts into thin slices. Arrange all the ingredients attractively on serving plates and drizzle over the dressing just before serving. Scatter orange shreds over the top to garnish.

Serves 4–6.   SM

Duck breast and rocket salad with orange dressing

COURGETTE AND CHERVIL SOUFFLES WITH SMOKED SALMON

Curd cheese may be used instead of ricotta, but the flavour and texture are a little less delicate. The exact cooking time may vary from 10–15 minutes, depending on the accuracy of the oven thermostat.

> *6 thin slices of smoked salmon*
> *6 oz (175 g) finely grated small, young*
> *   courgettes*
> *8 oz (250 g) ricotta cheese*
> *Approximately 1½ tablespoons chopped chervil*
> *Salt and freshly ground black pepper*
> *3 egg whites*
> *Crusty wholemeal or granary bread to serve*

Line 6 ramekin dishes with the smoked salmon. Pat the courgettes with absorbent kitchen paper to remove excess moisture (there should not be much with young courgettes). Mix with the ricotta and

19

chervil and season with pepper and a little salt. Whisk the egg whites until stiff, but not dry, then lightly fold into the ricotta.

Divide the mixture between the ramekin dishes, place in a baking tin and surround with boiling water. Cook in an oven preheated to 350°F (180°C, gas mark 4) until very lightly set – about 15 minutes. Garnish with chervil and serve.

Serves 6.   HW

SOLE AND RED PEPPER JELLIES WITH RED PEPPER SAUCE

These are rather involved to make, but the results, illustrated on page 99, are stylish and celebratory of the right kind of appreciative guests.

FISH BROTH
3 lb (1.5 kg) bones and heads from lean fish:
    Dover sole (best), lemon sole, plaice
1 large onion, peeled and sliced
2 leeks, cleaned and sliced
8 parsley stalks
4 tablespoons lemon juice
1 large glass dry white wine
½ teaspoon salt

FISH JELLIES
Vegetable oil for moulds and peppers
7–8 leaves gelatine
2½ pints (1.5 litres) fish broth (see above)
Whites and crushed shells of 2 eggs
Dry white wine
Salt and freshly ground black pepper
4 sweet red peppers
8 skinned fillets fresh Dover sole
Handful fresh basil leaves
¾ of a 1¾ oz (50 g) container of red 'caviar'

RED PEPPER SAUCE
Flesh of 2 red peppers (above)
10 oz (300 g) Greek-style yoghurt
Salt and black pepper
Fresh basil

To make fish broth, wash fish bones and heads; remove and discard gills. Chop carcases into convenient sizes and put these into a large, deep pot with onion, leeks, parsley, and lemon juice. Cover with 4½ pints (2.5 litres) cold water, bring this to simmer over a low heat, skim thoroughly, add wine and salt, and simmer, uncovered, for 30 minutes. Strain broth through a colander lined with muslin, cool and refrigerate for several hours.

To begin the jellies, lightly oil 12 oval, metal moulds of 3 fl oz (90 ml) capacity each; put these in the refrigerator to chill. Soak 7 leaves (8 if the weather is hot) of gelatine in a jug of cold water.

Carefully ladle 2½ pints (1.5 litres) chilled fish broth away from its sediment; the liquid should be fairly clear, but it will almost certainly be necessary to clarify it further. To do this, pour all but ½ pint (300 ml) of the broth into a clean pot and place this over a medium heat. Mix egg whites and shells with remaining ½ pint (300 ml). As liquid comes to the boil, whisk in the egg white mixture and continue whisking, slowly and thoroughly, until the broth boils across its surface.

Remove pot from the heat and let it stand, undisturbed, for 10 minutes. Then bring contents just to the boil, twice more, without whisking, leaving 10 minute intervals between each boil. The egg protein forms bonds with fish particles in the broth and draws them out of solution.

Line a large, fine sieve with a triple thickness of muslin and gently ladle in the clarified broth, keeping base of sieve well above surface of the strain liquid. Let contents of sieve drain, undisturbed, for 5 minutes, then discard whites and debris. Lift flavour of the broth with some dry white wine and salt, if necessary, to taste, and ladle 2 pints (1.2 litres) of this into a clean saucepan. Add softened, drained gelatine, and gently heat contents of pan until gelatine has dissolved. Cool.

Meanwhile, lightly oil surface of the 4 peppers and roast them whole under a medium grill, turning as skins blister and blacken all over. Cool under wet kitchen paper to trap steam that loosens their skins, and peel these away. Cut open peppers to remove cores and seeds, wash and dry flesh. Cut the two firmest peppers into small dice and place these in a medium bowl.

Venison liver pâté

VENISON LIVER PATE

The flavour of this dish improves with a day's rest, to allow the flavours to blend.

1 lb (500 g) sliced bacon
1 lb (500 g) chicken liver
2 tablespoons oil or clarified butter
1 medium onion, diced
Grated rind and juice of 1 orange
5 sprigs fresh rosemary (2 whole, the leaves from
*   the others chopped)*
4 fl oz (120 ml) whisky (possibly more)
1 lb (500 g) venison liver
10 oz (300 g) pork fat
1 egg white
Salt and pepper
3½ fl oz (100 ml) cream (or less)

Line a large terrine dish generously with slices of bacon, extending them over the sides. Set the dish aside and cover.

Brown the chicken livers in oil or clarified butter. Then remove from the pan and pour off the excess fat, leaving any sediment. Add diced onion, orange rind and juice, chopped rosemary and whisky to the pan. Return to the heat, and flame off whisky, reducing the contents of the pan by half. Remove from the heat.

Mince or process both livers until smooth and then add pork fat in small pieces, again beating or processing until smooth. Add the contents of the pan and beat or process again, then add egg white and beat or process once more. Season to taste, and add more whisky if you want a stronger flavour. Finally, add the cream, beating until it is just incorporated.

Spoon the pâté into the lined dish, smoothing it into the corners, then fold the bacon ends over and place the remaining rosemary sprigs on top. Cover and seal with lightly greased foil, and place in a roasting dish half full of water. Bake in a pre-heated oven at 425°F (220°C, gas mark 7) for 40–45 minutes, or until the pâté is firm in the centre. Leave in the tin until completely cold, then remove the sprigs of rosemary and turn out.

Serves about 10.   PM

Trim sole fillets, press the flat of a large, heavy knife down the length of each, score the membrane side – several times across – with a sharp knife (these measures reduce distortion in cooking) and gently poach fish in some of the unclarified broth until cooked through. Drain and dry fillets, and when they are cold, cut into small dice and add to the peppers in the bowl.

Chop basil, and put this, plus red 'caviar', among peppers and fish, season with black pepper, mix carefully with hands – the 'caviar' is fragile and breaks easily – and taste; salt will probably not be necessary.

Ladle a thin layer of cooled jelly into each chilled mould and return these to the fridge. When liquid has set, divide sole mixture among the 12 moulds, fill them carefully with jelly and chill till quite firm.

To make the sauce, purée remaining red pepper flesh in food processor; beat purée, to taste, into the Greek yoghurt and season well.

To serve jellies, run a blunt knife round side of each mould, dip briefly into hot water and turn out. Serve 2 per person, garnished with basil, and pass sauce separately.

Serves 6 as a first course.   AWS

Buckwheat blinis with crème fraîche and 'caviar'

BUCKWHEAT BLINIS

Serve with real caviar if you can, but otherwise these little buckwheat pancakes go well with lumpfish roe and crème fraîche. Iced vodka would be the traditional accompaniment.

1 oz (25 g) fresh yeast
¾ pint (450 ml) scalded milk cooled to 85°F
8 oz (250 g) sifted buckwheat flour
1 tablespoon sugar
3 eggs, separated
1 tablespoon melted butter
1 teaspoon salt

Dissolve the yeast in milk, and stir into 6 oz (175 g) of the flour, and 1 tablespoon sugar. Cover the bowl and set aside in a warm place to rise for about 1½ hours.

Beat egg yolks with melted butter, and stir in remaining flour with salt. Add to yeast sponge, beat well, and leave to rise for another 1½ hours, or until almost doubled in bulk.

Whip the egg whites until stiff but not dry and fold into the batter. Allow to stand for 10 minutes, then cook the pancakes, dropping a small amount at a time onto a hot greased skillet or griddle. Turn to brown lightly on the other side.

Place the blinis on serving plates, with a spoonful of red and black lumpfish roe and crème fraîche. Garnish with chives.

Makes 24 × 2″ (5 cm) blinis. CW

ASPARAGUS WITH ORANGE, WALNUT AND HONEY DRESSING

A light starter that is more refreshing than asparagus served with the usual rich butter dressings.

1 to 1½ lbs (500–750 g) fresh asparagus,
trimmed or bases peeled

DRESSING
Juice 1 orange
Juice ½ lemon
2 teaspoons grated orange rind
2 tablespoons extra virgin olive oil
1 tablespoon sunflower oil
1 teaspoon coarse-grained mustard
1 tablespoon clear honey
1 teaspoon grated onion (optional)
Salt and ground black pepper
2 oz (50 g) chopped walnuts

Mix all the dressing ingredients together in a screw topped jar and shake well.

Poach or steam the asparagus until the bases are just tender but still of good texture and the heads are not overcooked. If you have a microwave oven, asparagus is excellent cooked in this. Follow your manufacturer's instruction booklet for times, as these can vary.

Drain the asparagus and cool until lukewarm, then arrange on serving plates, coated with honey and orange dressing.

Serves 4.

NOTE This dressing is particularly good tossed into a mixed salad of bitter and astringent leaves, such as sorrel, chicory, Good King Henry, red orach and chives, with the sweetness of the honey and orange juice complementing them nicely. RD

A PATE OF BORLOTTI BEANS AND CHEESE

Well-flavoured beans are a suitable substitute to add body to a meatless pâté. This recipe is for a good basic pâté to which you could add your own variations—mould pâtés in baby savarin rings, for example, filling the centres with a salad – raw mushrooms or even more beans.

> *8 oz (250 g) borlotti beans, soaked and cooked, or one 15 oz (425 g) can, drained*
> *1 large clove garlic, crushed*
> *6 oz (75 g) soft goat's cheese, or ricotta or cream cheese*
> *2 oz (50 g) butter, melted*
> *2 tablespoons fresh chopped parsley*
> *1 tablespoon fresh chopped thyme or dill*
> *Grated rind of ½ lemon*
> *Salt and ground black pepper*

> TO SERVE
> *Diced salad vegetables, or some extra beans or raw button mushrooms*

For dried beans, soak overnight, drain, rinse and simmer in water for 50–60 minutes or until they are cooked.

Blend the beans in a food processor or liquidizer, then add the remaining ingredients, blending until quite smooth.

Spoon into four oiled individual moulds or cups and chill until firm. (The pâté will not be as firm as a meat or fish pâté.)

Dip the moulds briefly into hot water to loosen them, and shake out onto serving plates. If the edges look a little rough, simply smooth them with a blunt knife.

Spoon diced salad, or more beans or mushrooms, dressed in a little vinaigrette, into the centre of the moulds and serve attractively garnished with slices of toasted, garlic-flavoured baguette.

Serves 4.

NOTE The pâté can be spooned into a 1 pint (600 ml) dish until firm, then served in spoonfuls on leaves of radicchio, or frisée for example, sprinkled with fresh chopped herbs.   RD

BROAD BEAN TIAN

This is the favourite springtime dish in Provence.

> *¾ lb (350 g) young broad beans, in their pods*
> *½ lb (250 g) spinach or Swiss chard leaves*
> *6 eggs*
> *¼ pint (150 ml) cream or milk*
> *3 oz (75 g) freshly grated Parmesan*
> *1 teaspoon chopped savory or marjoram*
> *2–3 chopped spring onions*
> *1 teaspoon salt, freshly-milled pepper*
> *1 tablespoon olive oil*

Prepare the broad beans; as they are young and tender, string and chop them as for runner beans. Rinse and shred the greens.

Beat the eggs lightly with the cream or milk, grated cheese, herbs, spring onions, salt and pepper. Stir in the beans and the shredded greens.

Oil a shallow heatproof, earthenware dish (diameter about 7–8", 18–20 cm) and pour in the mixture. Bake the *tian* in a medium oven 350°F (180°C, gas mark 4) for 45 minutes, until the egg is set but still creamy. Serve with bread, black olives, a tomato salad and red wine.

Serves 6–8.   EL

A pâté of borlotti beans and cheese

HOT SOUPS AND COOL SOUPS

From shimmering, savoury jellies, served chilled
as the opener to a summer dinner, to robust
platefuls of steaming winter vegetables, there are
soups for all seasons and every occasion

CHILLED TOMATO ORANGE SOUP

Despite their everyday use, tomatoes and oranges
are rarely partnered. Here they make a wonderfully
refreshing and fragrant summer soup that is almost
exotic for its unusual combination.

*1½ lb (750 g) ripe tomatoes (or 2½ cups canned
    Italian plum tomatoes with liquid)*
2 large oranges
1 lemon
1 small white onion, chopped
*2 tablespoons chopped fresh dill or other fresh
    herb*
Salt and freshly-ground black pepper to taste
Sour cream or yoghurt for garnish

First, drop tomatoes into a pot of boiling water for
30 seconds or so, depending on their ripeness. Cut
in half and squeeze each half over a bowl fitted with
a sieve to hold the seeds, catching the juice below.
Slip off the skins and discard them with the seeds.
Coarsely chop the flesh and combine it with the
tomato juice in a food processor or blender.

Grate the zest from the oranges and lemon,
and squeeze the juice. For a more refined soup,
blanch the zest in boiling water for 2 minutes to
remove the bitterness, then drain. Add the citrus
zest and juice to the tomatoes with the onion and
dill. Combine well, but leave a little texture. Season to taste with salt and pepper. Cover and chill
thoroughly in the refrigerator until serving time.

Serve the soup in glass bowls, garnished with a
dollop of sour cream or yoghurt.
Serves 4.   ER

KISIEL (STRAWBERRY SOUP)

This Northern European dessert soup can be made
with various red fruits, as well as peaches and
nectarines, but fresh, ripe strawberries are undoubtedly the favourite.

Served chilled with whipped cream, it makes
an excellent finale to a summer meal, and would
also be delicious for a late Sunday breakfast.

2 tablespoons cornflour
½ pint (300 ml) white wine
2 oz (50 g) sugar or to taste
1 lb 6 oz (675 g) fresh strawberries, hulled
2 tablespoons lemon juice
2 tablespoons grated lemon zest
2 tablespoons Cointreau
*Unsweetened whipped cream and unsalted
    pistachios chopped fine for garnish*

Right *(clockwise from top) Chilled tomato orange
soup; chlodnik (a summer borsch, page 27); jellied
cucumber lime mint soup, page 26; kisiel (strawberry
soup); courgette, leek and yoghurt soup, page 26*

Using just enough water, make a paste with the cornflour in a pot. Stir in the wine, ½ pint (300 ml) water and the sugar. Bring to the boil and stir: the mixture will thicken. When cool, purée with the strawberries in the food processor or blender. Add the lemon juice, zest and a little more sugar if needed. Chill thoroughly, covered.

Just before serving, stir in the Cointreau. Ladle the strawberry soup into pretty bowls. Float a little whipped cream on top of each and dust with finely chopped pistachios.

Serves 6. ER

JELLIED CUCUMBER LIME MINT SOUP

This is a delicate soup, illustrated on page 25, to precede an elegant main course of salmon or trout, for a light summer dinner – not a robust peasant pottage for lusty appetites. The amount of gelatine is just enough to hold the soup together without making it bounce; to increase yield, double the entire recipe.

1 envelope unflavoured gelatine
2 fl oz (60 ml) water
¾ pint (450 ml) good chicken stock, preferably home-made, with all fat removed
1 large cucumber
3 spring onions, green tops included, chopped
2 fl oz (60 ml) lime juice or more
4 tablespoons chopped fresh mint
2 tablespoons chopped fresh parsley
Salt and pepper to taste
Lime for garnish

Soften the gelatine in the water for a few minutes, then dissolve it in the chicken stock over low heat, stirring. Coarsely chop the cucumber, then combine it in a food processor or blender with the chicken stock, onions and lime juice. Combine the ingredients well, but do not reduce them to a fine purée: a little texture is desirable. Season with herbs and salt and pepper, and taste; sharpen with more lime juice if needed. Pour the mixture into a bowl,

cover and refrigerate for at least 3 hours, until the gelatine is set.

To serve, mix up the jellied soup to redistribute the solids, scoop it into bowls and garnish with thin slices of lime.

Serves 6. ER

COURGETTE, LEEK AND YOGHURT SOUP

This wholesome vegetable soup, illustrated on page 25, is both satisfying and versatile. Make it thick or thin; serve it hot or cold; spice it with cumin, curry or other pronounced seasoning. It is an excellent way to use up giant courgettes, and freezes well if you add the yoghurt later.

3 tablespoons vegetable oil
8 oz (250 g) leeks, trimmed, quartered lengthwise, and chopped
1 lb (500 g) courgettes, chopped
2 pints (1.2 litres) chicken stock
1 large lemon
5 fl oz (150 ml) plain yoghurt
1 tablespoon cumin, or to taste
Salt and freshly-ground pepper to taste
More yoghurt and fresh coriander leaves for garnish, if desired

In a large pot, heat the oil over medium heat and sweat the leeks, stirring, for about 5 minutes. Add the courgettes and stock. Cut six very thin rounds from the centre of the lemon for garnish, and reserve. From the lemon ends, grate the zest and add, with the juice, to the pot. Bring to the boil and simmer, covered, for about 15 minutes.

Cool the soup, then purée in a food processor or blender with the yoghurt. Season to taste with cumin (start with a small amount and increase), salt and pepper. You may thin it with more stock. Cover and chill thoroughly.

To serve, ladle the soup into individual bowls and swirl in more yoghurt on top. Garnish with the reserved lemon and coriander leaves if you like.

Serves 6. ER

CHLODNIK (SUMMER BORSCH)

The brilliant deep magenta colour is reason enough to make this summer borsch from Poland, illustrated on page 25. The authentic soup is made with raw beetroot and tops, but this puréed version uses pre-cooked roots that are more readily available. Just be sure to use untreated ones, that is, un-vinegared. By saving the broth to add after cooking, the colour stays beautifully intense.

2 lb (1 kg) cooked beetroot (not vinegared)
4 tablespoons or more wine vinegar
4 oz (125 g) fresh young beet tops (or spinach or
Swiss chard)
1 large carrot, scrubbed and shredded
4 spring onions, green tops included, chopped
3 tablespoons chopped fresh dill, or to taste
For the garnish: chopped cucumber, sliced spring
onions, hard-boiled egg and sliced lemon
Sour cream
Seasoning

Grate a quarter of the beetroot over a large pot to catch all the juice. Add 2 tablespoons vinegar and 2 pints (1.2 litres) boiling water. Bring slowly to the boil, then cool. Strain, reserving the broth.

In another pot, combine the carrot and onions with 5 fl oz (100 ml) water. Bring to the boil, then add the greens. Cook for 10 minutes, stirring occasionally, until the greens are wilted and tender. Let the vegetables cool.

Meanwhile, grate the remaining beetroot, again keeping all the juice. When the vegetables have cooled, purée them with their liquid in a food processor or blender. Add the grated beetroot and reserved broth – just enough to give a thick but not semi-solid texture. Season to taste with more vinegar and dill. Chill thoroughly, covered.

To serve the chlodnik, ladle it over an ice-cube placed in the bottom of each serving bowl. Garnish with cucumber, spring onion, quartered hard-boiled egg and a slice of lemon. Pass the sour cream on the side.

Serves 10 or 12.   ER

Hampshire watercress and bacon pottage, topped with swirls of cream and crumbled crisp bacon

HAMPSHIRE WATERCRESS AND BACON POTTAGE

For centuries pottage was the universal food of the peasants. A thick broth containing vegetables, herbs, and usually a grain, such as oats or barley, it could be left to simmer in a large pot over an open fire. Any meat added was almost inevitably bacon, which provided not only a small amount of valuable protein, but also some additional flavour. This is certainly a more refined version than would have been available in the Middle Ages, but it is a recipe with ancient origins.

4 rashers streaky bacon
1 oz (25 g) butter
1 medium onion, peeled and chopped
1 large potato, peeled and chopped
2 bunches watercress
1½ pints (900 ml) chicken or vegetable stock
¼ pint (150 ml) single cream
Salt and freshly milled black pepper

Cut the rind off the bacon. Melt the butter in a pan and gently fry the bacon rinds with the onion for 5 minutes. Add the potato to the pan and cook for 3 minutes. Cut about 1 inch (2.5 cm) off the watercress stalks, then roughly chop the remainder. Add to the pan and cook for about 2 minutes. Pour over the stock and bring to the boil. Cover the pan and simmer gently for 20 minutes. Do not overcook or the soup will lose its vivid green colour. Remove the bacon rinds, then sieve the soup or purée it in a blender or food processor. Tip back into the saucepan, reheat gently and adjust the seasoning.

Meanwhile grill the bacon until it is crisp, remove from the pan and roughly crumble. Pour the soup into a tureen, pour the cream round in a swirl and sprinkle with the bacon. Serve immediately, piping hot.

Serves 4.   JR

and add to the soup to thicken it. (If using egg yolks, beat them into the soup at this stage.) Heat gently but do not boil. Adjust seasoning, add butter and cream and heat again. Pour into a warm tureen when almost ready to serve.

Cut slices of crust from the sides of the rolls and stick almond slices into the crust so that they look like spiky hedgehogs. Grill briefly to toast the almonds, and float the 'hedgehogs' on the soup. Serve immediately.

Serves 8.

NOTE If you possess a Thermomix, all the soup ingredients except the cream can be placed together in the machine, using half the required quantity. Switch on for 15 minutes, empty the soup into another container and repeat with the remaining half of the ingredients. Add the cream and seasoning and serve as above.   KD

HEDGEHOG SOUP

This is one of the oldest of soup recipes, which has its roots in Roman cookery. Often called white soup, and originally thickened with egg yolks, it has a subtle and delicate flavour. If you prefer the idea of egg yolk thickening to cornflour, use 3–4 yolks, beaten into the soup, which must then be heated gently, not boiled.

4 oz (125 g) ground almonds
3 pints (1.75 litres) good white stock
1 pint (600 ml) milk
2 tablespoons cornflour or 4 egg yolks
2 oz butter
½ pint (300 ml) single cream
3 bay leaves
Salt, freshly ground pepper

GARNISH
3 small round French rolls
1 packet sliced almonds

Heat ground almonds with the stock, milk and bay leaves. Simmer gently for about 15 minutes, and liquidize. Slake the cornflour in a little cold water,

Hedgehog soup, with floating almond 'hedgehogs'

POTAGE OF LEEKS, CELERIAC AND POTATOES

This is not a refined soup for an elegant evening but an earthy *potage* with the elusive flavour and celadon colour of celery. Chicken stock is used here rather than water; it slightly masks the celeriac colour and flavour but adds another note. Either way, the soup benefits from the contrasting sharpness of its garnish. Instead of caraway, you might try dried fennel seeds, rye bread croûtons, crumbled bacon, or bits of salty country ham.

2 medium leeks
1 large celeriac bulb, about 1 lb (500 g)
2 large potatoes, about 1 lb (500 g) total
2 tablespoons butter
Water or chicken stock to cover, about 2½ pints
    (1.5 litres)
1 pint (600 ml) rich milk
Salt to taste
White pepper to taste
Caraway seeds for garnish

Chop off the root end of the leeks and most of the green tops. Slice lengthwise in quarters almost to the root and rinse out any grit under cold running water. Shake off excess water and chop the leeks coarsely. Peel the celeriac and potatoes and cut both into cubes.

Melt the butter in a large pot over medium low heat. Add the leeks and cook, stirring, until wilted. Add the celeriac and potato together with water or stock barely to cover. Put on a tight-fitting lid and simmer slowly for about 40 minutes, until cooked through. Cool somewhat, then purée in a food processor or blender in batches. This much may be done in advance.

Return the soup to the pot, add 1 pint (600 ml) of rich milk, and heat it nearly to boiling point but do not let it actually boil. Season to taste with salt and white pepper, and thin with a little more milk if you prefer. Serve the soup piping hot in bowls, each garnished with half a teaspoon of caraway seeds or your chosen alternative.

Makes about 3 pints (1.75 litres) of warming winter soup.   ER

COLD TOMATO AND SWEETCORN SOUP

For the ripest, most flavourful summer tomatoes and the freshest sweetcorn only. Add some Italian, sun-dried tomatoes for their concentration of colour and flavour. (See illustration page 96.)

VEGETABLE BROTH
2 carrots, peeled
1 medium onion, peeled
1 leek, washed and trimmed
2 long sticks celery
½ potato, peeled
1 head of garlic, peeled
Bouquet of thyme, bay leaf, parsley
¼ teaspoon salt
4 pints (2.25 litres) cold water

SOUP
2½ lb (1.25 kg) large ripe tomatoes
½ large onion, peeled and sliced
3–4 sun-dried tomatoes, washed
1½ pints (900 ml) broth (above)
Salt
9 oz (275 g) sweetcorn kernels, cut from corn
    ears with small knife
Freshly ground black pepper
2–3 fl oz (60–90 ml) buttermilk
Plain yoghurt

To make the broth, quarter the 5 vegetables and place in a deep pot with the garlic, bouquet garni, salt and water. Bring to the boil and simmer, lid ajar, for 1¾ hours. Cool and strain the broth.

To make the soup, peel, seed, and chop the fresh tomatoes, putting flesh and all exuded juices into a medium pot with the onion, the sliced, sun-dried tomatoes, broth, and a little salt. Bring to the boil and simmer for 10–12 minutes, adding 4 oz (125 g) of the sweetcorn for the last 5 minutes.

Purée the soup until very smooth, and season to taste. Reheat with the remaining sweetcorn, simmering for 1 minute. Cool, add buttermilk to sharpen, check seasoning and chill for several hours. Serve each bowlful with a swirl of yoghurt.

Serves 6.   AWS

SUCCOTASH CHOWDER

Succotash is a Narragansett Indian word meaning something that is broken into bits. Nowadays, Americans use it to describe a stew of fresh lima beans, corn and other foods.

It can be made with canned or frozen corn and beans if necessary, and is hearty enough for a winter lunch, served with country bread. This version contains no meat (more traditional recipes use bacon grease) and is suitable for vegetarians.

> 2 cobs of fresh sweetcorn
> 1½ oz (40 g) butter
> 2 cloves garlic, crushed
> 1 medium onion, chopped
> 2 sticks celery, chopped
> 1 teaspoon fresh chopped basil
> 1 teaspoon fresh chopped thyme
> 2½ pints (1.5 litres) warm milk
> 2 teaspoons tamari soy sauce
> 12 oz (350 g) fresh or frozen lima beans or 4 oz
>   (125 g) dried weight, soaked and cooked

Succotash chowder

> Salt and ground black pepper
> Fresh chopped parsley and chives, or a few small
>   sage leaves

Stand the cobs upright and with a sharp knife strip the kernels off.

Melt the butter in a large saucepan and gently fry the garlic, onion and celery until softened, about 5 minutes. Add the corn and cook for a further five minutes then blend in the basil, thyme, milk, tamari and lima beans. Season well and heat gently until quite hot but not boiling. Serve hot, sprinkled with chopped herbs.

Serves 4–6.   RD

PUCHERO

This recipe from the Philippines is a close relation of Spanish *cocida*. It is best served in wide-brimmed soup plates, either the soup first, followed by the vegetables and meat – as in a French *pot au feu* – or together, as described here.

Chicken, pork and chorizo are combined with chickpeas, sweet potato, plantain and Chinese leaves in this one-pot dish, and a garlicky aubergine sauce is stirred in at the last minute.

> 8 oz (250 g) chickpeas, soaked overnight in
>   water
> 3 lb (1.25 kg) chicken, jointed into 8 pieces
> 12 oz (350 g) lean pork belly, rind removed and
>   cut into chunks
> 2 medium onions, chopped
> 4 pints (2.25 litres) water
> 4 tablespoons groundnut oil
> 3 cloves garlic, crushed
> 1 can (14 oz, 400 g) chopped tomatoes
> 3 tablespoons tomato purée, or to taste
> 2 chorizos (Spanish sausages)
> 2 sweet potatoes, or equivalent in pumpkin or
>   potato if liked, peeled and cubed
> 1–2 plantain (bananas for cooking), peeled and
>   sliced
> 6–8 Chinese leaves, finely shredded
> 6 spring onions, shredded to garnish

(Clockwise from top) puchero; Lancashire hot pot (recipe on page 81); Genoese minestrone

AUBERGINE SAUCE
1 large aubergine
1 small onion, chopped
2 cloves garlic, crushed
2 spring onions, trimmed and chopped
Salt and pepper to taste

Place the drained and rinsed chickpeas in a large pan with chicken pieces, pork belly, one chopped onion, and water to cover. Bring to boil, skim if necessary, half cover and cook gently for 45 minutes or until meats are tender.

Set oven to 400°F (200°C, gas mark 6). Score the aubergine with a knife and place in oven for 40–50 minutes till wrinkled on the outside. Strip off skin with a knife, holding the aubergine gently with an oven-glove. Scoop flesh into a food processor with the onion, garlic and spring onions. Beat to a pulp, season and transfer to a serving dish.

Fry remaining onion gently in hot oil, with the garlic, till soft and transparent. Add chopped tomatoes and then the purée, and stir into the meat mixture along with the peeled and sliced chorizos, cubes of sweet potato and plantain. Season to taste, then cook gently for 15–20 minutes.

Just before serving, bring to the boil and add Chinese leaves. Cook for 2 minutes only and scatter with the spring onion before you take the *puchero* and the prepared sauce (which is stirred into helpings of the soup) to the table.

Accompany with fresh bread.

Serves 6–8.   SM

GENOESE MINESTRONE

This is traditionally served with spoonfuls of rich green pesto floating on the surface. Other vegetables in season – carrots, cauliflower, aubergine, potato, for example – can be used, but they will need more cooking than celery and tomatoes.

1 large onion, peeled and chopped
3 cloves garlic, crushed
1 can (1¾ oz, 45 g) anchovy fillets
3–4 tablespoons groundnut oil
2 sticks celery, finely chopped
4–6 oz (125–175 g) French beans, cut into
    short lengths
Sprigs marjoram and parsley tied together
2 × 14 oz (400 g) cans chopped tomatoes
2 × 15 oz (425 g) cans borlotti beans
2–2½ pints (1.2–1.5 litres) chicken stock,
    home-made or from a cube
4–6 oz (125–175 g) tiny shell or bow-shaped
    pasta cooked according to packet directions
Salt and freshly ground black pepper

PESTO
1 cup fresh basil leaves, or continental parsley,
    plus 2–3 teaspoons dried basil
2 cloves garlic, crushed
2–3 oz (50–70 g) pine-nuts or walnut pieces
½ pint (300 ml) sunflower or groundnut oil
2–3 tablespoons Parmesan cheese
Seasoning

31

Fry the onion and garlic in the drained oil from the anchovies and the groundnut oil till soft and transparent. Chop the anchovies and add to the pan with celery, French beans, herbs and tomatoes. Cook together for 3–4 minutes.

Add the drained and rinsed beans and the stock, and cook for 10–15 minutes. Add pasta shapes and cook for a further 2–3 minutes. Taste for seasoning and remove herbs if liked.

Meanwhile, make the pesto by placing the herbs, garlic and nuts in a food processor with oil and blending till smooth. Add cheese and season to taste. The pesto should be quite runny, so you may need to add a little boiling water.

Serve the soup in a tureen, drizzle some of the pesto into the centre and serve the remainder separately so that each person spoons a little onto the individual helping. Serve with chunks of warm bread or rolls.

Serves 6–8.   SM

Soup of meat and red beans

CREAM OF SPINACH SOUP

This delicious soup (illustrated on page 87) can be made in minutes with the aid of a liquidizer.

> 6–7 tablespoons chopped shallot
> 1½ oz (40 g) butter
> 1 lb (500 g) fresh, washed spinach leaves
> ½ teaspoon salt
> 1½ oz (40 g) flour
> 2½ pints (1.5 litres) chicken stock
> 2 egg yolks
> 5 fl oz (140 ml) double cream
> ½–1 oz (15–25 g) softened butter

Soften the shallots in the first measure of butter in a covered pan; do not let them brown. Stir in the spinach and salt. When the spinach has wilted, stir in the flour and cook slowly for 4–5 minutes. Add the boiling chicken stock off the heat. Stir to incorporate, then simmer for about 5 minutes.

Blend the egg yolks and cream in a bowl. Beat in ½ pint (300 ml) of hot soup, little by little to prevent curdling. Then gradually add the rest of the hot soup. Pour back into the saucepan, and stir over a moderate heat for 2 minutes; do not let it boil. Purée the soup in a liquidizer. Bring to simmering point and stir in the softened butter gradually.

Serves 4–6, hot or cold.   BGM

SOUP OF MEAT AND RED BEANS

> 1¼ lb (625 g) very lean beef (chuck or shin)
> 1 oz (25 g) butter or margarine
> 18 oz (500 g) dried red kidney beans, soaked in
>   water overnight
> 2 tins tomato juice, about 18 fl oz (500 ml) each
> Salt and pepper

Cut the meat into bite-size cubes. Melt the butter or margarine in a large pan and brown the meat slowly. When lightly browned, add the drained beans and heat through. Pour in the tomato juice, and simmer for 3 hours. Season and serve.

Serves 6.   PF

FRESH TOMATO SOUP WITH BORAGE FLOWERS

This dish looks particularly striking – the vibrant red of the tomato soup with borage blue. Borage (*Borago officinalis*), the bee plant, has a flavour of cucumber and, as such, marries well with salad vegetables. This is a no-cook soup, served cold, which does need overnight marinating.

> 2 lb (1 kg) ripe tomatoes, skinned, seeded and chopped
> 1/3 cucumber, peeled, seeded and chopped
> 2 spring onions or 2 tablespoons fresh chopped chives
> 1 tablespoon chopped red or yellow pepper
> 1/2 pint (300 ml) light stock
> 2 tablespoons cider vinegar
> 3 leaves of borage
> About 24 borage flowers, with hairy sepals removed
> Salt and white pepper
> Single cream, to serve

Blend or process everything together except the flowers and cream. Chill overnight and check the seasoning when cold.

Serve, if possible, on a bed of crushed ice and trail whispers of cream into the soup, then scatter over the borage flowers. Naturally, the flowers are best picked just before serving.

Serves 6.   RD

SOPA MORELLANA

The walled medieval town of Morella in Spain has given its name to this clear, strongly-flavoured broth, which is topped with tiny floating choux buns called *buñuelos*.

FOR THE STOCK
1 ham bone (best from Parma ham)
1/4 chicken
1/4 boiling fowl
Small beef or lamb bone

FOR THE CHOUX PUFFS
1 oz (25 g) butter
1/4 pint (150 ml) milk
2 oz (50 g) flour
2 egg yolks, plus 1 white
Pinch of salt

Place the stock ingredients in a large pot, cover well with cold water, bring to the boil, and simmer, covered, for 4–5 hours. Skim the surface occasionally and top up with more water if required. Strain and leave the stock in a basin in the fridge overnight. Skim fat off the surface.

To make the choux puffs, place butter, milk and salt in a small saucepan, and bring to the boil. Add flour, blend well and stir over gentle heat until it forms a mass and the inside of the pan is clean. Remove from heat, cool slightly, and beat in egg yolks one at a time, followed by the egg white. Allow to cool completely before piping the mixture (or spooning, if preferred) into small balls onto a baking tray. Bake at 325°F (170°C, gas mark 3) for about 15 minutes, until golden brown.

Reheat broth, check seasoning, and float *buñuelos* on top to serve.

4 pints (2.25 litres) serves 6–8.   MJS

CARROT SOUP WITH CARDAMOM AND JUNIPER

This highly aromatic pair of spices surprises and enhances the decidedly unexotic qualities of the carrot. Prepare the soup a day in advance to allow the flavours to mingle and give its character time to mature.

> 16 green cardamoms
> 3 large juniper berries
> 1 oz (25 g) butter
> 1 large onion
> 1 1/2 lb (750 g) carrots
> 3 pints (1.75 litres) chicken broth
> Salt
> Freshly-ground black pepper
> Double cream

Open and discard the cardamom pods, crush their seeds with the base of a heavy knife handle; crush and chop the juniper berries and drop both spices into a large, heavy pot with the just-melted butter.

Add the peeled and sliced onion and carrots and let all sweat over a low heat, the pot's lid ajar, for about 10 minutes, until vegetables have softened and the spices' fragrance is well-developed. Stir often.

Add broth and a little salt and let simmer until vegetables are cooked. Half-cool the mixture and liquidize, seasoning to taste, until the soup is very smooth and spices are well pulverized. Reheat to serve, swirling a drop of cream round the centre of each bowlful.

Serves 6.   AWS

CARROT, CELERY, POTATO AND LOVAGE SOUP

Fresh lovage leaves, with their pungent, slightly maverick flavour of celery, lift a comfortable, everyday soup into one of unusual interest, and (illustrated on page 99) make a small adornment.

1 medium onion, peeled and sliced
10 oz (300 g) carrots (peeled weight), sliced
12 oz (350 g) celery, sliced
1 oz (25 g) butter
6 oz (175 g) potato (peeled weight), cubed
2¾ pints (1.6 litres) home-made chicken broth
Salt and freshly ground black pepper
Leaves of fresh lovage

Using a large, heavy pot, sweat onion, carrots, and celery in butter until softened, stirring occasionally. Add potato, broth, a dash of salt; bring liquid to the boil and allow broth to simmer until vegetables have cooked – a period of some 10 minutes from boiling point.

Remove pot from heat and add 6–7 chopped lovage leaves – these vary in impact and you can always increase their number – cool soup slightly and liquidize, seasoning to taste. Judge whether to

add more lovage – it should be quite evident, but not overpowering – and liquidize again until smooth.

Reheat soup to serve, garnishing each bowlful with a frond of lovage.

Serves 6.   AWS

PARTAN BREE WITH CRÈME FRAÎCHE

This classic Scottish soup takes on a tangy creaminess if crème fraîche is stirred in just before serving.

3 shallots, finely chopped
1 stick celery, finely chopped
1 oz (25 g) butter
2 tablespoons flour, optional, to thicken soup
½ pint (300 ml) milk
1½ pints (900 ml) fish or chicken stock
8 oz (250 g) crab meat, fresh or frozen
Sprig fresh rosemary
A good pinch cayenne pepper or few drops hot pepper or Worcestershire sauce
2 tablespoons brandy
Freshly grated nutmeg
Salt and ground black pepper
4 tablespoons crème fraîche plus a little extra for garnish, beaten until smooth
Fresh chopped parsley, to garnish

Gently sauté the shallots and celery in the butter for 10 minutes in a large saucepan until softened. Stir in the flour, if using, and cook for a minute. Then gradually stir in the milk and stock.

Bring to the boil, stirring, add the crab meat, rosemary and seasoning. Cover and turn down to a gentle simmer for 20 minutes. Remove rosemary, and stir in brandy and nutmeg, then blend in the crème fraîche. Reheat just a little but don't boil.

Serve the soup in warm bowls and spoon in some extra cream. Scatter over the parsley.

This can be made in advance and kept chilled or frozen up to the stage of adding the crème fraîche. Finish off before serving.

Serves 6–8.   RD

CREAM OF TURNIP SOUP

The distinctive flavour of turnips seems to blend particularly well with game stock. Piquant orange croûtons add a nice finishing touch.

12 oz (350 g) peeled turnip
2 shallots or 1 small onion
1¼–1¾ oz (32–45 g) butter
½ teaspoon caster sugar
1¾ pints (1 litre) game or chicken stock
1 tablespoon potato flour
3–4 fl oz (75–125 g) cream or milk
Little fresh chopped parsley
Salt and pepper

CROUTONS
3–4 slices white or brown stale bread, cut into
* tiny squares*
1 tablespoon oil
½ oz (15 g) butter
½–1 teaspoon curry paste or powder
Grated rind of ½ orange or clementine

Cream of turnip soup

Finely chop the onion and cut the turnip into thin slices. Sweat in ¾ oz (20 g) of the butter in a heavy pan, sprinkle with sugar and cook gently, without browning, for 20–30 minutes (add a tablespoon or so of stock if the pan gets too dry). Season, add the stock and simmer for 20 minutes, or until completely tender, then purée and return to the rinsed-out pan.

Mix the potato flour with the cream or milk, add to the pan and bring to the boil, stirring. Correct the seasoning and simmer for a minute or two before drawing off the stove. Stir in the remaining butter in little bits to enrich and further thicken the soup, and serve immediately with the croûtons, parsley and some fine shreds of orange or clementine zest.

To make the piquant orange croûtons, heat butter and oil in a frying pan, add the curry paste or powder, orange rind and the squares of bread and fry, tossing, until golden brown. Drain on absorbent kitchen paper and keep warm or reheat before serving.

Serves 4–6.   NC

GERMAN PUMPKIN SOUP

This delicate amber soup has its own fresh innocent flavour; don't be tempted to stir in cream.

1½ lb (750 g) piece pumpkin
¾ pint (450 ml) water
3 cloves
Small piece cinnamon stick
2 tablespoons wine vinegar
2 oz (50 g) butter
Salt, pepper, sugar

Peel the pumpkin, and scoop out the seeds and fibrous middle. Cut the flesh into 1″ (2.5 cm) cubes and put them in a saucepan. Pour in the water – it may appear too little, but pumpkin is very watery.

Stick the cloves and the stick of cinnamon into a piece of the pumpkin flesh so that you can remove them easily. Stew gently with the spices for 20–30 minutes, until the pumpkin is soft. Take out the spices, then purée the pumpkin with its cooking liquid. Stir in the wine vinegar. Heat again and beat in the butter. Season with salt, plenty of freshly milled black pepper, and a little sugar.

Serves 4.   EL

FISH AND SHELLFISH

The most healthful and versatile of foods, fish and shellfish lend themselves to a thousand different treatments, from chowders to kedgeree, terrines to tartares, crêpes to croquettes

MILLE-FEUILLE OF SALMON AND POTATOES

Alternate layers of salmon and potato, with a cream and lemon sauce.

4 medium-sized potatoes
1 lb (500 g) fresh salmon
7 fl oz (200 ml) double cream
Juice of 1 lemon
Salt, pepper, small bunch of chives

Peel the potatoes, and slice thinly. Heat a heavy frying-pan, and coat the base thinly with oil. Arrange slices of potato over the base of the pan, overlapping the slices, so that the potatoes adhere during cooking, until the base is covered. Keep any remaining potato for cooking later. Cook the potatoes for 5 minutes on each side, turning in one piece like a pancake, until cooked through and lightly browned. They should form a solid disc when cooked. Using a 3" (6 cm) circular cutter, make rounds of potatoes and set aside. Repeat until all the potato slices are cooked and cut into rounds. Keep potato discs warm whilst cooking the salmon.

Slice the salmon into escalopes about ½" (1 cm) thick, season and cook in an oven at 300°F (150°C, gas mark 2) for 4 minutes.

Remove the salmon from the oven, and cut into rounds with the same circular cutter. Arrange alternate layers of salmon and potato rounds on serving plates in the style of a mille-feuille.

Mix together the cream, lemon juice and chopped chives. Season and pour the sauce around the mille-feuilles to serve.

Serves 4.   CP

CABBAGE LEAVES STUFFED WITH PIKE

Pike is difficult to find in England, unless you have an enlightened fishmonger, or angling friends who are prepared to part with their catch.

6 cabbage leaves

STUFFING
1 lb 4 oz (635 g) fillet of pike, skinned
1 lb (500 g) double cream
1 egg white
Salt, pepper

SAUCE
1 lb (500 g) peas, shelled
Knob of butter
Fresh tarragon
Salt, pepper, pinch of sugar

Right *(Clockwise from top) tartare of trout (see page 38); cabbage leaves stuffed with pike; and mille-feuille of salmon and potatoes*

To make the stuffing, first pulverize the fish thoroughly, and pass through a sieve to remove any bones which may remain. Gradually incorporate the cream and egg white bit by bit, blending well, to obtain a smooth, creamy consistency.

Blanch the cabbage leaves, refresh under cold water, and cut away the stalk from each leaf.

Cook the peas with a little boiling water, butter, salt, pepper and sugar, for 10 minutes. Blend in the liquidizer with fresh chopped tarragon, to make a fairly liquid sauce.

Divide the pike mixture between the 6 cabbage leaves, placing a spoonful on each, and wrap the leaves up to form neat parcels. Bake, covered, in the oven for 15 minutes at 325°F (175°C, gas mark 3).

Serve hot, with the pea sauce poured around.
Serves 6. CP

TARTARE OF TROUT

An elegant starter, using really fresh trout.

TARTARE
1 lb (500 g) fresh trout, filleted and skinned
Juice of 1 lemon
Small bunch of chives
2 dessertspoons olive oil
Salt, freshly ground white pepper

RED PEPPER SAUCE
2 red peppers
½ pint (300 ml) olive oil
Salt, pepper

With a sharp knife, chop the trout finely and season with lemon juice, salt and pepper. Finely chop the chives; add to the trout mixture, together with the two spoonfuls of olive oil. Blend well and refrigerate for a couple of hours.

To make the sauce, place the red peppers in a very hot oven for 15 minutes to loosen the skins. Peel and deseed, then purée the flesh in a blender. Slowly add the olive oil to the red pepper purée, blending all the time, as if making mayonnaise.

Season to taste.

To serve, pour a pool of sauce onto each serving plate. Using two dessertspoons, make egg-shaped *quenelles* of the trout mixture. Place one *quenelle* on each plate, and serve decorated with fresh chives.
Serves 4. CP

FRESH TUNA WITH GINGER VINAIGRETTE

Fresh tuna is becoming increasingly available from the wet fish counters in good supermarkets, as well as from go-ahead fishmongers. However, if it is not available, the dressing might be served with salmon steaks.

1" (2.5 cm) piece fresh ginger, peeled and finely
*   chopped*
2 large spring onions, white and some of the
*   green parts, thinly sliced*
8 fl oz (225 ml) olive oil
Juice of 2 limes
2 tablespoons soy sauce
2 tablespoons sesame oil
Salt
Freshly ground black pepper
1 bunch fresh coriander or flat-leaved parsley,
*   finely chopped*
6 × 5–6 oz (150–175 g) tuna steaks
Coriander or flat-leaved parsley leaves and slices
*   of lime for garnish*

To make the vinaigrette, stir together the ginger, spring onions, vinegar, olive oil, lime juice and soy sauce, then whisk in the sesame oil and seasonings. Finally, add the coriander or parsley. Grill the tuna under a high heat (or over a barbecue) for 3½–4 minutes on each side, or a little longer for more well-cooked fish.

Spoon some of the dressing onto 6 plates. Add the fish and garnish with coriander or parsley leaves and slices of lime. Serve with crisp salad of mixed lettuce leaves.
Serves 6. HW

Scallop stir-fry with rice

SCALLOP STIR-FRY

The ultimate fast food – once the ingredients are prepared, cooking takes less than five minutes.

A Californian interpretation of the Chinese style of cooking, it uses ingredients which are readily available in most supermarkets today, not just the Chinatown emporia of large cities.

6 oz (175 g) fresh raw prawns
6 oz (175 g) scallops, sliced in two horizontally
Oil for frying
1 carrot, cut in julienne strips
1 stalk celery, in julienne strips
1 oz (25 g) shitake mushrooms, sliced
1 small red onion, sliced
1 tablespoon soy sauce
2 tablespoons oyster sauce (available from Chinese foodstores)
3–4 teaspoons sugar
1/2 teaspoon sesame oil
1/4 teaspoon black pepper
2 teaspoons dry sherry
1 slice fresh ginger, shredded
1/2 teaspoon finely chopped garlic
2 spring onions, trimmed and sliced

Heat oil in wok, and sauté carrot, celery, mushrooms and red onion for about 1 minute. Remove from oil, set aside. Add prawns and scallops to wok. Sauté until scallops turn white and firm and prawns turn pink – about 1½ minutes. Add soy sauce, oyster sauce, sugar, sesame oil, pepper, sherry, ginger, garlic and spring onions. Stir in vegetables and sauté for about another 30 seconds. Serve with plain rice.

Serves 2.   CW

STEAMED FRESH SCALLOPS WITH GARLIC

This is a speciality of the Bayee House, an excellent Chinese restaurant in Putney, whose manager, Albert Siu, described the method. Quantities given are *per person* as a first course.

3 large fresh scallops, with their coral and rounded half-shells
1 teaspoon minced garlic per scallop
Vegetable oil
Salt
Freshly ground black pepper

Have your fishmonger clean the scallops and shells; carefully detach coral (the Bayee House does not serve this, but it adds interest and colour) and remove any extraneous tissue from around the side of each white muscle. Put the muscle, with coral, into a rounded half-shell, and top the scallop with a teaspoon (or less, if this is too much) of minced garlic mixed with a little oil and seasoning.

Set each shell in the top of a steamer, or on a rack placed inside a pot large enough to hold the scallops well above the level of simmering water. Cover with a snug-fitting lid and gently steam the fish for 10–15 minutes, or until each scallop is cooked right through and has made its own delectable broth.

Carefully remove each shell from the steamer – so as not to spill the broth – season the contents, and eat without delay.

Serves 1.   AWS

Salt cod with sweet red peppers

SALT COD WITH SWEET RED PEPPERS

Salt cod is a great favourite in Spain, and is used in hundreds of ways. This appetizer, called *pericana*, comes from the region of Valencia.

2–3 dried sweet red peppers
About 8 oz (250 g) dried salt cod
6–7 cloves fresh garlic
Olive oil

Soak the salt cod in cold water for 24 hours, changing the water twice.

Heat a pan of olive oil, remove from heat and 'blanch' the peppers in the hot oil very briefly, taking care not to allow them to burn. Remove and set aside.

Using a heavy frying-pan or griddle, roast peeled garlic cloves until tender and slightly blackened on the outside. Remove and set aside. In the same pan, sweat the salt cod, without oil, until cooked. Flake the fish, discarding skin and bones, and chop the garlic finely. Crumble the fried red peppers, and mix cod, garlic and peppers together in a bowl. Pour over olive oil to taste, check seasoning and serve with crusty bread.

Serves 4. MJS

SMOKED HADDOCK SOUFFLE CREPES

This is a very popular dinner-party starter.

CREPES
2 eggs
4 oz (125 g) plain flour
½ pint (300 ml) milk
Salt and ground black pepper
Oil, for greasing

FILLING
1 lb (500 g) Finnan haddock
¾ pint (450 ml) milk
1 large bay leaf
2 oz (50 g) butter
1 shallot or small onion, chopped
1 clove garlic, crushed
1 teaspoon curry powder or paste
1½ oz (40 g) flour
5 tablespoons Parmesan cheese
2 egg yolks
3 egg whites
Some flaked almonds, to sprinkle

Blend the crêpe eggs with the flour, milk and seasoning, in a blender or food processor, until the mixture is smooth.

Using a 7″ (18 cm) omelette pan, lightly grease the base and make a batch of lacy thin crêpes, heating the pan well in between each one. Stack the crêpes and keep warm in a clean tea towel.

Meanwhile, poach the haddock in the milk with the bay leaf and black pepper, for about 10 minutes, until it just flakes. Skin, bone and flake with a fork. Discard the bones and skin but strain and reserve the milk.

Melt the butter in a large saucepan and sauté the chopped onion and crushed garlic for about 5 minutes. Stir in the flour and curry powder and cook for another minute.

Gradually blend in the reserved fish milk, stirring until smooth and thickened. Season and add the 2 egg yolks. Stir in the flaked fish and 3 tablespoons of the cheese.

Whisk the egg whites until forming stiff peaks. Beat a spoonful into the mixture, then carefully fold in the rest.

Divide the soufflé mixture into 6, and spoon down the middle of 6 crêpes. Flip over the two edges and place the crêpes down the centre of a large, oval ovenproof dish. Sprinkle over the remaining cheese and almonds, and bake uncovered at 400°F (200°C, gas mark 6) for 20–25 minutes, until risen and slightly crispy. Serve at once – make sure your guests are sitting down first.

Serves 6.

NOTE Despite being a soufflé mixture, the filling is surprisingly adaptable as it can be prepared in advance and baked 25 minutes before you sit down. Any leftover crêpes can be interleaved, wrapped and frozen. RD

FISH PIE IN FILO PASTRY

This exquisitely delicate pie, which can serve as a starter or main course dish, is at its best when served within half an hour of cooking. However, it is perfect for dinner parties, as it can be assembled a couple of hours in advance and cooked just before it is to be served.

FILLING
8 oz (250 g) mushrooms, rinsed and dried
1 leek (only its white part), trimmed, chopped and rinsed
2 carrots, scraped and chopped
1 oz (25 g) butter
1 lb 6 oz (675 g) fresh fillet of cod, skinned and boned
2 spring onions, trimmed and rinsed
2 tablespoons chopped fresh dill
1 tablespoon chopped parsley
3 eggs
2 tablespoons single cream or creamy milk
Salt

PASTRY
1 lb (500 g) packet filo pastry
6 oz (175 g) melted butter

Make a *mirepoix* by putting carrots, leek and mushrooms through the sharp mincing blade of a food processor and processing briefly until the mixture has the consistency of large-sized crumbs. Melt the butter, add the minced vegetables and sauté over medium heat, turning over until all the moisture has evaporated; about 3–4 minutes. Season and keep aside.

Process the remaining filling ingredients until finely chopped and well amalgamated.

Butter a rectangular or square roasting dish, about 15″ × 11″ × 3″ (39 × 28 × 8 cm) or slightly smaller. Unfold the stack of pastry and brush its top layer with melted butter; lift it and line the oven dish as neatly as possible, removing excess length but allowing 2″ (5 cm) overhang on all sides in order to enclose filling. Continue in the same manner until about half of the pastry has been used, which will be about 6–7 sheets. Spread the fish filling evenly into the dish, then top with the *mirepoix*. Fold all four sides of the pastry over the filling, enclosing it and preventing it from spilling. Cover neatly with sheets of pastry that have been brushed with butter as before, until all the pastry has been used. Brush top sheet liberally and trim any excess edges with scissors. Score only the top sheets of pastry carefully and light-handedly – otherwise the filling might spill – into diamond or square serving portions. Sprinkle with a little cold water with your fingertips to prevent the edges of the pastry from curling upwards, and cook in an oven preheated to 375°F (190°C, gas mark 5) for 45 minutes until the top is crisp, puffed up and light golden. Take out and let it stand for 5–10 minutes to solidify and make it easier to serve.

Serves 8 as a starter; 6 as a main course.   RS

NEW ENGLAND CLAM CHOWDER

Fresh clams are difficult, though not impossible to obtain through a fishmonger. Only those that are closed or close when touched should be used.

1 quart fresh soft shell clams or 2 × 6½ oz cans
3 oz (75 g) salt pork or green bacon, diced

1 onion, sliced
1 lb (500 g) potatoes
Fresh bay leaf
1 pint (600 ml) milk, scalded
1 oz (25 g) butter
Salt and ground black pepper

If using fresh clams, steam open, remove from shells, then mince. Reserve any juice. If using canned, reserve juice and mince the flesh.

In a large saucepan, gently fry the diced pork until the fat begins to run. Add the onions and fry until golden brown.

Cut the potatoes into dice and add to the pan together with the clam juices and enough water to cover. Season well and add the bay leaf. Simmer until just tender. Add the clams and simmer for about 10 minutes (less if using canned clams).

Just before serving, add the hot milk and butter. Stir until melted. If possible store for 24 hours in a fridge before re-heating and serving.

Serves 4–6.   RD

SALMON, CUCUMBER AND CORN CHOWDER

A hearty main course soup with a pleasing contrast of sweet and salty flavour.

1 tail piece fresh salmon, about 1¼ lb (625 g)
4 oz (125 g) smoked salmon
2 fresh corn cobs
1 cucumber, skinned, seeded and chopped
1 onion, chopped
1 oz (25 g) butter
3 tomatoes, skinned, seeded and chopped
2 medium potatoes, chopped
1″ (2.5 cm) cube fresh ginger, grated
Salt and ground black pepper
A little fresh fennel, to garnish

Right *(from top) three seafood chowders: snapper and squid chilli, page 44; salmon, cucumber and corn; New England clam chowder*

Fillet and skin the salmon tail, then make a stock with the bones, skin, onion peelings and seasonings in about 3 pints (1.8 litres) of water. Cook for 20 minutes and strain.

Dice the fresh and smoked fish. Stand the corn cobs upright and with a sharp knife strip the kernels off by cutting downwards. Sauté the vegetables in the butter with the ginger for about 5 minutes then add the stock and seasonings. Simmer for about 15 minutes and add the fresh and smoked salmon. Cook for a further five minutes. Serve hot garnished with fennel.

Serves 6.   RD

SNAPPER AND SQUID CHILLI CHOWDER

This is based on a Bahamas recipe, where fresh chillies feature strongly in the native cuisine. Red snapper, a most delicious fish, can be found not only in speciality fish shops but also on fish stalls in city markets supplying West Indian communities.

About 1 lb (500 g) whole red snapper
1 lb (500 g) squid, prepared and skinned
8 oz (250 g) white crab meat
2 limes
2 fresh green or red chillies, seeded and chopped
4 oz (125 g) salt pork or green bacon, diced
1 medium onion, chopped
1 large clove garlic
1 green pepper, diced
1 lb (500 g) potatoes, peeled and diced
Sprig fresh thyme
1 bay leaf
½ teaspoon ground mace
Salt and ground black pepper
Fresh parsley, to serve

Fillet the snapper and skin it (or ask the fishmonger to do this for you).

Put the bones into a large saucepan with onion skins and seasonings. Make a fish stock from this, draining after 15 minutes. Reserve.

Cut the fish and squid into bite-size portions

and marinate with the crab in the lime juice with the chillies for an hour or so. (Take care though when cutting chillies as they can sting, and never, never rub your eyes with chilli-stained fingers!)

Fry the pork gently until the fat runs, then add the chopped onion and garlic. Sauté gently for about 5 minutes.

Add the green pepper and potatoes together with the marinated fish, snapper stock, herbs and mace. Season and simmer for about 5 minutes. Serve garnished with little fresh parsley.

Serves 6.   RD

COTRIADE BRETONNE

This is very popular seafood dish from Brittany which has its origins in the days when the fisherfolk went out to sea with very limited cooking facilities on board their fishing boats.

However, with true French flair and expertise, they were able to produce a dish, some would say a feast, fit for a king.

1½ lb (750 g) fresh fish – cod, haddock or
*   monkfish – skinned and cut into chunks*
3 lb (1.5 kg) fresh mussels
1½ lb (750 g) potato, peeled and diced
2 onions, peeled and chopped
3 leeks, cleaned and sliced
3 oz (75 g) butter
2 cloves garlic, crushed
Seasoning to taste
8 oz (250 g) spinach leaves, finely shredded, or
*   equivalent of frozen spinach*
A little grated nutmeg
½ pint (300 ml) single cream
Chopped parsley

FISH STOCK
A few fish bones from the fishmonger
2½ pints (1.5 litres) water
1 small onion, peeled and quartered
1 stick celery
Salt
Black pepper

Cotriade bretonne

Make the fish stock first. Wash fish bones well, then place in a large pan with water, onion, celery and seasoning. Bring to the boil, skim and simmer gently for 20 minutes. Cool and strain. Reserve 1¾ pints (1 litre) for soup.

Prepare fish and set aside. Clean the mussels by scraping off barnacles with a small knife and pulling away beards. Discard any mussels which are broken or open.

Choose a very large pan with a tight-fitting lid. Fry the potato, onions and leeks in melted butter without browning. Add garlic and cook gently for 3–5 minutes. Pour in fish stock and seasoning, simmer for 8–10 minutes, then add the fish and cook for 4–5 minutes only.

When ready to serve, bring to the boil and add the spinach, nutmeg, cream and mussels. Cover and cook over high heat for 4 minutes till all the shells are open, shaking the pan from time to time.

Serve from the pan into wide soup plates sprinkled with parsley, and eat with French bread.

Serves 8.   SM

HADDOCK AND HAZELNUT CROQUETTES

These are ideal for preparing ahead and, after sealing in hot oil, can be reheated later (next morning, for breakfast, for example) in a moderate oven.

1 small onion, chopped
1 oz (25 g) butter
¼ teaspoon curry powder
12 oz (375 g) Finnan haddock, cooked, skinned and flaked
1 lb (500 g) floury potatoes, boiled and mashed
2 tablespoons fresh chopped parsley
2 teaspoons grated lemon rind, optional
2 egg yolks
Salt
Pepper
Oil, for deep frying

TO COAT
Plain flour, for dusting
1–2 eggs, beaten
3 oz (75 g) natural dried breadcrumbs
2 oz (50 g) hazelnuts, chopped

Sauté the onion in the butter for 5 minutes, then add the curry powder and fry for a few seconds.

Mix with the fish, potato, parsley, lemon rind (if using), egg yolks and plenty of seasoning. Chill.

Shape into 8 rolls, using wet hands if the mixture is sticky.

Prepare three bowls with the flour in one, beaten eggs in another and the crumbs and nuts mixed in a third. Coat the rolls in flour, then egg, and finally the crumb mixture. Set aside on a plate.

Pour enough oil to come a third of the way up a deep-fat frying-pan and heat to 375°F (190°C) or until a cube of white bread browns in half a minute. Deep fry the croquettes 2 or 3 at a time until crispy and browned, then drain. Reheat the oil in between batches. If the croquettes show signs of breaking up in the pan, the oil is not hot enough.

Reheat on a baking tray at 375°F (190°C, gas mark 5), for about 15 minutes. Serve with a home-made tartare sauce.

Serves 6–8.   RD

Bouillabaisse, the classic fish soup of the Mediterranean

BOUILLABAISSE

This classic Mediterranean dish is really a soup, but sufficiently filling to be served as a main meal. The important thing to remember is to boil rather than simmer the liquor, to mix the oil and water together. Choose from a good mixture of firm, rich seafood and white fish.

About 4 lb (1.75 kg) fish total weight from the
*   following. Choose at least five types: sea*
*   bass, whiting, monkfish, John Dory, conger*
*   eel, squid, langoustines, clams, crabs,*
*   crawfish*

2 large onions
3 cloves garlic
2 large tomatoes
Pinch saffron filaments
Sprig fresh thyme
3 sprigs fresh fennel
2 bay leaves
2 pieces thinly pared orange rind
Salt
Ground black pepper
¼ pint (150 ml) olive oil
¼ pint (150 ml) dry white wine
Fresh chopped parsley
Slices French bread

Trim and cut the fishes into good-sized chunks. Skin the squid, pick over the shellfish. Put the firm fish and shellfish on one plate, the white on another. Make a court bouillon, if liked, with the heads, trimmings and any onion peelings. Simmer 15 minutes, then strain. Slice the onion, crush the garlic, skin and chop the tomatoes.

Put the firm fish into a large cast iron casserole, sprinkle over the onions and garlic; tomatoes, saffron, herbs and orange rind. Pour over the oil, wine and cover with court bouillon or water.

Bring to the boil and boil well for 5 minutes. Add the other fish and then boil again for a 5 further minutes.

Serve piping hot, ladled on top of bread slices and sprinkled with parsley.

Serves 6. RD

MONKFISH CASSOULET

A classic bean dish using monkfish fillets, instead of the traditional ingredients of preserved goose, pork and sausage.

> 6 oz (175 g) dried haricot beans or 15 oz
>   (425 g) can of cannellini beans, drained
> Pinch saffron threads
> 1 lb (500 g) monkfish tail, filleted
> 1 pint (600 ml) water or fish stock
> 1 large bay leaf
> 1 onion, sliced
> 1 small bulb fennel, sliced
> 4 oz (125 g) salt pork or ham, diced
> 2 oz (50 g) smoked bacon, diced
> 1 oz (25 g) butter
> ¼ pint (150 ml) dry cider or white wine
> ½ teaspoon ground mace
> Sprig each of fresh thyme, rosemary and savory
> 4 tomatoes, skinned and quartered
> Salt
> Ground black pepper

> TOPPING
> 6 tablespoons fresh white breadcrumbs
> 3 tablespoons chopped parsley

If using dried beans, soak overnight, and simmer in seasoned water until soft. Reserve. Soak the saffron in a few tablespoons of warm water.

Poach the monkfish in the water with the bay leaf and seasoning until firm; about 10 minutes. Cut into bite-size pieces. Reserve the stock.

Sauté the onion, fennel, pork and bacon in the butter until softened, about 5 minutes.

Add the cider or wine and reserved stock. Stir in the beans, herbs, mace, saffron with its soaking water and the tomatoes. Season.

Bring to the boil, then cover and simmer gently for 20 minutes. Add the fish, and a little extra liquid if you feel it is needed.

Spoon into a shallow gratin dish, sprinkle with the crumbs and herbs then put into an oven at 375°F (190°C, gas mark 5) for about 25 minutes until the topping is crisp. This dish can be made in advance and the oven reheating done when ready to serve. Ideal with warm, crusty baguettes and a salad.

Serves 4. RD

SPAGHETTI ALLE VONGOLE

Mediterranean clams or *vongole* – the small whitish, smooth variety – are cheap and make a delicious meal in the Italian manner that will bring you foreign tastes, smells and even sounds, as this is a dish found in every small restaurant of central and southern Italy. Sometimes chopped and skinned ripe tomatoes are added.

Make sure the pasta is neither overcooked, nor dry, but glistens with a good olive oil, and the dish will be mouthwatering.

> 3 lb (1.5 kg) clams
> 7 tablespoons olive oil
> 3 spring onions, trimmed, rinsed and sliced finely
> 2–3 cloves garlic, peeled and crushed
> 3 tablespoons parsley, finely chopped
> 3 tablespoons fresh dill, finely chopped
> Freshly ground black pepper
> 12 oz (350 g) spaghetti
> Salt

47

Place the clams in a large bowl of cold water and let their grit sink. Lift clams out and repeat the process until the water is perfectly clear. In the meantime, pick out and discard any clams that remain open even after they are tapped.

Heat the oil in a large frying-pan or casserole and sauté the onion gently without browning it; add the garlic and parsley, and sauté briefly until aromatic. Turn heat up, add the clams and stir continuously, coating them in the oil, until they open; about 2–3 minutes.

Remove from heat and let them stand for 1–2 minutes until slightly cooler. Working quickly, pick half the clams out of their shells using your fingers and discard the shells; keep the rest in their shells. In the meantime, discard any that may not have opened. (At this stage, the clams can wait up to 10 minutes, but no longer as they will lose their fresh flavour and become leathery.)

In the meantime, boil the spaghetti in plenty of lightly salted water for about 8 minutes, making sure it is not overcooked, and strain. Heat the clams up, stirring continuously, add pepper and the fresh dill and, after a few seconds, the cooked spaghetti. Mix well, coating the pasta in the oil for a few seconds, and withdraw from heat. Serve immediately on hot plates.

Serves 4 as a starter; 2 as a main course. RS

RICE WITH SALT COD, GARLIC AND SPINACH

Rice is grown on the plains around the Spanish town of Valencia and forms the basis of dozens of local specialities.

4 oz (125 g) salt cod
14 oz (400 g) shortgrain rice
1 lb (500 g) spinach
4 tablespoons olive oil
10–12 spring onions, trimmed and cut in half
2–3 garlic cloves, unpeeled
1 teaspoon paprika
5–6 strands of saffron
Salt and pepper

Soak the dried salt cod for 24 hours, changing the water twice. Drain, dry the cod, and flake, discarding skin and bones.

To prepare the saffron either roast in a hot pan for a few minutes and crumble, or soak in a little hot water. Heat the oil in a fireproof dish (the Spanish use terracotta, prepared for use on the hob) and brown the cloves of garlic in the oil. Remove and discard. Wash the spinach thoroughly, discard tough stems, and add to the garlicky oil, together with the spring onions. Stir around on gentle heat for 2–3 minutes. Measure the volume of rice in a cup, and set aside double that volume of water.

Add the flaked cod and the rice to the spring onions and spinach, and continue to cook for another 3–4 minutes. Heat the water which was set aside, and add, together with the saffron. Bring to the boil, then place in a medium oven 350°F (180°C, gas mark 4) for about 20 minutes, or until the rice is cooked, taking care not to let it dry out through over-cooking. Check seasoning.

Serves 6 as a first course, or as a light supper or lunch dish. MJS

Rice with salt cod, garlic and spinach

PAN-FRIED SALMON WITH A QUICK QUARK SAUCE

One of the benefits of pan-frying is that you can make an excellent sauce with the juices in just a few minutes. Quark, a soft cheese with a very low fat content, can be stirred into sauces as a lighter, more tangy alternative to double cream – ideal for fish. Do not, however, allow the sauce to boil after it has been added, or it will curdle. Fromage frais, soured cream or crème fraîche could also be used.

1 oz (25 g) butter
1 tablespoon olive oil
4 salmon fillets, about 6 oz (175 g) each, e.g. from the tail end
Chopped fresh herbs of your choice such as thyme, parsley, dill or basil
2 tablespoons chopped shallots
4 tablespoons dry white wine
½ pint (300 ml) fish stock (use the skin and bones from filleting)
Juice ½ small lemon or 1 lime
4 tablespoons quark
A little fresh chopped parsley or more herbs, to garnish
Salt
Ground black pepper

Heat the butter and oil in a wide, heavy-based frying pan and fry salmon fillets for about 4 minutes each side, sprinkling with some herbs if liked. Do not overcook. Season lightly and remove.

Add the shallots to the pan (with a little extra butter if need be) and cook for 2 minutes. Pour in the wine and cook until reduced. Add the stock. (This can be made by boiling the skin and bones from filleting in seasoned water for 20 minutes, if you don't have any to hand!)

Bring to the boil, add the lemon or lime juice and seasoning. Simmer for a few minutes. Mix the quark until smooth then stir into the sauce, reheating but not allowing to boil.

Serve the salmon fillets on warm plates with the sauce and maybe some broccoli florets and a sprinkling of more herbs to garnish.

Serves 4.   RD

BOURGEOIS IN THE F.T.

A good dish for serving to city slickers, this is a high protein, low cholesterol meal wrapped up in the latest financial news. Your guests could even check their share prices whilst negotiating the bones. Bourgeois (or Red Admiral) is a tropical game fish which is imported from the Seychelles and can be ordered from good fishmongers, given a little notice. However, you may have to be prepared to take a whole fish of about 4 to 5 lbs (1.75 to 2.25 kg) in which case, have it all cut into steaks and freeze the remainder for another dinner party. Of course, the recipe can easily be used for salmon, turbot, halibut and even cod steaks. This dish can be prepared in advance.

6 cutlets of Bourgeois, about 6–8 oz (175–250 g) each
2 carrots, peeled and cut in thin julienne strips
1 small bulb fennel, sliced thinly
2 oz (50 g) pack ready-made herb and garlic butter, or 3 tablespoons extra virgin olive oil
2 spring onions, sliced thinly
¼ pint (150 ml) dry white wine
6 tablespoons single cream, optional
Salt and ground black pepper

First prepare 6 single sheets of newspaper – whichever is appropriate for the occasion. Line them with a sheet of lightly greased greaseproof paper. Check the fish for any large bones and remove, but try to keep the skin intact. Place the fish in the centre of each sheet and season lightly.

Blanch the carrot and fennel in boiling water for 3 minutes, then drain and toss in the butter or oil with the onion shreds. Spoon on top of each fish steak, sprinkle over with the wine and cream if using, and season lightly again. Wrap up well, keeping the joins on top if possible, then place on a baking sheet and bake at 375°F (190°C, gas mark 5) for about 30–35 minutes or until the fish feels firm.

Serve the parcels as they are, for your diners to unwrap, accompanied by sprigs of fresh fennel, if you have any, new potatoes and a green vegetable such as mangetouts.

Serves 6.   RD

SKATE IN LIME AND SAFFRON

The delicate taste of this dish, with the fresh aroma of lime, makes it very special. If you have enough time, the dish is infinitely better when the fish has been marinated for a couple of hours.

> 4 (or 8 if they are small) pieces of skate wing;
>   about 2 lb (1 kg)
> 2 limes
> 2 tablespoons olive oil
> 1 oz (25 g) butter
> ¼ pint (150 ml) dry white wine
> 2 large pinches saffron, crumbled
> Salt and black pepper

Wipe the skate clean and arrange in one layer in a *gratin* dish. Rinse and dry limes. Cut 6–7 strips of zest from a lime, cover with film and keep aside. Squeeze 1½ limes and pour the juice over the skate. Use remaining lime for garnish.

    Heat oil and butter gently in a saucepan, add the wine and bring to boil. Add seasoning and the saffron, and bubble for 2–3 minutes until the liquid is brightly coloured. Pour over the fish, cover with foil and let it marinate for 2 hours.

    Half an hour before serving baste the fish, replace foil, and cook in an oven preheated to 375°F (190°C, gas mark 5) for 20–25 minutes. Baste the fish once or twice during cooking time.

    Pour the juices in a small saucepan, add the reserved lime zest and boil rapidly for 1–2 minutes, until it thickens lightly. Place skate on hot plates and coat with the sauce. Decorate with lime slices.

    Serves 4.   RS

A CREAMY KEDGEREE

It is intriguing that an Indian peasant dish, *khichiri*, of rice, lentils, eggs and spices, became a British Raj breakfast dish containing smoked haddock. For breakfast, this dish can be made the night before, without the raw egg, reheating and finishing before serving, as spicy hot as you like.

> 1 lb (500 g) smoked Finnan haddock
> Parsley stalks and a bay leaf
> 1 small onion, chopped
> 1½ oz (40 g) butter
> 1 teaspoon turmeric
> 8 oz (250 g) cooked long grain rice, preferably
>   Basmati
> 2 large eggs, one hard boiled and one raw and
>   beaten
> 2 tablespoons fresh chopped parsley or coriander
> Salt, pepper and cayenne or hot pepper sauce

Poach the fish in water to cover, with the parsley stalks, bay leaf and pepper, until just cooked: about 10 to 15 minutes. Drain, skin and flake the fish.

    Sauté the onion in the butter for 5 minutes, then add the turmeric and fry for a few seconds. Mix in the rice, fish, seasoning, cayenne or pepper sauce to taste, and reheat.

    Chop the hard egg white and sieve or very finely chop the yolk. Mix the chopped white into the kedgeree.

    Just before serving, mix in the fresh herbs and beaten egg and serve topped with the sieved yolk.

    Serves 2–3.   RD

SALMON, SAMPHIRE AND DILL SALAD

This is ideal for those who like to serve salmon when entertaining but don't feel up to garnishing a whole fish. Sea bass could also be used, and when samphire is out of season, use blanched asparagus or thin Kenya beans instead, although the flavour is, of course, quite different.

> 2 lbs (1 kg) fresh salmon, on the bone (a large
>   tail piece would be suitable)
> 2 tablespoons wine vinegar
> Small onion, sliced
> Bay leaves, peppercorns and sprigs of dill – for
>   the court bouillon
> 4 oz (125 g) fresh samphire, rinsed
> 4 spring onions, sliced
> Seasoning

SAUCE
¼ pint (150 ml) soured cream
2 egg yolks
1 teaspoon horseradish relish
Grated rind and juice of a small lemon
2 tablespoons fresh chopped dill
Salt and ground black pepper

Poach the fish for about 15 minutes in 1 pint (600 ml) water, with the vinegar, onion, bay leaves, peppercorns and dill sprigs. Season lightly. Leave to cool in the court bouillon, if possible. Strain the liquor off and boil down to about 4 tablespoons. Cool and reserve.

Skin and flake the fish into bite-size chunks. Mix with the samphire and onion.

Blend all the dressing ingredients together with the reserved fish stock, then mix into the fish. Chill the salad, and serve garnished with a few sprigs of samphire and dill. This is delicious served with hot, buttered new potatoes.

Serves 4.   RD

Terrine of smoked eel and leeks

TERRINE OF SMOKED EEL WITH LEEKS

An excellent combination of flavours and textures, which looks stunning when sliced through.

TERRINE
12 young leeks
1 lb (500 g) smoked eel, skinned and filleted, but
   in one piece
2 red peppers
7 fl oz (200 ml) aspic jelly

SAUCE
Juice of ½ lemon
3 fl oz (100 ml) olive oil
Salt, pepper

Trim the leeks, washing thoroughly and discarding all the tough greenery and leaving only the tender white part. (The trimmed leeks should approximately equal the length of the terrine in which the dish is to be made.) Cook in plenty of salted, boiling water for about 6 minutes. Remove and refresh in cold water, then drain and set aside.

Make the aspic jelly. Pour a small amount of warmed jelly into the base of a terrine, then cover with a layer of leeks, laid lengthwise. Leave in the refrigerator to set.

Place the red peppers in a very hot oven for 15 minutes to loosen the skins. Peel and cut in half lengthwise, remove the seeds, and wrap the pieces of pepper around the smoked eel.

Place the smoked eel, wrapped in red pepper, on top of the leeks. Pour in more aspic. Fill the terrine with the rest of the leeks, packing them around the eel, and remaining aspic.

Leave the terrine in the fridge, weighted on top, overnight to set.

Make the vinaigrette with olive oil, lemon juice, salt and pepper. It should be sufficiently sharp to offset the richness of the smoked eel.

To serve, turn the terrine out onto a serving plate, and, with a very sharp knife, cut slices about 1" (2.5 cm) thick. Serve the slices with the vinaigrette sauce poured around.

Serves 6.   CP

POULTRY AND GAME

Quail, duck, goose and even rabbit or chicken all have the makings of dinner-party fare when combined with the fresh fruits, herbs and aromatics which are their natural partners

ROAST QUAIL WITH GRAPES

For this straightforward and subtly-flavoured dish, the quail are wrapped in vine leaves and pork fat, and roasted with grapes and a moistening of semi-sweet Vouvray wine from the Loire.

This preparation (or any other, for that matter) is not worth making with anything other than the best young quail: freshly-killed, dry-plucked fowl, raised by small producers who feed their birds with a mixture rich in grain and protein, and rear them in clean, non-intensive conditions.

In London, worthwhile fresh quail are available at Harrods, and from restaurant suppliers Snipe & Grouse who welcome private customers at their shop in the Chelsea Farmers Market. It is wise to telephone first (01-376 8514) in order to ensure that the necessary quail are available.

In certain parts of the country, it is possible to find poulterers selling birds of quality, and in addition, good small producers.

Unsalted butter
4 best quail, weighing 3–4 oz (75–125 g) each, oven-ready and trussed
12 fresh vine leaves (if available), washed and dried
4 rectangles of thinly-sliced pork back fat
Small bunch white or 'flame'-coloured grapes
½ pint (300 ml) semi-sweet, non-sparkling young Vouvray
Salt and freshly-ground black pepper

Butter breast and thighs of each bird, wrap a stemless leaf round each breast, and tie on a piece of back fat. Place birds, breast up, in an ovenproof dish with a low side.

Halve and, if necessary, seed grapes, and place half of these in vessel with the quail. Pour on about one third of the wine, and centre dish in a 450°F (230°C, gas mark 8) oven. Put remaining grape halves into a small, heavy saucepan with the rest of the wine, and simmer for several minutes until fruit has just cooked. Retrieve grapes from the saucepan with a slotted spoon and keep in a warm place.

After quail have roasted for 15 minutes, carefully cut string that secures their barding fat, remove this – together with vine leaves – and return birds to the oven for 10 minutes, to allow their breasts to brown attractively.

When quail are ready, reserve them in warmth, add grapes from the ovenproof dish to the previously-simmered quantity and set aside. Add roasting juices to the saucepan containing wine and grape juice, degrease, and reduce the liquid by one third. Then, as this simmers briskly, beat in about 1 oz (25 g) butter and season sauce to taste.

Cut trussing string from quail, season birds, and serve 2 per plate on the optional vine leaves, flanked by grapes. Pass sauce separately.
Serves 2.   AWS

Right *Roast quail with grapes, and (above) matuffi, a dish of polenta and meat sauce (see page 101)*

COLD STUFFED QUAIL

Stuffed quail are better poached than roasted. Poaching in stock keeps them plump and moist. Buy frozen boned quail for this recipe, which is then quite quick and not at all difficult. A lick of aspic improves their appearance.

12 boned quail
1 small onion, chopped
1 oz (25 g) butter or 2 tablespoon oil
½ oz (15 g) dried porcini mushrooms (boletus edulis)
6 oz (175 g) fresh mushrooms, finely chopped
1 small chicken breast, diced
Chopped tarragon and parsley
Salt and freshly-ground black pepper
1 pint (600 ml) chicken stock
1 packet aspic
1 tablespoon balsamic or red wine vinegar
4 tablespoons madeira
12 leaves flat parsley

Cold stuffed quail

Cook the onion in the butter until it is soft, but not brown. While the onion is cooking, put the dried *porcini* in a bowl and pour ½ pint (300 ml) boiling water over them. Leave them to soak.

Add the chopped fresh mushrooms to the onions, and when they have cooked down a little, add the chicken. Turn the mixture on a medium heat until the chicken is cooked and the mushrooms have given off some liquid and reabsorbed it. Drain and add the dried mushrooms, saving their soaking liquid. Season the mixture quite strongly with tarragon, parsley, salt and pepper – remember the taste will fade when the stuffing is cold. Turn the stuffing into a food processor and process it briefly. It should be very finely chopped, not a cream.

Open out the quail. Put about a tablespoon of stuffing into each bird, then reform them, closing them top and tail with wooden cocktail sticks.

Heat the stock and mushroom soaking liquid in a large shallow pan; when it boils, add the quail. Reduce the heat to simmering and cover the pan. Poach the quail for 15 minutes, drain and set aside to cool.

Make up the aspic, substituting the vinegar and madeira for part of the liquid specified on the packet. The aspic is ready when it has cooled to the syrupy stage and is just about to solidify. This can be achieved in moments if a small amount of warm aspic is put in a bowl resting in iced water. Paint the cold quail with aspic. Place one parsley leaf on each bird and give them another coat. Chill to serve.

Pour the remaining aspic into a dish to a depth of about ¼" (0.5 cm). This can be cubed and scattered between the quail on the serving dish.

Serves 6.   SCP

ROAST QUAIL IN BUCKWHEAT NOODLE NESTS WITH PINENUTS

Allow 1–2 birds per person, depending on appetites and menu.

4–6 quail (or poussin or young partridge)
2 tablespoons pinenuts
Sprigs of celery or bunch watercress

MARINADE
1 teaspoon sugar
½ teaspoon salt
1 tablespoon soy sauce
1 tablespoon vermouth or sherry
½ teaspoon grated fresh root ginger
1 teaspoon finely chopped shallot
1 teaspoon oil

BUCKWHEAT NOODLES
2 oz (50 g) buckwheat flour
8 oz (250 g) strong white flour
2 eggs
2 yolks
1 teaspoon pinenut, hazelnut or olive oil
1 teaspoon salt
1–2 tablespoons cold water if necessary

A little pinenut, hazelnut or olive oil

Roast quail in buckwheat noodle nests

Wipe the birds dry. Mix up the marinade, rub the birds with it and leave to marinate, turning from time to time, for 1–2 hours.

To make the buckwheat noodles, process the flours, eggs and yolks, oil and salt in a food processor until crumbly, then gradually drip in water as the mixture processes until it forms polystyrene-like granules which can be pressed together to form cohesive lumps. Press into 4–5 lumps and keep in a polythene bag.

Roll each piece through the pasta roller, set at its widest, until smooth; then progressively through thinner rollers to the thinnest-but-two setting. Lay on a cloth while you repeat with remaining pieces. Leave to dry for half an hour before cutting if you wish, or cook at once. Then pass through the fine noodle cutter and toss in piles on a tray. Alternatively make up the pasta by hand; knead for 5–10 minutes then roll out very thinly, flour well, roll up and cut into fine noodles. Shake out onto a tray.

Roast the quail for 18–20 minutes until done in a hot oven at 400°F (200°C, gas mark 6), brushing with marinade frequently. If necessary, they can be left in a switched-off or very low oven (under 200°F, 95°C, gas mark ¼, so the birds do not go on cooking or dry out) for up to half an hour.

Fry the pinenuts in a little oil until golden.

At the last minute, toss the noodles into plenty of boiling, salted water to which a teaspoon or so of vegetable oil has been added. Boil for 3–5 minutes until 'al dente' then drain. Toss the noodles, seasoning and pinenuts with their oil in the roasting pan juices. Form mounds of noodles into nests on a serving dish and top each nest with a roast bird. Tuck in sprigs of celery leaf or watercress and serve at once.

Serves 4–6.   NC

CHICKEN BREASTS WITH FRESH CORIANDER SAUCE

Simply cooked chicken with a positively-flavoured, low fat sauce.

6 chicken breasts, with skin
Salt and freshly ground black pepper
¾ pint (450 ml) chicken stock
3 fl oz (75 ml) dry vermouth
1 shallot, finely chopped
12 oz (350 g) fromage blanc
Leaves and fine stems from a small bunch (about
    ¼ oz or 7 g) fresh coriander
Salt and freshly ground black pepper

Season the chicken breasts and grill skin-side uppermost for 4 minutes. Turn them over using tongs and grill for a further 4 minutes.

Meanwhile, boil the vermouth with the shallot in a frying pan until only 1 tablespoon remains. Add the stock and boil until the liquid is reduced to 1½ fl oz (45 ml).

At the same time, chop about a third of the coriander and purée with the fromage blanc. Lower the heat beneath the stock and stir in the fromage blanc purée until warmed through, but do not allow it to boil. Season to taste. Cover and remove from the heat.

Skin the chicken and slice or leave whole, as preferred. Spoon some of the sauce onto 6 warmed plates, place the chicken on top and trickle the remaining sauce over the breasts. Garnish with the rest of the coriander leaves, and serve with new potatoes and young broad beans.

Serves 6.   HW

VINEGAR CHICKEN

Volaille au vinaigre is one of the classic dishes of France. The trick is in the properly jointed chicken (you could buy these ready-prepared, but not just quarters) and in the professional finish to the sauce. This is a typical reduction sauce from which the cooking butter is skimmed and fresh butter whisked in to 'monte' or thicken the reduced juices. It is a principle that can be applied to any sauté dish, meat or fish, and well worth accomplishing. Serve with fresh tagliatelle.

> *2 × 2½ lb (1.2 kg) chickens jointed into 8*
>   *pieces*
> *4 cloves garlic – crushed*
> *4 oz (125 g) butter*
> *5 tablespoons wine vinegar*
> *5 tablespoons white wine*
> *1 tablespoon tomato purée*
> *5 tablespoons stock*
> *Salt*
> *Pepper*

Season the chicken joints and sauté quickly with the garlic in the butter, turning to brown lightly. Remove from the pan. Deglaze the pan with the wine and wine vinegar. Add tomato purée and stock to the pan and return the chicken joints. Cover and simmer gently for 30 minutes till tender but firm. Remove pieces and skim surplus butter (use a jug so that you can see the butter floating on the top). Reduce remaining liquid by half at the most. Add 2 oz (50 g) butter in small pieces, whisking as for *hollandaise* or *beurre blanc*. Pour the sauce over arranged pieces of chicken and sprinkle with a little chopped parsley.

Serves 8.   AN

CHICKEN BREASTS IN WATERCRESS SAUCE

At its best in early spring and summer, the peppery flavour of watercress adds a tangy freshness to this simple dish.

> *12 oz (350 g) chicken breasts*
> *3 oz (75 g) butter*
> *1 tablespoon oil*
> *2 bunches watercress*
> *6 tablespoons double cream*
> *1 teaspoon lemon juice*
> *Salt*
> *Pepper*

Cut across the chicken breasts to give 1″ (2.5 cm) slices. Heat 1 oz (25 g) butter with the oil and cook the chicken pieces over low heat until cooked through and slightly golden. Meanwhile, remove the base of the stems from the watercress, and cook the rest in boiling water for 5 minutes. Drain and dry well and chop finely.

Lift the chicken pieces on to a warm serving dish. Add the watercress to the cooking juices in the pan, with the remaining butter. Simmer for 3 minutes. Stir in the cream, lemon juice, salt and pepper. Pour over the chicken pieces and serve at once with rice or vegetables.

Serves 4.   MN

SWEET SOY CHICKEN

This is a simple and delicious way to transform an average chicken into a tasty dish. Ideally, marinate it in the sauce for a couple of hours, or overnight if more convenient.

3½ lbs (1.5 kg) fresh chicken, jointed into 4 or 8
Salt and ground black pepper

MARINADE
4 tablespoons light soy sauce
3 tablespoon clear honey
2 tablespoons dry sherry
2 cloves garlic, crushed
1 tablespoon fresh grated root ginger
2 tablespoons sesame oil
1 tablespoon sunflower oil

Mix all the marinade ingredients together, then pour over the chicken joints. Rub well in, cover and leave to marinate in the fridge.

Place the joints and marinade in a wide shallow ovenproof dish. Season and bake at 375°F (190°C, gas mark 5) for 30 minutes, turning occasionally and basting with the juices, which should gradually reduce down to a dark golden syrup.

Serve the joints hot or chilled with a salad, ideally one containing some unusual salad leaves.

Serves 4.

NOTE This is also an excellent barbecue sauce, but will burn easily if cooked for too long, so par-bake in the oven for half the time and finish over glowing charcoal.   RD

CASSEROLE OF PARTRIDGE WITH RED CABBAGE

Casseroled partridge with cabbage is a dish that appears in many Continental recipe books, from Spain through to Poland. It is particularly suitable for older birds or ones that have been frozen for some months, as the vegetables and liquids help to prevent the birds from becoming too dry. Pheasant can be cooked in the same way.

2 large partridges
2 oz (50 g) butter
Salt and ground black pepper
1 small red cabbage
1 onion
1 small cooking apple
About 8 juniper berries, crushed
¼ pint (150 ml) dry red wine
¼ pint (150 ml) game or poultry stock
2 teaspoons sugar

Truss the birds, then place in a large casserole and smear with the butter, particularly over the breast. Season well. Roast uncovered at 400°F (200°C, gas mark 6) for about 15 minutes until browned.

Shred the cabbage and blanch in boiling water for a minute or two. Drain. Slice the onion, core and slice the apple.

Remove the partridges from the casserole, place the cabbage, onion and apple on the base and scatter over the juniper berries and sugar. Pour over the wine and stock, then season.

Return the birds to sit on top of the vegetables. Baste with any juices and pour over the wine and

Sweet soy chicken with bitter salad leaves

stock. It helps to cover the breasts with butter paper during cooking to stop them from drying out. Cover and return to the oven at 350°F (180°C, gas mark 4) for at least another 30 minutes or until tender. This will depend on the age of the birds.

Cut the birds in half along the breast to serve. Drain the cabbage mixture and thicken the sauce with a little cornflour, if liked, or simply serve the vegetable mixture unthickened. Creamed or boiled potatoes or fresh pasta will accompany this winter dish nicely.

Serves 4.   RD

CHICKEN AND HAM BURGOO WITH CORN BREAD

The traditional dish of the American state of Kentucky, burgoo should really be made with squirrel meat, for the sake of authenticity. However, chicken and ham seem more acceptable substitutes for this hearty one-pot meal. It can be cooked outside, in keeping with the American tradition of cook-outs, but is probably easier to cook indoors and reheat over the barbecue in a flameproof pot.

Chicken and ham burgoo with cornbread

1 × 2 lb (1 kg) joint smoked collar bacon
1 × 2½ lb (1.25 kg) chicken
½ teaspoon cayenne pepper
8 oz (250 g) carrots, sliced
8 oz (250 g) potatoes, diced
1 large onion, chopped
3 sticks celery, sliced
14 oz (400 g) can tomatoes
8 oz (250 g) broad beans
4 oz (125 g) cabbage, shredded
8 oz (250 g) sweetcorn kernels
8 oz (250 g) okra, scrubbed and trimmed
1 tablespoon Worcestershire sauce
1 small green pepper, diced
Fresh chopped parsley, to garnish

If the bacon is not lightly cured, you may need to soak it overnight in cold water. Cover the meats with at least 6 pints fresh water, bring to the boil and simmer for about 1 hour. Allow the meats to cool in the liquid, then remove, dice and reserve. Skim any fat from the top.

Return the stock to the pan with the cayenne, carrots, potatoes, onions, celery and tomatoes. (No need for salt as the stock will have salt from the bacon.) Simmer for 15 minutes then add the other vegetables (except the green pepper), the diced meats and Worcestershire sauce. Simmer for a further 10 minutes. Stir in the green pepper, ladle onto plates sprinkled with parsley and serve with slices of buttered cornbread.

Serves 8.

CORNBREAD
7 oz (200 g) yellow cornmeal
3 oz (75 g) plain flour
4 teaspoons baking powder
1 teaspoon salt
3 teaspoons caster sugar
2 size 3 eggs
½ pint (300 ml) milk
2 tablespoons oil

Blend everything to a smooth batter in a processor or blender. If made by hand, beat the liquid ingredients gradually into the dry.

Pour into a well-greased, 8″ (20 cm) sandwich

tin and bake at 400°F (200°C, gas mark 6) for approximately 30–35 minutes. RD

CHICKEN BREASTS BRAISED WITH BACON, CELERIAC, CARROTS AND PEARL ONIONS

In this simple, braised dish, the celeriac mingles with all the other ingredients so that their flavours enhance each other. You can prepare it mostly ahead and do the final braising soon before serving.

4 strips streaky bacon, diced
2 large chicken breasts, halved and boned
8 pearl onions
1 large carrot
½ celeriac bulb
¼ pint (150 ml) chicken stock
¼ teaspoon dried thyme
2 tablespoons chopped fresh parsley

Cook the bacon in a flameproof casserole or pan, tossing to brown it on all sides. Drain and reserve. In the remaining fat and over medium heat, cook the chicken breasts on both sides until the skin is golden brown.

Meanwhile, peel the onions and cut a shallow cross into the root ends. Peel and cube the carrot and celeriac; each should measure about 6 oz (175 g) in weight. When the chicken is browned, reserve it on a plate. Leaving 2 tablespoons of fat in the pan, lower the heat and brown the onions, stirring to colour them evenly. Put them with the chicken. Cook the root vegetables in the fat (add a little butter if necessary), stirring until lightly browned.

Pour in the stock and stir up to deglaze the dark crusty bits on the bottom. Return the chicken to the pan and surround with the bacon, vegetables and herbs. Cover with a lid or piece of foil and simmer 10 minutes. Uncover and simmer about 10 minutes longer, until the chicken is cooked through but still tender and springy to the touch.

Arrange the chicken on warm serving plates and, with a slotted spoon, put the vegetables and bacon around. Over high heat reduce the braising liquid until concentrated in flavour and thickened in texture. Nap the chicken with this sauce and serve with boiled potatoes or another starch.

Serves 4. ER

SAFFRON-SCENTED WHOLE CHICKEN

Even tiny quantities of saffron have the ability to give striking yellow-orange colour and a warm, flowery sweetness to huge dishes of risotto, paella and bouillabaisse. Here it imparts the same qualities to a whole chicken.

This dish is delicate, delicious and very simple. Saffron adds such a taste of luxury that you need not hesitate to serve it for a special meal.

3 lb (1.5 kg) fresh chicken
¼ teaspoon saffron threads
Pinch of salt
2 oz (50 g) unsalted butter, softened
1 small carrot, quartered
1 shallot, halved
1 small stick of celery
Bouquet garni
Sprigs of chervil for garnish

Gently heat the saffron in a heavy non-stick pan for about 5 minutes. Crush the saffron and beat it into the butter. Place a knob of the saffron-flavoured butter in the cavity of the chicken and rub the remainder over the skin. Place the chicken in a steaming basket and cover with a tight-fitting lid. Steam the chicken over about 440 ml/14 fl oz of gently boiling water – to which the vegetables and bouquet garni have been added – for about an hour. Place the steaming basket, with the chicken still inside, on a large warm plate and keep warm.

Strain the liquid and taste to see if it should be reduced to concentrate the flavours. Check and adjust seasoning.

Slice the chicken and serve accompanied by the juices and garnished with sprigs of chervil.

Serves 4. HW

POULET EN COCOTTE A L'AIL

A true French bourgeois dish with a glorious aroma of garlic. Use the best corn-fed chicken you can find (though this is a marvellous treatment for any chicken) and firm fresh garlic. You can get this all prepared and leave it ready for the oven. Then pop it in and forget it until ready to serve. The garlic is surprisingly delicate treated in this way so don't be afraid of using this quantity.

3½ lb chicken
1–2 heads garlic
4–5 tablespoons olive oil
¼ teaspoon Pernod
3–4 slices stale French bread
A good bunch of herbs (3 sprigs fennel, 2 sprigs
*   rosemary, 3 sprigs thyme and a little*
*   marjoram)*
1 bay leaf
Salt and pepper

HUFF PASTE
8 oz (250 g) plain flour
5 fl oz (150 g) water
½ teaspoon salt

Whisk together 2 tablespoons oil and the Pernod. Dry the bread in a low oven until crisp. Rub 1–2 cloves of garlic, cut in half, over both sides of the bread, then moisten them with the Pernod-oil, season with salt and pepper and pop inside the chicken. Rub the dry chicken all over with the remaining Pernod-oil.

To make the huff paste, mix the flour, salt and water to a stiff paste, knead until smooth and use to seal the casserole.

In a casserole (preferably earthenware) place 2–3 tablespoons olive oil just to cover the bottom. Make a bed of herbs on this and scatter over the cloves of garlic, separated but unpeeled. Lay the chicken on this, breast up, season with salt and pepper and cover with the lid. Seal the lid in place with huff paste. Set the casserole to cook in a hot oven at 450°F (230°C, gas mark 8) for 1¼ hours. Remove the lid of the casserole at the table so that

Poulet en cocotte à l'ail

you catch the wonderful trapped aroma, and carve the chicken. Serve 2–3 of the cloves of garlic with each serving. Pressed from its paper skin, the purée is mild and delicious.

Serves 4–6.   NC

CHICKEN IN A BOTTLE OF WORCESTERSHIRE SAUCE

Although fairly spicy, this dish is no hotter than a medium-strength curry or Mexican chilli. It is simply chicken breasts marinated in a bottle of Worcestershire sauce, which can be done before you shoot off to work, and then baked in the oven just before the guests turn up.

6 chicken breasts, boned and skinned
5 fl oz (142 ml) bottle Worcestershire sauce
About 4 tablespoons sesame seeds
2 oz (50 g) butter, melted

Put the chicken breasts in a polythene food bag and pour in the sauce. Rub well in, seal the bag and leave to marinate in the fridge for about 6–8 hours.

Drain off the Worcestershire sauce and discard, then coat the breasts on both sides with sesame seeds, pressing them well in. (It doesn't matter much if they are not completely covered.) Lay them in a shallow roasting dish and dribble over the melted butter.

When you are nearly ready to sit down and eat, bake the breasts at 375°F (190°C, gas mark 5) for about 20 minutes, until just cooked.

Cut each breast into slices for an attractive presentation. Baked potatoes, or a bowl of buttered basmati rice, together with an interesting green salad, would be appropriate accompaniments.

Serves 6.   RD

GOOSE LEGS WITH CABBAGE

This hearty winter casserole is an especially popular dish in North Germany.

2 goose legs
1 oz (25 g) fat or goose dripping
2 large onions, chopped
2 lb (1 kg) white cabbage, finely sliced
1 tablespoon wine vinegar
1 dessertspoon brown sugar
4 crushed juniper berries
¼ pint (150 ml) white stock
¼ pint (150 ml) dry white wine
Pepper and salt

Brown the legs in the fat. Add the onions, and continue cooking until they have softened. Add all the other ingredients, season then simmer until the legs are tender. Take out the legs, remove all the bones then dice the meat and put it back in the pot. Reheat and serve with plenty of boiled potatoes.

Serves 4–5.   BGM

GOOSE NECK SAUSAGE

In Eastern and Northern Europe, this is considered one of the best ways to enjoy goose liver. A similar dish exists in the Quercy region of France.

1 goose neck

STUFFING
1 goose liver
8 oz (250 g) streaky bacon
1 small onion
2 tablespoons cooked rice
1 beaten egg
Pepper and salt
3 fl oz (90 ml) sherry or Madeira
Strong stock for cooking

Clean and bone the neck, then sew up one end. Stiffen the liver in a little fat, and mince together with the streaky bacon and onion. Add the rice, mix well together, bind with the egg, and season to taste. Stir in sherry or Madeira. Stuff neck loosely and sew up the open end.

Simmer neck gently in the stock for 50–60 minutes. Remove and allow to cool. Flatten slightly by leaving the sausage between two boards with a weight on top. Slice when cold, having pulled out the sewing threads first.

Serve as a starter, for 6–8.   BGM

PRESERVED GOOSE

Confit d'oie is the basis of cassoulets. It can be used to give a unique flavour to casseroles and stews.

2 lb (1 kg) uncooked, jointed goose legs and
  wings
1 oz (25 g) sea salt
1 dessertspoon allspice or mixed spice
Fat, preferably goose fat or pure pork lard

Mix salt and spice together. Rub it well into the meat. Put the meat in a container, cover with foil and leave in a cool place for at least 48 hours.

Brush off surplus salt and spice mixture. Arrange the meat in a terrine, and pour over enough melted fat to cover the joints. Cook with the lid on at 240°F (120°C, gas mark ¼) until the meat is tender – about 2½–3 hours.

Drain joints and arrange in an earthenware

storage jar. Strain the fat over the meat to cover it completely – make certain the fat is at least ¼" (0.5 cm) above the joints to seal them hermetically. Cover the confit and store in the refrigerator.

The goose will keep for several months but, when using only one or two pieces of the confit, make sure that the rest is covered with the fat so it will keep. Duck can be preserved in the same way.

BGM

COUNTRY CASSOULET

A French bean and meat casserole with many local variations, this is best made the day before eating, and then reheated.

> 1–1½ lb (500–750 g) haricot beans
> 4 oz (125 g) smoked ham rind cut in ½" (1 cm) squares
> 2 medium onions, chopped
> 2 cloves of garlic, crushed
> 2 lb (1 kg) diced stewing lamb
> 4 oz (125 g) streaky bacon, chopped
> 1 lb (500 g) Toulouse or other spicy sausages, cut in thick slices
> 8 oz (250 g) preserved goose (confit d'oie)
> Goose fat or lard
> ½–1 pint (300–600 ml) strong meat stock
> Pepper and salt
> 3 tablespoons tomato purée
> Bouquet garni
> Fine white breadcrumbs for topping

Soak the beans overnight in unsalted water. Fry the ham rind until the fat runs, add the beans and the water in which they were soaked, and simmer gently for about 1 hour – the rind should disintegrate during cooking, but adds flavour.

In the meantime, soften the onions and garlic in a heavy, fireproof casserole. Add all the meats and brown lightly. Add the beans, their liquor, and enough meat stock to cover. Stir in the tomato purée and put in the bouquet garni. Season highly. Cover closely, and cook slowly in the oven at 240°F (120°C, gas mark ¼) for at least 2 hours. Check

from time to time and add more stock if necessary.

Remove lid, cover with the breadcrumbs, dot with fat and cook until topping is brown. A hearty red wine accompanies this well.

Serves 6–8.

BGM

SWEDISH ROAST GOOSE

This method of cooking goose keeps the flesh moist without retaining too much fat.

> 1 young goose weighing 6–8 lb (3–4 kg)
> Pepper and salt
>
> STUFFING
> 1 lb (500 g) cooking apples, peeled, cored and chopped
> 15–20 prunes, pitted and stewed
> 1 teaspoon powdered cloves
> 1 finely chopped onion, parboiled for 10 minutes in a little water
> Pepper and salt

Remove neck, giblets and wing tips from goose, and set aside for use in other dishes. Cut out surplus fat from inside vent end (to be rendered and used for pastry or as a spread).

Rub the inside of the bird with pepper and salt. Mix stuffing ingredients together and use to stuff goose body. Sew up, or skewer. Prick the breast all over to allow fat to escape. Heat the oven to 400°F (200°C, gas mark 6). Start roasting with the breast down on a grid over a little water in the meat dish. After half an hour, when the fat runs, pour the liquid off, pour in more hot water, and continue roasting with the breast up. Cook until tender, about 2–2½ hours, basting frequently.

When nearly done, pour 4 tablespoons ice-cold water over the breast, and leave oven door slightly open to make the skin crisp. The Swedes

Right (from top) Country cassoulet; Swedish roast goose; ingredients for country cassoulet; goose eggs

carve the breast in strips, reassemble it, reheat, and serve with red cabbage and roast potatoes.

NOTE Alternatively, roast the goose as above but stuff with 5 or 6 large leeks, chopped and seasoned to taste. Serve the leeks with the bird.

Serves 6–8. BGM

RABBIT IN FILO PASTRY WITH BACON AND RED ONION SAUCE

Crisp parcels of filo pastry enclosing flavoursome rabbit morsels.

1 rabbit
1 medium onion, chopped
1 medium carrot, chopped
1 stick celery, chopped
2 bay leaves
12 fl oz (350 ml) white wine
2 oz (50 g) butter

Rabbit in filo pastry with bacon and red onion sauce

2 oz (50 g) flour
12 sheets of filo pastry
Clarified butter or oil
3½ oz (100 g) bacon, cut in thin strips
3½ oz (100 g) red onion, thinly sliced
1 oz (25 g) butter
½ pint (300 ml) cream

Place the rabbit in a suitably-sized casserole dish with the chopped onion, carrot, celery and bay leaves. Add the white wine, and top up with water if necessary just to cover. Cover and braise for 2–2½ hours.

Reserve 1 pint (600 ml) of the stock, and leave the rabbit to cool. Remove the flesh from the rabbit, cover and refrigerate. Melt the butter and add the flour to make a roux. Cool slightly, add the reserved stock, bring to the boil and simmer for 10 minutes, then cool and refrigerate. When sauce and rabbit are chilled, combine the two.

Lay 3 sheets of filo pastry on top of each other. Brush the top sheet with melted, clarified butter (oil is a perfectly suitable alternative), then fold the bottom edge of the 3 sheets back over about 2″ (5 cm). Place a quarter of the rabbit mix on the folded section, fold the sides over, brush with clarified butter, and roll up. Brush the top with clarified butter and place on a baking tray.

Repeat with the remaining ingredients, to finish with 4 parcels. Bake for 20–25 minutes at 400°F (200°C, gas mark 6).

For the sauce, sauté the bacon and red onion for one minute with a touch of butter. Then add the cream and reduce. Season to taste.

Serves 4. PM

RABBIT WITH MUSTARD

The British are not very adventurous when it comes to eating rabbit, but the French, especially in the rural areas, enjoy rabbit dishes a great deal. The meat is fresh, lean and succulent, as well as being cheap and readily available.

Rabbit is particularly well complemented with a creamy mustard sauce.

2 tablespoons vegetable oil
6 rabbit portions, thawed if frozen
8 oz (250 g) green streaky bacon
8 oz (250 g) shallots, peeled
1 tablespoon flour
¼ pint (150 ml) light stock or water
2 tablespoons Dijon mustard
Salt and ground black pepper
¼ pint (150 ml) single cream
Sprigs fresh tarragon or parsley

Heat the oil in a large frying-pan, and brown the rabbit portions. Remove to a casserole dish. Add the streaky bacon rashers, cut in half if liked, and the shallots. Brown lightly and add these to the casserole. Sprinkle in the flour, stir up and pour in the wine, stock or water, mustard and seasonings. Bring to the boil, stirring well. Allow to simmer for a minute or two, then pour over the rabbit. Cover and cook at 350°F (180°C, gas mark 4) for about 1 hour.

When tender, remove the rabbit to a serving dish and pour the cream into the sauce. Stir well, reheat gently but do not allow to boil, then serve spooned over the rabbit. Looks pretty garnished with fresh tarragon or parsley.

Serves 4–6.   RD

COLD DUCK WITH ORANGE AND MINT JELLY

The amount of gelatine you will need for this recipe depends on how jellied the stock is. After the gelatine has been added, spoon a small amount of the liquor onto a saucer and place it in the refrigerator to set (the jelly should be very light).

4 tablespoons dry white vermouth
5 fl oz (150 ml) Seville orange juice
Finely grated rind of 1 Seville orange
7 fresh mint leaves, broken
1 pint (600 ml) jellied chicken stock
1 egg white
1 egg shell, crushed
3–4 teaspoons clear honey, to taste

Approximately 2 teaspoons gelatine
1 cooked duck, about 4½ lb (2 kg), jointed or
   boned
Mint leaves for decoration

Boil vermouth until syrupy. Stir in orange juice and rind, mint and stock. Whisk in egg white and shell, and bring slowly to the boil, whisking constantly. Take off heat and leave for 5 minutes. Carefully make a hole in crust on the surface of the liquor, then ladle out the liquor, taking care not to disturb the crust.

Dissolve honey in a little of the heated liquor, then stir into the remaining liquid. Place gelatine in a small bowl, stir in a little liquor, and leave for 5 minutes. Place the bowl over a saucepan of hot water until the gelatine has melted, then, off the heat, stir in the remaining liquor. Add seasoning, and more honey, if necessary, to taste. Leave until just on the point of setting.

If the duck you are using has been jointed, put the pieces on a rack placed over a tray, and spoon a little of the liquor over the meat. Leave aside to set.

Position the mint leaves for the decoration on the portions, and apply 2 or 3 more coats of still just-liquid liquor, allowing each to set before adding the next. Leave any remaining liquor to set, then chop and serve around the duck.

If the duck flesh is off the bone, put the pieces of duck into a bowl, spoon the liquor over and fork through the duck gently. Leave until the liquor is just beginning to set, then carefully transfer the duck to 4 serving plates. Garnish with mint, warm the remaining liquor so it is just liquid and spoon over the duck. Leave to set before serving.

Serves 4.   HW

DUCK BREASTS WITH ORANGE, ONIONS AND TURNIPS

This recipe uses French boned duck breast – magret – and, with a vegetable accompaniment, all it needs is a little pasta or crusty rolls to mop up the juices, and perhaps a watercress and chicory salad.

Hannah Glasse's dressed duck (at left); lamb tagine (see page 81); rabbit with mustard (see page 64)

6 boned duck breasts
1 large Spanish onion, peeled and chopped
8 oz (250 g) baby turnips, topped and tailed,
    then diced
1 clove garlic, crushed
1 orange, strips of peel from half the fruit and all
    the juice
3 tablespoons dry sherry
Good pinch dried sage
Good pinch sugar
Salt and ground black pepper

Heat a large, heavy-based frying pan without oil,
until it feels really quite hot when you hold your
hand above it. Slash the duck breasts a number of
times on the skin side, then place skin side down in
the pan. This ensures that the fat runs out (there is
no need for any extra) and gives a nice dark
browned skin. Fry for about 5 minutes, then flip
over and cook on the other side, for about 3 minutes if you like your duck pink, or longer if you
prefer it more cooked. Season lightly in the pan,
then take off the heat and keep warm in a low oven.

Pour off all but about 2 tablespoons of the fat
that has run out and sauté the onions, turnips and
garlic for 3 minutes, stirring once or twice. Meanwhile, scrape the pith off the orange peel and cut
into julienne strips. Add these to the pan along with

the juice, sherry, sage, sugar and seasoning.

Bubble up the sauce, cover and cook gently for another five minutes or until the turnips are just cooked. Serve the vegetables spooned alongside the duck breasts.

Serves 6. RD

HANNAH GLASSE'S DRESSED DUCK

We seem to think of cooking with lettuce as rather French, yet the eighteenth-century English cookery writer, Hannah Glasse, in her *Art of Cookery Made Plain and Easy*, uses lettuce when slow-cooking a duck. She specified a whole duck, but few modern frying-pans are large enough to brown a large duck, so use quarters instead.

4 duck quarters or 5 lb (2.25 kg) duck, quartered
Flour, to dust
1 oz (25 g) butter
1 dessertspoon vegetable oil (not in the original recipe, but it does stop the butter from burning)
1 firm round lettuce, shredded
12 oz (350 g) garden peas
½ pint (300 ml) good gravy, or strong giblet stock flavoured with a little dry sherry
A small bunch sweet herbs – marjoram, thyme, parsley and sage
½ teaspoon ground mace or nutmeg
Salt and ground black pepper
1 egg yolk
3 tablespoons double cream
Few sprigs fresh mint, to garnish

Remove as much loose fat as possible from the duck quarters, then dust with flour. Heat the butter and oil in a large heavy frying-pan and brown the quarters. Remove and drain well.

Sprinkle the base of a large casserole dish with the shredded lettuce and peas and lay the duck on top. Pour over the gravy or stock, snip over the fresh sweet herbs (out of season, use a good pinch of dried marjoram, thyme and sage but fresh par-

sley), sprinkle over the mace or nutmeg and season well. Cover and cook at 350°F (180°C, gas mark 4) for about ¾ to 1 hour or until tender.

With a slotted spoon, remove the duck and vegetables to a large serving platter. Pour the stock into a small saucepan.

Beat the egg yolk and cream and blend into the stock. Reheat gently, stirring continually until slightly thickened, but do not allow to boil. Pour over the duck. Garnish with chopped mint.

Serves 4. RD

BARBARY DUCK WITH GREEN OLIVES

A classic dish from Provence.

1 Barbary duck weighing 10 lb (4.5 kg)
7 oz (200 g) green olives
3½ oz (100 g) smoked bacon, diced
7 oz (200 g) button mushrooms, sliced
2 large onions, peeled and minced
4 cloves garlic, chopped finely
Olive oil
Bouquet garni; herbes de Provence
1 bottle white Côtes de Provence

Clean and section the duck. Place 4 tablespoons of olive oil in a fireproof casserole and brown duck on all sides. Remove duck and pour away oil. Lightly cook bacon in the same casserole and remove, discarding the fat produced. In the same casserole toss the minced onion. Cook mushrooms gently in a separate pan with a little oil, allowing their juice to evaporate. Set aside.

When onions are golden, add 1 tablespoon flour, stir and cook for 1 minute, then add the wine, stirring well. Season and add 2 pinches of *herbes de Provence* and a bouquet garni. Return duck, mushrooms and bacon to casserole, stir gently then simmer, uncovered, in a slow oven for 1–1½ hours. Half-way through cooking, add olives and garlic. When cooked, remove duck, skim fat from sauce, reduce if necessary, and serve.

Serves 6–8. SJW

MAINLY MEAT

Here are aromatic lamb dishes from Morocco
and the Middle East, traditional English ways
of cooking pork, and some inspired ideas
for capturing the richness of wild boar

POTTED RILLONS OF WILD BOAR

Boar is a seasonal meat, its dusky savour well suited to the winter months; a jarful of small morsels, preserved in the age-old manner, effectively extends the season and would make a distinctive Christmas, or Twelfth Night, present. Stay with the suggested cuts – the method ensures tenderness and intensity of flavour.

> 2–3 lb (1–1.5 kg) belly or shoulder of boar
> 4 oz (125 g) additional back-fat
> 1 tablespoon juniper salt
> 3 tablespoons water
> 1 fat, unpeeled clove of garlic
> 1 blade of mace
> 4 allspice berries
> 1 fresh or dried bay-leaf
> 2 sprigs of fresh thyme

Cut the meat into 1½″ (3.5 cm) cubes, trimming it carefully of any gristle and membrane. Dice the back-fat quite small. Mix both meats thoroughly with the juniper salt, cover and keep cool for 24 hours. After dry marinating the meat, discard any large pieces of juniper and any liquid which may have formed. Place the meat with the remaining ingredients in a flame-proof pot and bring the water to the boil. Include any bones removed in trimming the meat. Simmer the meat very gently – the liquid should hardly bubble – on top of the stove or in a low oven, 300°F (150°C, gas mark 2)

for 3 to 4 hours, or until the meat offers little resistance to a small skewer.

Once the meat is tender, drain the contents of the pan, reserving the fat but discarding the bones, mace, allspice and herbs. Transfer the meat to a heavy-based frying pan and toss quickly over a fairly high heat to caramelize the surface appetizingly (the flavour can take the addition of very little light, raw sugar at this stage, for a more pronounced caramel note). Either serve immediately – with sautéed potato or root vegetable purées and a sharpish sauce, or a hunk of good country bread and a little salad – or pot up for future use in the traditional manner.

Pack the browned meat into stoneware pots or glass jars and cover lightly until ready to coat with rendered fat. Strain reserved fat and juices through a fine sieve and cool, until the fat can be separated off and poured over the potted meat. Aim to cover the meat with a ½″ (1 cm) layer of fat. Cover and keep chilled until ready to use, when the fat should be melted down and the chunks of meat reheated in a little of the fat. Serve as above.

Serves 8 as a snack. SD

Right A feast of wild boar (clockwise from bottom right): Boar liver cooked in red wine and herbs; boar chops sauced with morello cherries and liquorice (centre) page 71; wild boar sausage with pickled walnuts and mushrooms; gilded apples, page 72; terrine of forest boar, page 70; leg of roast boar

TERRINE OF FOREST BOAR

Use an inexpensive, fat-rich cut for the forcemeat layer, lean fillet for the strips of marbling, It would be as well to order caul fat a week in advance.

2 lb (1 kg) boar loin, or other lean meat
1 lb (500 g) boar belly or shoulder
12 oz (350 g) flare fat ⎱ from
8 oz (250 g) smoked, streaky ⎰ range-reared
   bacon ⎰ pork
8 oz (250 g) caul fat
2 tablespoons juniper salt

WINE MARINADE
½ pint full-bodied red wine
1 tablespoon red wine vinegar
1 tablespoon virgin olive oil
2–3 diced, aromatic vegetables – white of leek,
   celery, carrot, parsnip as available
2 shallots, peeled and sliced

1 large garlic clove, peeled
6 juniper berries
2 allspice berries
2 black peppercorns
1 blade of mace
1 cinnamon stick
12 oz peeled, cooked chestnuts, soaked in
   3–4 tablespoons brandy
2 oz (50 g) dried forest mushrooms, soaked,
   rinsed, drained and chopped
1 small truffle, peeled and diced (optional)
2–3 peeled cloves of oven-baked garlic
12 juniper berries, crushed
½ teaspoon ground mace
½ teaspoon ground allspice
Grinding of milled black pepper
1 teaspoon sea salt

GLAZE
2 tablespoons Madeira
A little concentrated game stock
1 sheet leaf gelatine

Potted rillons of wild boar; recipe on page 68

Dice lean meat finely and cube fat meat roughly. Coat each type of meat with the juniper salt and store separately, cool and covered, for 12–24 hours.

Meanwhile, place wine marinade ingredients into a non-reactive saucepan, bring to the boil, and simmer gently for 15 minutes (the diced vegetables may be caramelized lightly in the oil before adding to the marinade, if time allows). Keep cool until needed.

Brush or rinse excess juniper salt off the meats, and strain the marinade over each type of meat, still keeping the two meats separate. Marinate meats for 12–36 hours as convenient.

Dice 8 oz (250 g) of the flare very finely and set aside. Soak the caul in vinegared warm water for 15 minutes to soften and deodorize, drain and pat dry, stretch it out gently and drape into a 2 pint (1.2 litre) terrine dish. Drain the marinaded meats thoroughly, discarding all but a spoonful of the wine marinade.

Mix together the diced lean meat, diced flare, and truffle, if using, and set aside.

Mince together finely the cubed fat meat,

remaining flare, smoked bacon, and about 4 oz (125 g) of the crumblier chestnuts, drained. Blend in (a food processor may be used for this stage as for the mincing) the garlic, spices and seasoning, reserved marinade and chestnut-soaking brandy, then gently stir in remaining chestnuts – whole if possible – and mushrooms. Layer the two types of meats in the terrine, beginning and ending with the minced meat, and mounding up in the centre. Bring the caul over and around the meat, tucking edges down the sides of the terrine.

Bake in a water-bath in a medium-hot oven, at 350°F (180°C, gas mark 4) for about an hour, or until juices run clear when a skewer is inserted, and the meat has pulled away from the sides of the dish.

Cool, then pour off and retain juices. Chill the terrine and juices separately. The terrine may be weighted if wished; this will make it easier to cut and serve, but the compacted meat will be a little less juicy. Strain off any juices and reserve.

To make the glaze, degrease reserved juices (which will probably have set). Heat and melt these gently and make up to ¼ pint (150 ml) with the Madeira and additional stock. Soak the leaf gelatine in a little warm water, and dissolve the softened gelatine thoroughly in the hot (but not boiling) juices. Chill until almost setting, then spoon over the terrine. Chill until one hour before serving.

Serves 12.   SD

CHOPS OR CUTLETS OF WILD BOAR SAUCED WITH MORELLO CHERRIES AND LIQUORICE ROOT

A simple treatment for any small, tender cuts and one which ensures the meat keeps well both before and after cooking, if need be. Dried morello cherries from America are now widely available at wholefood stores and good grocers.

4 chops or cutlets of boar, about 8 oz (250 g)
*   without bone, 10–12 oz (300–350 g) with*
*   bone*
1 tablespoon juniper salt (optional)

WINE MARINADE
½ pint (300 ml) full-bodied red wine
1 tablespoon balsamic vinegar
1 tablespoon muscovado sugar
1 stick liquorice root
1 fat clove of garlic, peeled
1 shallot, peeled and sliced
1 fresh bay leaf
6 juniper berries
2 allspice berries

MORELLO SAUCE
1 tablespoon dried morello cherries, soaked in
*   5 tablespoons red wine with ½ stick cinnamon*
½ pint (300 ml) game stock, or good chicken
*   stock*
1" (2.5 cm) piece unsweetened liquorice stick (or
*   2 small pieces sweetened liquorice)*
1–2 tablespoons wild fruit jelly
Salt and pepper
4 oz (125 g) stoned fresh morello cherries,
*   lightly cooked (optional)*

Trim meat of any excess fat and coat with juniper salt if wished. Meanwhile, make up the marinade by bringing all the ingredients to the boil, then simmering gently for about 15 minutes in a non-reactive saucepan. Wipe any salt off the meat and cover with cooled marinade. Keep covered and cold for 1–3 days.

Heat a little light oil in a heavy-based, deep frying pan. Drain and dry the meat, discarding the marinade. Sear and caramelize the chops or cutlets quickly over a fairly high heat, then fry gently for about 10 minutes on each side until nicely browned. Cover the pan and continue to cook the meat in its own juices over the lowest possible heat until tender – another 30 to 40 minutes, depending on thickness. Meanwhile simmer the soaked cherries and cinnamon gently in the wine for about 5 minutes and strain, separately reserving cherries and wine.

Transfer cooked meat to a warm plate and rest, covered, in a low oven. Deglaze the frying pan with the wine, scraping any sediment into the liquid. Add the stock and liquorice and reduce, stirring, until liquorice is dissolved, and the sauce a

Gilded apples

8 Cox Pippin apples, or sound Golden
   Delicious when necessary
8 oz (250 g) boar sausage-meat
2 oz (50 g) seedless raisins, soaked in
   2 tablespoons sweet Madeira
1½ oz (40 g) pinenuts, lightly toasted
1 teaspoon balsamic vinegar
Good pinch of powdered cinnamon
Good grating of nutmeg
1 rounded teaspoon muscovado sugar
A little boar-lard or butter
1 dessertspoon maple syrup or honey
Additional Madeira
1 yolk of egg, beaten with ½ teaspoon water
1 generous pinch powdered saffron

Core the whole apples, but do not peel. Score the skin of each once round the circumference and twice vertically from the top to the circumference line. Beat together the sausage-meat (remove skins from sausages and break down the filling), drained raisins, nuts, vinegar, spices and sugar and divide this filling between the apples, packing down until all the mixture is used up. Place the apples in a greased fireproof dish and pour in a spoonful of water. Dot the top of each apple with a little boar-lard or butter and dribble on maple syrup or honey and Madeira. Bake in a medium-hot oven for 35–55 minutes, until soft but not collapsed. Remove the dish from the oven and carefully strip the top half of peel off each apple. Beat together the egg yolk and saffron and brush this over the (peeled) top half of each apple. Replace in the oven for 5 minutes to 'gild'. Serve hot with roasts and hams, or on their own, with any rich juices collected in the dish.

Serves 8.   SD

little syrupy. Strain through a fine sieve into a fresh saucepan, add the reserved cherries and a little fruit jelly, and season to taste (unsweetened liquorice will demand more fruit jelly to balance flavours than will sweetened). Add any fresh, cooked cherries to the sauce, heat through, and transfer chops and sauce to a hot serving dish.

The chops will become more succulent for 15–20 minutes' resting. If making the dish in advance, cool cooked chops and sauce quickly and store in the refrigerator, reheating gently to serve.

Serves 4.   SD

GILDED APPLES

This recipe is in keeping with a centuries-old British predilection for blending the sweet and the savoury; use boar sausages for the filling, and make sure to 'dore with the yolks of eyroun', or brush with egg yolk for the effect of gilding.

MARTINMAS STEAKS

The feast of Martinmas, the patron saint of horsemen and all domestic animals, was celebrated in great style in Scotland until comparatively recently. November was the farmworkers' annual holiday, and the Saint's Day on the 11th heralded its beginning. The more benevolent farmers and landowners would kill a steer and distribute it among their employees and tenants and, for many of the poorer families, this was the only time they ate beef all year. A traditional dish for the richer elements of society was steaks made from minced venison and pork, dipped in egg and breadcrumbs, fried and served with redcurrant jelly or Cumberland sauce.

8 oz (250 g) venison
8 oz (250 g) pork belly
1 small onion
1 teaspoon dried thyme or 1 tablespoon fresh
*   thyme*
4 crushed juniper berries
1 tablespoon malt whisky
Salt and freshly milled black pepper
2 tablespoons seasoned flour
1 egg, beaten with 1 tablespoon water
3 oz (75 g) fresh white breadcrumbs
Oil or fat for frying

Finely mince the venison and pork or process thoroughly in a food processor. Grate the onion and add to the meat with the thyme, juniper berries, whisky and seasoning. Mix well and form into 4 flat cakes, about ½" (1 cm) thick.

Dip each steak in the seasoned flour, then the egg and finally the crumbs, so that they are evenly coated. Fry in shallow oil or fat over a medium heat for 12-15 minutes until golden brown. Drain well and serve piping hot with redcurrant jelly or Cumberland Sauce.

Serves 4.   JR

OSSO BUCO

This classic Italian casserole of shin of veal with wine and tomatoes is nothing without cremolata. Although cremolata is no more than a finely chopped mixture of parsley and garlic with grated lemon zest which is sprinkled onto the slowly cooked veal when it is served, the effect is astonishingly vibrant.

The freshness of the lemon is essential to the taste of the dish.

1 oz (25 g) clarified butter
3 lbs (1.5 kg) shin of veal cut in slices at least 1"
*   (2.5 cm) thick*
1 large tin (about 2 lbs/1 kg) Italian plum
*   tomatoes*
½ bottle dry, white Italian wine
Salt and freshly-ground black pepper
1 small clove garlic, very finely chopped
6 tablespoons finely chopped parsley
Finely grated zest of 1 lemon

Heat the butter in a large, heavy casserole and brown the veal pieces on both sides in two or three batches. Pack them into the casserole in one layer – so that the bone marrow which is one of the high spots of the dish does not slip out when the veal is cooked – and add the wine. Boil briskly until the wine is reduced by approximately half, then add the tomatoes and their juice. Leave the tomatoes whole and just pinch out the cores with your fingers. Add salt and pepper and cook, covered and very slowly on top of the stove or in a cool oven, at 275°F (140°C, gas mark 1) until the meat is melting off the bones.

Combine the garlic, parsley and lemon zest to make the cremolata.

Traditionally, osso buco is served with a saffron-flavoured risotto made with arborio rice. If you decide to serve it this way, you may wish to reduce the liquid in the casserole by fast boiling. However, it is excellent with creamed potatoes and with the sauce left pretty liquid. Either way, sprinkle each serving of meat with a generous spoonful of the cremolata.

Serves 6.   SCP

COLD VEAL WITH A LIGHT APRICOT SAUCE

Veal is excellent cold, especially served slightly pink, with a tangy fruit sauce. Use a rolled shoulder or fillet joint for this, not breast which tends to be rather fatty.

This dish is perfect for buffets, or after-theatre suppers, as it can be prepared ahead.

> *2–3 lb (1–1.5 kg) rolled joint of veal*
> *12 dried apricots*
> *½ pint (300 ml) light stock*
> *½ pint (300 ml) dry white wine*
> *1 teaspoon dried thyme*
> *About 6–8 thin rashers streaky bacon, derinded*
> *1 onion, sliced thinly*
> *1 tablespoon mango or other fruit chutney*
> *2–3 tablespoons fromage frais or natural yoghurt*
> *Salt and ground black pepper*
> *A few halved unsalted pistachios, to garnish*

Soak the apricots overnight in the stock and wine, then drain, reserving the liquid, and chop.

Season the joint, sprinkle over with half the thyme and press half the chopped apricots on top. Cover tightly with the bacon rashers.

Put the remaining apricots, onions and thyme in the base of a roasting pan and place the veal on top. Pour in the reserved liquid. Cover with foil. Roast at 375°F (190°C, gas mark 5) for 30 minutes per lb if you like your veal pink, plus 30 minutes for well done. Uncover the veal to brown for the last 20 minutes or so. Remove the veal and cool. Strain the pan liquid into a jug, cool and skim off any fat. Reserve the apricots and onion.

Purée the liquid with the pan apricots, onions and chutney, then adjust the seasoning. Stir in the fromage frais or yoghurt. Serve the veal sliced, with sauce, and scatter over the pistachios.

Serves 4–6. RD

QUICK SAUTE OF VEAL KIDNEYS

Kidneys are very much part of the traditional English breakfast, and delicious for lunch or supper.

> *1 veal kidney, about 8 oz (250 g)*
> *1½ oz (40 g) butter*
> *Juice 1 small orange*
> *1 teaspoon coarse grain mustard*

> *2 tablespoons medium dry sherry*
> *2 tablespoons single cream*
> *Salt and pepper*

TO SERVE
> *4–6 rashers lean streaky bacon, rinded*
> *1 large tomato, halved*
> *Olive oil, preferably garlic flavoured*
> *Fresh chopped parsley*

Peel the thin membrane from the kidney, cut into ½″ (1 cm) slices and snip out core with scissors.

Roll the bacon rashers neatly and skewer together. Halve the tomato, brush with oil and season. Grill both, turning the bacon once, then keep them warm.

Heat the butter in a sauté pan until foaming, then fry the slices of kidney for 2 to 3 minutes, turning occasionally until just done. Take care not to overcook.

Add the juice, mustard, sherry and seasoning. Simmer for two minutes until reduced by a third, then stir in the cream.

Serve immediately.

Serves 1–2. RD

SHROPSHIRE COLLARED PORK

There are a number of different ways of 'collaring' meat. Often the joint is simply sprinkled with a few herbs or spices, rolled up, tied with a piece of tape or string (like a collar) and boiled. Sometimes the meat is brined prior to cooking, or else, as in this recipe, it is brined for 24 hours after cooking.

FOR THE STUFFING
> *6 oz (175 g) fresh white breadcrumbs*
> *Grated rind of 1 lemon*
> *2 tablespoons chopped parsley*
> *2 teaspoons chopped fresh marjoram*
> *6 anchovy fillets, finely chopped*
> *1 teaspoon grated nutmeg*
> *1 egg, beaten*
> *Salt and freshly milled black pepper*

Quick sauté of veal kidneys

FOR THE MEAT
3 lb (1.5 kg) boned lean pork belly
1 pig's trotter
1 carrot, sliced
1 leek, sliced
1 stick celery, roughly chopped
About 12 peppercorns

FOR THE BRINE
1½ pints (900 ml) water
½ (300 ml) malt vinegar
1 oz (25 g) salt
1 oz (25 g) soft brown sugar
6 cloves

First make the stuffing. Put all the ingredients into a basin, bind with the egg, and season to taste.

Lay the meat out flat, spread evenly with the stuffing to within 1″ (2.5 cm) of the edge, then roll up and tie with string. Put into a pan with other meat ingredients, cover with water and bring to the boil. Skim off any scum, then cover and simmer gently for 2½ hours. Remove from the heat and allow to cool in the cooking liquor.

Heat brine ingredients gently until sugar has dissolved. Remove from heat. Place pork in a deep bowl, pour over cold brine and leave for 24 hours. Drain thoroughly and serve pork cold with salad.
Serves 8–10.   JR

PORK CHOPS IN MINT

Mint is normally associated with lamb, but it goes equally well with pork, as this old recipe of Eliza Acton's proves. Chopped fresh mint is mixed with flour to form a thick crust round the chops, which keeps them very moist during grilling, as well as giving a superb flavour.

¼ pint (150 ml) milk
2 oz (50 g) chopped fresh mint
2 oz (50 g) flour
Salt and freshly milled black pepper
4 pork chops

Pour the milk into a shallow plate. Mix together the mint, flour and seasoning. Dip each chop in the milk and then thickly coat with the flour and mint mixture. Put under a moderate grill and cook for 15 minutes, turning once.
Serves 4.   JR

SUFFOLK SOPS

Sops, or Spread Toasts as they are also known, are a direct descendant of medieval trenchers. Before platters were in general use in manor houses, large pieces of bread known as trenchers, about 5″ (13 cm) × 8″ (20 cm) and 1″ (2.5 cm) thick were used instead. The meat etc. was placed on them and the juices, gravies and sauces would soak or 'sop' into them.

The trenchers were not, however, generally eaten by those lucky enough to dine in such a grand manner, but were kept and handed on to the poor. Indeed, it was considered very bad manners to bite into your trencher and thus spoil the dinner of the less fortunate.

Ideally you should use sweet-cured Suffolk ham for this recipe, but failing that (and it is not easy to obtain) use a good quality cooked ham or even gammon off the bone.

Should you then have access to free-range eggs as well, you will have a feast of great simplicity fit for a king.

6 oz (175 g) cooked ham (see above)
4 tablespoons double cream
4 thick slices of bread
2 oz (50 g) butter
10 eggs
Salt and freshly milled black pepper

Finely chop the ham and put into a small saucepan with the cream. Heat gently. Toast the bread on both sides, then spread with the ham mixture and put into a warm oven while preparing the eggs. Melt the butter. Beat the eggs and season with a little salt and pepper. Add to the pan and scramble lightly, then quickly spoon the eggs over the ham mixture and serve at once.
Serves 4.   JR

GEORGIAN MARBLED TONGUE AND HAM

Potting meat, i.e. pressing it into a pot and then sealing it with clarified butter, lard or suet, was one of the earliest methods of food preservation. The addition of Worcestershire sauce is a modern adaptation, but it does improve the flavour.

8 oz (250 g) cooked tongue
8 oz (250 g) cooked ham or gammon
6 oz (175 g) softened butter
¼ teaspoon grated nutmeg
2 teaspoons Worcestershire sauce
Salt, if necessary, and black pepper

Finely mince the tongue and ham, or process separately in a food processor. Divide the butter in half, put into separate bowls and beat lightly. Add the tongue to one and the ham to the other and mix well. Season the tongue with the nutmeg and pepper. Add the Worcestershire sauce to the ham and

Right *(clockwise from right) Martinmas steaks, page 72; pork chops in mint; Suffolk sops (in foreground); pommes dorées, page 78; Georgian marbled tongue and ham; Cornish chicken and gammon pie, page 80*

beat again. Season both with salt if necessary.

Lightly butter a small dish. Spread a third of the tongue over the base, then cover with half the ham in small lumps, about the size of a walnut. Spread over another third of the tongue, then the last of the ham in lumps, and finally spread with the remaining tongue. Cover with a sheet of greaseproof paper or clingwrap, place a weight on top and leave for at least 4 hours in a cool place.

Serves 8 as a starter with hot toast or 6 as a main course with salad.   JR

POMMES DOREES

A medieval dish which, despite meaning golden apples in French, has nothing whatever to do with fruit. The origin is Norman, the *pommes* being little spicy balls of cooked pork and *dorées* referring to the practice of making food golden.

Pommes dorées were made golden by being dipped in crisp batter. It was usual for half the balls to be dipped in plain batter and the other half either to have parsley added to the batter or to be dipped in parsley after frying so that they were a brilliant green against plain gold.

> 1 lb (500 g) cooked pork
> 2 oz (50 g) currants
> ½ teaspoon ground ginger
> ¾ teaspoon ground mace
> 1 teaspoon soft brown sugar
> Salt and freshly milled black pepper
> 2 eggs, beaten
>
> FOR THE BATTER
> 3 oz (75 g) plain flour
> 1 oz (25 g) self-raising flour
> 1 egg
> ¼ pint (150 ml) milk
> 3 tablespoons very finely chopped parsley
> ½ teaspoonful salt

Finely mince the pork, add the currants, ginger, mace and soft brown sugar. Season well and bind

with the eggs. Lightly flour your hands and form the mixture into balls about 1½″ (4 cm) in diameter. Sift the flours with the salt. Make a well in the centre, add the egg and half the milk and beat to a smooth batter, then beat in the remaining milk. Divide the batter in half and stir the parsley into one half. Dip the pork balls into the batter then fry in deep fat until golden brown and crisp.

Serves 4.   JR

AMERICAN SUGAR-GLAZED HAM

A delicious treatment for a special home-cooked ham is to baste it during the final period of roasting with a sweet spicy glaze. The flavours are wonderfully complementary.

Quantities given are sufficient for a 10–12 lb (4.50–5.50 kg) ham joint; adjust proportionally for larger or smaller joints.

American sugar-glazed ham; ham and spinach roll; ham rolls à la basquaise

6 oz (175 g) muscovado or dark soft brown
  sugar
3 tablespoons maple syrup or clear honey
2 tablespoons cider vinegar
1 tablespoons mustard powder
Juice of 2 small oranges
Whole cloves, to stud

Mix all the glaze ingredients together well.

Cook the ham as usual. About three-quarters of an hour from the end of cooking, cut off the rind, score the fat with a sharp knife in a criss-cross pattern and stud with cloves.

Spoon over the glaze and return to the oven, basting about three times.

Cool the joint out of the pan. The glaze and juices can be used again if covered with a thin layer of melted fat and stored in the fridge for up to three weeks.   RD

HAM AND SPINACH ROLL

Served cold, this delicious pie is ideal for picnics or summer buffets.

1 × 13 oz (375 g) pack frozen puff pastry,
  thawed
8 oz (250 g) fresh spinach leaves, washed
8 oz (250 g) raw pork, minced
8 oz (250 g) lean raw ham, minced
1 medium onion, finely chopped
2 tablespoons fresh chopped parsley
½ teaspoon dried thyme
½ teaspoon dry sherry
3 tablespoons dry sherry
Grated rind ½ lemon
Salt and ground black pepper
3 hard-boiled eggs, peeled
Beaten egg, for glazing

Roll the pastry out thinly to a rectangle roughly 14 × 12″ (36 × 30 cm). Place on a baking sheet.

Cook the spinach briefly, then drain very well, squeezing dry between two dinner plates, and chop finely. Cool.

Mix all the ingredients together except for the pastry, eggs and glaze.

Spoon half down the centre of the pastry. Place the whole hard-boiled eggs on top in a line, cover with the rest of the filling and mould around the eggs.

Slash the pastry edges at intervals, slanting diagonally, and brush the tips with glaze.

Now, pull the strips over the meat alternately in a criss-cross fashion and press well to seal each strip, and the two ends. Brush all over with glaze.

Bake in a preheated oven at 400°F (200°C, gas mark 6) for about 25 minutes until golden brown, then reduce the heat to 350°F (180°C, gas mark 4) for a further 35 minutes to cook the meat.

Remove, cool on the tray and slide off onto a wire tray to get quite cold.

Serves 6.   RD

HAM ROLLS A LA BASQUAISE

A Mediterranean dish for slices of ham. Grilling the peppers imparts a delicious flavour and is well worth the effort.

1 large red pepper
1 large green pepper
2 tablespoons olive oil
1 onion, sliced
4 fresh tomatoes, skinned and chopped
1 tablespoon tomato paste
Salt and ground black pepper
1 sprig fresh thyme
2 sage leaves, chopped
2 tablespoons fresh chopped parsley
6 green olives, stoned and sliced
6 black olives, stoned and sliced
12 thin slices ham

Grill the peppers under a high heat until the skins burn and split, turning frequently. Peel the skins off, core, de-seed and slice.

Heat the oil and gently fry the onion and pepper strips, then add the tomatoes, paste, seasoning and herbs. Simmer for 10 minutes.

Add the olives, then divide the mixture between the 12 ham slices and roll up. Spread any leftover mixture on the base of a baking dish and put the rolls on top.

Bake at 375°F (190°C, gas mark 5) for about 15 minutes until well heated through. Serve hot with crisp bread and a green salad.

Serves 4. RD

CORNISH CHICKEN AND GAMMON PIE

There are numerous Cornish recipes for pies which are filled with cream after baking. Likky pie, which was similar to this one, but used only bacon and leeks, was served on high days and holidays. Chicken breast fillets would not, of course, have been used originally.

12 oz (350 g) shortcrust pastry
3 boneless chicken breast fillets, weighing in total about 12 oz (350 g)
2 thick gammon steaks, weighing in total about 12 oz (350 g)
2 oz (50 g) chopped parsley
1 small onion, very finely chopped
¼ teaspoon ground mace
Salt and freshly milled black pepper
¼ pint (150 ml) chicken stock
Milk for glazing
¼ pint (150 ml) double cream

Roll out just over half the pastry to line an 8 " (20 cm) diameter deep-pie plate. Cut each chicken fillet into three and lay in the base of the pastry-lined plate. Season well with salt and pepper. Cover with the parsley, then scatter over the onion. Cut the gammon into about 6 pieces and lay them on top. Sprinkle with mace and more pepper. Pour over the chicken stock. Damp the pastry edges.

Roll out the remaining pastry for the lid and place in position. Seal the pastry edges, then trim and flute them. Roll out any pastry trimmings and make into leaves to decorate the pie. Make a hole in

the top of the pie for the steam to escape, then brush all over with milk. Bake in a moderately hot oven, 375°F (190°C, gas mark 5) for 1¼ hours, then remove from the oven.

Bring the cream to just below boiling point in a small saucepan, then pour into the pie before serving, using a funnel if necessary. Serve hot, as soon as possible once the cream has been added.

Serves 4–6. JR

BOEUF A LA MODE

A potentially tough piece of beef is larded with pork fat and then cooked slowly in delicious, tenderising liquids.

About 3–4 lb (1.5–1.75 kg) piece rolled beef – e.g. brisket, or top rump or aitchbone or unsalted silverside
4–6 oz (125–175 g) pork or bacon fat, cut into thin strips
1 onion and 3 carrots, sliced
2 bay leaves, sprig each fresh thyme and rosemary
1 calf's foot, sawn into three
½ pint (300 ml) red wine
½ pint (300 ml) good beef stock
3 fl oz (100 ml) brandy
Salt and ground black pepper

With a larding needle, thread the pork fat strips through the meat. Secure the meat neatly.

Place the onions and carrots in the base of a large casserole and stand the meat on top. Sprinkle over the herbs and squeeze the calf's foot pieces around the sides. Pour over the wine, brandy and stock, season well, cover and bake at 325°F (170°C, gas mark 3) for about 3 hours or until quite tender.

Remove the meat and slice it up. Scoop any marrow jelly from the calf's foot into the sauce then discard the bones. Strain the stock and thicken if liked with a little cornflour, or liquidize with the vegetables and herbs. Pour a little over the meat and hand the rest separately in a sauce boat.

Serves 6. RD

LANCASHIRE HOT POT

There are many variations on the theme of the hot pot. Traditionally, it was often cooked in the residual heat of the local baker's oven after the day's bread had been baked. Lancashire hot pot, illustrated on page 31, is usually made in a deep earthenware casserole, glazed brown, with a domed lid, which can be removed toward the end of cooking to allow the potatoes to brown.

> 3 lb (1.5 kg) best end neck lamb chops (there
>   should be about 12)
> 3 lamb's kidneys, halved and skinned
> 1 oz (25 g) seasoned flour
> 3 lb (1.5 kg) potatoes, peeled
> 2 onions, peeled and sliced
> 3–4 carrots, peeled and sliced
> 2 sticks celery, sliced
> 2–3 bay leaves
> ¾ pint (450 ml) lamb or chicken stock
> 1 oz (25 g) butter, melted
> Parsley to garnish

Trim any excess fat from the lamb, then toss in seasoned flour. Snip core from each kidney with scissors and toss in remaining flour.

Prepare vegetables. Slice the potatoes neatly and place in a pan of cold water. Bring to the boil and cook for 2 minutes. Drain well, then place a layer of potato slices (about half) on the base of a large ovenproof casserole, followed by onion, carrots, celery and bay leaves. Season to taste. Place kidneys and lamb chops on top, fitting in the pieces like a jigsaw. Finally, cover with neat slices of overlapping potato. Pour the prepared stock down the side of the dish. Brush potato slices with melted butter, and lay a piece of buttered greaseproof paper on top. Cover with a well-fitting lid and set in moderate oven 375°F (190°C, gas mark 5) for about 1¾ hours.

Remove lid and paper, then brush with remaining butter and return to a slightly hotter oven for 30–45 minutes to brown and crisp the potatoes. Scatter with parsley before serving if liked, and serve straight from the casserole.

Serves 6.   SM

LAMB TAGINE WITH ARTICHOKES AND FENNEL

In Morocco and Algeria, rich aromatic stews are cooked in conical earthenware pots called *tagines* (see page 66). The shape of the lid is supposed to encourage steam to drop back into the stew to help moisturize it. However, any casserole with a slightly domed lid should achieve excellent results.

> 2 tablespoons oil
> 1 medium onion, grated
> ½ lemon
> 1½ (750 g) lean stewing lamb (e.g. boned
>   shoulder)
> 1" (2.5 cm) cube fresh ginger, grated, or
>   1 teaspoon ground
> Salt and ground black pepper
> 3 young globe artichokes
> 4 tomatoes, skinned and chopped
> 2 medium heads fennel
> 3 tablespoons fresh chopped coriander leaves
> ¼ pint (150 ml) water
> Some black olives, to serve

Heat the oil in a large cast-iron casserole and gently fry the grated onion. Cut the lemon into thin slices and add to the pan. (This gives a pithy bitterness which Western palates may not like, so thinly pare the rind first, remove the pith, cut the flesh into slices and add rind and flesh only.)

Cut the lamb into bite-size chunks and add to the pan with the grated ginger and seasoning. Cook until browned, about 15 minutes.

Strip the leaves from artichokes, trim the bases of any woody bits, and scoop out the spiky choke with a spoon. Cut the bases into quarters and drop into cold water with a squeeze of lemon juice to prevent them from darkening. Dip the tomatoes briefly in boiling water, skin and chop; slice the fennel. Add the vegetables to the pan with the coriander and water. Cover and simmer gently for about another 20 to 30 minutes or until the meat is tender. Add the olives five minutes before the end of the cooking time. Serve with rice, couscous or simply chunks of sesame bread.

Serves 4–6.   RD

LAMB BIRIYANI WITH PUMPKIN CHUTNEY AND CUCUMBER

This is an adaptation of a southern Indian dish of spiced meat layered with rice – a kind of elaborate and subtly-flavoured pilaff. The original recipe came from a book called *Indian Regional Cookery* (now out of print) by Meera Taneja. This version, sharpened by chutney and cooled with cucumber, although no longer authentic, is, however, intriguing and delicious, and appropriate for a small crowd. For the chutney, advance planning is necessary; it should mature for at least a month.

LAMB BIRIYANI

2 lamb shoulders, boned by butcher
4 oz (125 g) ghee
3 large onions
18 oz (550 g) natural yoghurt
6 fresh green chillies, tops off
8 large cloves garlic, peeled
A 2" (5 cm) piece root ginger, peeled
Salt
2 teaspoons black cumin seeds
10 green cardamoms
9 cloves
A good handful each of fresh mint and coriander
*   leaves*
Strained juice of 6 lemons
1 lb (500 g) basmati rice

Trim lamb of excess skin, fat, and connective tissue. Cut into small cubes, and weigh out 4 lb (1.75 kg) of these; submerge them in cold water for an hour. Use any remaining lamb for another purpose.

Meanwhile, melt 3 oz (75 g) ghee in a wide sauté pan, mince onions and fry these slowly until golden-brown. Drain with a slotted spoon and mix with yoghurt, discarding used ghee.

Cut up chillies, garlic and ginger, and purée these to a paste – with the aid of a little salt – in the food processor. Drain lamb and press out water; smear meat with paste and leave for 1 hour.

Bruise cumin seeds with the base of a heavy knife-handle; add to yoghurt with whole cardamoms, cloves, chopped mint and coriander, lemon juice. In due course, add lamb and its paste and mix well. Cover and marinate meat for 5 hours, stirring occasionally.

Transfer all to a large, deep pot – such as a heavy stock pot, 10" (25 cm) across by 6" (15 cm) deep, with a close-fitting lid – salt mixture and simmer it slowly, atop the stove, for 30–40 minutes or until lamb is tender; keep pot half-covered and stir contents occasionally. There should be quite a lot of sauce. Rinse rice in 3 changes of cold water and blanch for 3 minutes in 1½ pints (900 ml) salted, boiling water; drain rice well and reserve.

When lamb is ready, taste for salt, remove meat and sauce from the pot and clean this; smear remaining ghee over bottom and half way up side. Line bottom of pot with ⅓ of rice, cover with half of meat and sauce. Strew with half of remaining rice, spread with the rest of meat and sauce, cover with rice. Top with a very snug lid and bake biriyani in a 375°F (190°C, gas mark 5) oven to finish cooking the grain. A gas oven will require some 30–40 minutes; a traditional electric one may take up to twice as long.

To serve, bring pot to the – well-insulated! – table, remove lid (beware of steam), fork up rice, and dig deep into layers.

Serves 10, with pumpkin chutney and cucumber as follows.

PUMPKIN CHUTNEY

The quantities given here fill two 2 lb (1 kg) jars, and one of 1 lb (500 g) capacity.

4¼ lb (1.85 kg) firm pumpkin (gross weight),
*   seeded, peeled, cut into ¾" (2 cm) chunks*
1½ large onions, peeled and chopped
3 large cloves garlic, peeled and chopped
3 oz (75 g) sultanas
2 teaspoons black peppercorns and 1 teaspoon
*   black mustard seeds, crushed together in a*
*   mortar*
A 1" (2.5 cm) piece root ginger, peeled and
*   grated*
1 stick cinnamon

Lamb biryani with pumpkin chutney and cucumber with mint; with Milleens cheese and salad to follow

2 teaspoons salt
1 lb (500 g) soft light brown sugar
1¼ pints (750 ml) white wine vinegar

Put everything into a deep, heavy pot, bring vinegar to the boil, and simmer contents – uncovered and skimming when necessary – until chutney thickens to a jam-like consistency; the process will take about an hour and 40 minutes. Stir constantly at the end or chutney will stick nastily. Leave it somewhat liquid and ladle immediately into hot, dry sterilized jars; cover with sterilized lids. Let the chutney ripen for at least 4–8 weeks before opening the containers.

CUCUMBER WITH MINT

Two 18 oz (550 g) cucumbers
Salt
1 small onion
A handful of fresh mint leaves

Peel, trim, and seed cucumbers. Cut flesh into ⅜″ (1 cm) cubes, salt these lightly and allow them to drain for an hour or so in a colander. Rinse well and drain again.

Peel and mince the onion finely. Toss cucumber with minced onion and mint.

Serves 10 as a condiment. AWS

83

Persian-style rice and lamb mould

PERSIAN-STYLE RICE AND LAMB MOULD

Rice moulds with their crisp 'skins' are a classic of Persian cuisine. They are made by pressing cooked rice round the base and sides of a mould, then baking with a filling. Although not strictly traditional, this is easier to turn out if the rice is first mixed with eggs and yoghurt.

> *12 oz (375 g) basmati rice, unrinsed*
> *2 egg yolks*
> *5 oz (150 g) tub thick natural yoghurt*
> *2 oz (50 g) butter or ghee, melted and cooled*
> *1 lb (500 g) minced lean lamb or beef*
> *1 tablespoon oil*
> *1 onion, chopped*
> *2 cloves garlic, crushed*
> *1 teaspoon ground coriander (optional)*
> *¾ pint (450 ml) stock*
> *2 tablespoons tomato purée*
> *6 dried apricots, chopped*
> *2 oz (50 g) raisins*
> *2 oz (50 g) walnuts, chopped*
> *Salt and ground black pepper*

It is important not to rinse the rice so that it is slightly sticky. Cook the rice in plenty of boiling water on a medium boil for 10 minutes. Drain but don't rinse. Cool.

Beat together the yolks, yoghurt and half the cool but still runny butter, then mix in half the rice. Mix the remaining half of rice with the rest of the runny butter and check the seasoning.

Brown the mince in the oil for 3 minutes in a large frying-pan, then add the onion, garlic and coriander, and fry, stirring for 3 minutes.

Stir in the stock, tomato purée, dried fruits and seasonings. Bring to the boil, then simmer, uncovered, for 15–20 minutes until the liquid has nearly gone. Mix in the nuts.

Grease a loose-bottomed 9″ (23 cm) round deep cake tin with a little butter, and line base with a circle of buttered foil or greaseproof paper.

Spoon in all the egg rice and, with the back of a spoon, work it up the sides of the tin, leaving sufficient on the base to cover. Pat well to firm.

Spoon in half the meat, then half the buttered rice. Repeat the layers finishing with rice, and cover with buttered foil. Stand the tin on a baking sheet and bake at 350°F (180°C, gas mark 4) for 1 hour. Allow it to stand for 15 minutes afterwards, dip the tin briefly in cold water, then invert onto a plate and shake out.

Top with onion rings fried gently in butter until golden, and some parsley or coriander leaves.
Serves 4.   RD

SPICED CURRIED LAMB

Despite the fact that they will eat steak tartare with no qualms at all, many people are slightly dubious about eating other meat raw and, while pork and all poultry should always be thoroughly cooked, lamb is delicious eaten raw. This particular recipe is for a very lightly spiced, curried lamb; however if you would like a slightly hotter mixture you could also add a very finely chopped green chilli as well. Although it can be served with any number of salads, it goes particularly well with cucumber mixed with yoghurt and a little fresh mint.

1 lb (500 g) lean lamb, preferably from the leg
4 rounded tablespoons mayonnaise
1" (2.5 cm) piece root ginger, minced
1 tablespoon garam masala
3 tablespoons chopped fresh coriander
Salt and freshly milled black pepper

TO GARNISH
Coriander sprigs (optional)
Lemon slices

Cut off any excess fat or sinew from the lamb and grind or mince finely. Turn into a bowl and add the mayonnaise, ginger, garam masala and two-thirds of the coriander. Mix well together and season to taste with salt and pepper. Make into 4 cakes and place on a serving dish. Sprinkle with the remaining chopped coriander and garnish with the coriander and lemon.

Serves 4. JR

LAMB WITH SALTED LEMON

Whole lemons preserved with salt are fundamental to the Moroccan kitchen and are used here in a stew of lean lamb and new potatoes which is flavoured additionally with saffron.

This is a boon recipe when time for preparation is tight because, unusually, the meat is not browned before the liquid is added, and, once the ingredients have been prepared, is left to simmer.

6 tablespoons olive oil
1 clove garlic, crushed
1 small piece (size of garlic clove) fresh ginger,
  crushed
¼ teaspoon powdered saffron
2 lbs (1 kg) boneless lamb, leg or neck fillet,
  cubed
2 Spanish onions, finely chopped
1 salted lemon
2 lbs (1 kg) scraped new potatoes
Salt
Freshly-ground black pepper

Put the oil, crushed garlic, ginger and saffron into a big, wide pan. Add the lamb and turn to coat it with the oil. Add the onions.

Divide the lemon into quarters, remove and discard the flesh and pith, and add the skin to the pan with enough water to cover the lamb. Bring to the boil, lower the heat and simmer until the lamb is almost tender. This may take up to two hours.

Add the potatoes and continue cooking until the potatoes are tender. If there is still too much liquid, take out the meat and vegetables and keep them warm, while reducing the sauce by fast boiling. Season with salt, if needed, and freshly-ground black pepper.

Lamb with salted lemon can be cooked in advance and reheated. It can also be frozen.

Hot French bread and a mixed green salad complete this easy meal.

Serves 4–6.

NOTE Free-range chickens, which have more flavour than battery birds, are also excellent cooked this way. Cut one bird into about 10 pieces and halve the cooking time. SCP

SALTED LEMONS

7 fresh, firm, thin-skinned lemons
7 tablespoons sea salt

Wait until you can find thin-skinned lemons before making this preserve, since coarse, pithy lemons are not nearly as good.

Scrub the lemons with warm water and a soft brush, and scald a Kilner or Parfait jar which is large enough to hold all the fruit.

Using a stainless-steel knife, cut six of the lemons lengthwise as if into quarters, but not right through. Pack a tablespoonful of salt into each one and pack them tightly into the jar. Add the remaining salt and strained juice of the seventh lemon. Top up with boiling water to cover the fruit. Close the jar tightly and leave it for two or three weeks in a cool, dark place.

Once matured, salted lemons keep well for many months. SCP

MAINLY VEGETABLES

Whether served as accompaniments to meat or
fish, or as main-course dishes in their own right,
these imaginative vegetable recipes are suitable, or
easily adapted, for vegetarians

PROVENCAL TIAN D'EPINARDS

A dessert made with spinach, this dates from the
seventeenth century. It is cooked in a *tian* – a
shallow red earthenware dish – and is still eaten in
Vaucluse at the end of a meal, but can also accompany savoury dishes. This traditional open tart
combines spinach with spinach beet, but it can be
made with spinach alone.

1 lb (500 g) spinach
½ lb (250 g) spinach beet
Pinch salt
Boiling water
2 oz (50 g) melted butter
1 oz (25 g) white breadcrumbs
2 oz (50 g) currants
1 oz (25 g) ground almonds
½ pint (300 ml) single cream
2 tablespoons sugar
Nutmeg
2 whole eggs
2 egg yolks
4 oz (125 g) puff pastry

Blanch spinach and spinach beet in a little lightly
salted boiling water for 1 minute. Drain and chop.
Mix in the melted butter. Stir breadcrumbs, currants and ground almonds into the cream. Then
mix in the spinach, sugar and nutmeg. Add the
beaten whole eggs and egg yolks. Line a 9″ (23 cm)
tian – if you have one – or a flan plate with the

pastry. Pour in the spinach mixture. Bake at 425°F
(220°C, gas mark 7) for 10 minutes, then lower heat
to 350°F (180°C, gas mark 4) and cook for a further
30 minutes. Serve hot.

For 6 people. BGM

SPINACH SOUFFLE

Delicately flecked with green, this classic soufflé is
seasoned with Parmesan and anchovy essence,
combined to give a pleasant saltiness.

1 tablespoon chopped shallot
½ oz (15 g) butter for frying
6 oz (175 g) blanched, chopped spinach

PANADA
1½ oz (40 g) butter
2 oz (50 g) flour
½ pint (300 ml) boiling milk
2 teaspoons anchovy essence
4 egg yolks, and 5 egg whites
Salt and pepper to taste
1½–2 oz (40–50 g) grated Parmesan cheese

Right *(from top right) Spinach soup (recipe on page
32); Provençal tian d'epinards; spinach soufflé; raw
spinach and hot bacon salad (recipe on page 111);
Bavarian ham and spinach torte, page 88*

Soften the shallot in melted butter, add spinach and stir and cook until moisture evaporates.

To make the panada, melt the butter and stir in the flour, then cook for 1–2 minutes; do not let it brown. Still stirring, add the milk off the heat, stir vigorously until smooth, then add spinach, anchovy essence and pepper. Stir and cook for about 1 minute. Remove from heat and beat in the egg yolks one by one. Check seasoning. Beat the egg whites and salt until stiff and dry. Add about a quarter to the panada, and stir in all except 1 tablespoonful of the cheese. Very gently fold in the rest of the egg whites.

Butter the bottom and sides of a 2½ pint (1.5 litre) soufflé mould. Pre-heat oven the 400°F (200°C, gas mark 6). Put the mixture into the prepared mould, and sprinkle the top with the remaining tablespoon of cheese. Place in the middle of the oven, and immediately turn heat down to 375°F (190°C, gas mark 5). Cook for 25–35 minutes, by which time soufflé should have risen and be a delicate brown.

Take out of the oven, and leave aside for 4–5 minutes to become firm, before serving.

Serves 4.   BGM

Filo roll with feta and spinach

BAVARIAN HAM AND SPINACH TORTE

A light lunch or supper dish illustrated on page 87, which, by omitting the ham, could be adapted for vegetarians.

> 7 oz (200 g) puff pastry, can be frozen
> 8 oz (250 g) cooked ham, coarsely chopped
> 1½ lb (750 g) minced cooked spinach mixed
>   with butter
> 3 hard-boiled eggs, chopped
> 5 fl oz (140 ml) light creamy béchamel sauce
> Pepper, salt
> Egg for glazing

Line a shallow, 9″ (23 cm) circular mould with half the pastry. Divide ham and spinach in half, season and arrange in alternate layers on top of the pastry. Put the eggs on top, then cover smoothly with the béchamel. Cover with the rest of the pastry, decorate with any trimmings, and make a hole in the centre. Glaze with beaten egg. Bake at 350°F (180°C, gas mark 4) for 40–45 minutes.

Serves 4.   BGM

FILO ROLL WITH FETA AND SPINACH

This classic Greek pie suits many occasions, from stand-up buffets to a first course for formal dinners. Make it up in advance, ready for baking, then cook it when required. However, it is equally good served cold.

> 5–6 sheets filo pastry, thawed
> 1½ oz (40 g) butter, melted
> 1 lb (500 g) fresh leaf spinach, blanched, or ½
>   lb (250 g) frozen
> 3 spring onions, chopped
> 7 oz (200 g) feta cheese, crumbled or grated
> 1 egg, beaten
> 1 tablespoon fresh chopped dill
> Sesame seeds, to sprinkle
> Salt and ground black pepper

Lay a sheet of pastry on a lightly greased baking sheet. Brush lightly all over with butter. Top with another two sheets of pastry, brushing in between with more butter.

Squeeze the spinach quite dry, then chop. Mix with the onions, cheese, egg, dill and seasoning. (Watch the salt, as feta cheese can be quite salty.) Spread the filling on the pastry, then top with the remaining pastry sheets, brushing in between with more butter.

Roll up like a Swiss roll and brush all over with the last of the butter. Scatter over sesame seeds. If you wish to bake this later, then keep it chilled until required. Bake at 375°F (190°C, gas mark 5) for about 25 to 30 minutes until golden and crispy. Allow to stand for a few moments before cutting into slices.

Serves 4.   RD

SPINACH AND RICOTTA

Rather like a flan without pastry, this vegetable dish can be served hot or cold, sliced like a cake.

1 oz (25 g) butter or margarine
18 oz (500 g) spinach
9 oz (275 g) ricotta
1 medium onion
1 oz (25 g) dried mushrooms (porcini)
3 eggs
1 oz (25 g) Parmesan
Chopped parsley
Breadcrumbs, and butter to grease tin

Put the mushrooms in a little hot water. Cook the spinach, well washed, in as little water as possible. Drain very well and chop. Slice the onion thinly and cook in butter in a heavy-based frying-pan until transparent, then add the drained mushrooms, finely sliced. Add a good pinch of chopped parsley, cover with a lid and cook slowly until the mushrooms are cooked. Remove pan from heat. Add the spinach, together with salt and pepper to taste and Parmesan cheese.

Put the ricotta in a bowl and break it up evenly

with a fork, then add to spinach mixture. Beat the eggs in a basin and add to spinach.

Butter a pie dish about 9″ (23 cm) in diameter, and sprinkle with breadcrumbs. Pour in the spinach mixture and spread it evenly. Sprinkle the top with breadcrumbs, dot with butter and bake in the oven (350°F, 180°C, gas mark 4) for 30–40 minutes. When cooked, turn it out and allow to cool on a cake rack. Serve hot or cold.

Serves 6.   PF

LENTIL AND SPINACH CREPE TIMBALE WITH TOMATO COULIS

A spectacular layered centre-piece that can be prepared ahead and re-heated when required.

CRÊPES
2 oz (50 g) each wholewheat and white plain
  flour
Salt
2 eggs
½ pint (300 ml) milk
A little oil

FILLINGS
12 oz (350 g) fresh spinach leaves, chopped
2 shallots, chopped
1 clove garlic, crushed
1 oz (25 g) butter
A little fresh grated nutmeg
8 oz (250 g) ricotta cheese
1 oz (25 g) fresh Parmesan cheese
6 oz (175 g) red lentils
1 small onion, chopped
2 medium tomatoes, peeled and chopped
¼ pint (450 ml) water or vegetable stock
Pinch dried basil
Salt and ground black pepper

Make the batter by mixing the crêpe ingredients in a processor or blender. Using a small pancake pan, make 12–14 thin crêpes about 8″ (20 cm) in diameter. Cool and cover.

Sweat the spinach, chopped shallots and garlic in the butter for about 5 minutes in a covered saucepan. The spinach should be wilted and soft. Stir in the nutmeg, ricotta and Parmesan cheeses. Season well.

Cook the lentils with the rest of the ingredients for about 25 minutes until quite soft. Season well. Set aside.

Grease a charlotte russe tin or 2-pint (1.2 litre) basin. Line the base and sides with crêpes, cutting to fit where necessary. Halving the crêpes helps.

Now make layers of the two fillings and crêpes, finishing with a crêpe. Fold over any crêpes from the sides, cover with greased foil, pressing the edges well to the sides.

Steam or boil the mould for about 1 hour. Unmould to serve, allow to stand for a few minutes before cutting into wedges. Hand the tomato coulis separately.

TO MAKE THE COULIS
Sweat 1 large chopped onion and 2 cloves of crushed garlic in 1 oz (25 g) butter and 1 tablespoon olive oil. Add 2 lbs (1 kg) of skinned and chopped fresh tomatoes, 1 teaspoon sugar, 2 teaspoons fresh chopped basil and plenty of seasoning. Simmer for 20 minutes, then strain and serve.

Serves 6–8.   RD

Carrot and ginger pilau in a spinach crown

CARROT AND GINGER PILAU IN A SPINACH CROWN

This could form the basis of a vegetarian main meal, or a more elaborate accompaniment to a simple grill or roast.

1 large onion, half sliced thinly, half chopped
3 tablespoons groundnut oil or ghee
2 cloves garlic, crushed
1" (2.5 cm) cube fresh root ginger, finely grated
1 fresh green chilli, seeded and chopped (optional)
2 carrots, peeled and coarsely grated
8 oz (250 g) basmati rice, rinsed
Good pinch saffron strands
¾ pint (350 ml) light stock or water
1 cinnamon stick
1 teaspoon ground coriander
1 lb (500 g) fresh leaf spinach, well washed and slightly chopped
1 teaspoon garam masala powder
Salt and ground black pepper

TO SERVE
Either some fresh pistachio nuts, chopped, or toasted almond flakes

Lightly fry the chopped onion in half the oil or ghee with one clove of garlic, the ginger and chilli, if using, for 3 minutes. Add the carrots and rice, stir well and cook for 2 minutes. Add saffron (crushing between fingers), the stock, spices and seasoning.

Bring to the boil, cover and turn down to a gentle simmer for about 12 minutes. Meanwhile, in a large saucepan sauté the sliced onion in the remaining oil or ghee, with the other clove of garlic, for 3 minutes. Add the spinach – it should not need any extra water as enough should be clinging to the leaves. Sprinkle over the garam masala and stir well to mix in. Cover and simmer on a low heat for about 5 minutes. Season.

Spoon the spinach around the edge of a serving platter and pile the rice in the middle. Scatter over the nuts and serve hot.

Serves 4–6.   RD

SPINACH PUFFS

Serves as a starter, as a hot canapé with drinks, or as a main course accompaniment.

2 lb (1 kg) spinach
2 level tablespoons flour
5 fl oz (140 ml) béchamel sauce
Pepper, salt
Pinch nutmeg
2 eggs, separated
Oil for deep frying

Cook, drain and purée the spinach. Put it in a pan over a low heat, and stir until all the liquid evaporates. Remove from heat, let it cool slightly, stir in the flour, then add the béchamel. Add egg yolks and seasoning. Beat egg whites until stiff and dry. Fold them in gently. Drop dessertspoons of the mixture into the hot oil and fry until the puffs are crisp. Serve immediately.
Serves 4. BGM

Potato and parsnip amandine (above; recipe on page 98); cucumber shells with creamed spinach

CUCUMBER SHELLS WITH CREAMED SPINACH

Cucumber makes an excellent hot vegetable, and when halved and seeded, a surprisingly good container for a filling.

2 cucumbers
1 lb (500 g) fresh leaf spinach
1 oz (25 g) butter
1 oz (25 g) flour
½ pint (300 ml) hot milk
Freshly grated nutmeg
Salt and ground black pepper

TOPPING
2 tablespoons dried breadcrumbs
2 tablespoons chopped nuts
2 tablespoons freshly-grated Parmesan

Cut each cucumber into three then peel, halve and scoop out the seeds. Steam or blanch the shells until just tender but still holding their shape. Drain well and stand in a shallow ovenproof dish.

Trim and wash the spinach then cook, with no extra water, in a covered saucepan for about 5 minutes. Drain well and squeeze dry. This can be done by pressing the spinach between two dinner plates held over a sink. Chop roughly.

Make a roux with the butter and flour and cook for 2 minutes, then gradually add the milk, stirring until smooth and thickened. Season well and add the nutmeg to taste. Simmer for 2 minutes then stir in the spinach. Spoon the spinach into the cucumber shells. Mix the crumbs, nuts and cheese and sprinkle over. The vegetables can be prepared to this stage for reheating later.

Before serving, bake at 375°F (190°C, gas mark 5) for about 20 minutes until bubbling and lightly browned.
Serves 6. RD

Gratin of crunchy vegetables

GRATIN OF CRUNCHY VEGETABLES

This dish can keep warm or be reheated (microwave is best) if the vegetables are kept underdone.

A mixture of: carrots, courgettes, celery, florence fennel, cauliflower and thick ends of Chinese leaf; about 1½ lb (750 g) altogether

SAUCE
½ teaspoon finely chopped ginger
1 teaspoon finely chopped shallot
2 tablespoons oil
8 fl oz (250 g) chicken or vegetable stock
2 tablespoons cornflour
2 tablespoons sherry or white wine
2 tablespoons cream
1 tablespoon light soy sauce
½ teaspoon sugar
¼ teaspoon salt
1 teaspoon chicken fat (optional)

Keeping the vegetables separate, cut up the carrots, courgettes and celery into thumbnail-sized bits and the florence fennel into small segments; break the cauliflower into florets and cut the Chinese leaves into thick slices. Steam the vegetables until nearly cooked but still nice and crisp; fennel, celery and cauliflower take longest, followed by carrot and courgette, while Chinese leaf takes the least time. Remove each vegetable as it's done. Mix together the stock and cornflour, the sherry, cream, soy, sugar, salt and chicken fat. Heat a wok or large pan and add the oil, ginger and shallot. Toss for about 30 seconds then add the vegetables; stir-fry until glistening then stir and add the sauce. Bring to the boil, stirring, and boil until the sauce thickens before turning into a shallow gratin dish.

Serves 4.   NC

AUBERGINE DHAL

Yellow split peas, or dhals, make the basis for wonderful, quickly cooked main meals with whatever seasonal vegetables, eggs, nuts and spices you have to hand. Serve with rice or bread – preferably Indian naan or chapatis.

8 oz (250 g) split peas
1 pint (600 ml) stock or water
2 onions, chopped
1 large bay leaf
2 teaspoons black mustard seeds
2 tablespoons oil or butter
1 clove garlic, crushed
1" (2.5 cm) cube fresh root ginger, peeled and grated
1 small green pepper, sliced
1 teaspoon turmeric
1 teaspoon mild curry powder or garam masala
1 medium aubergine, diced in chunks
2 large tomatoes, skinned and chopped
Salt and pepper

TO SERVE
2–3 hard boiled eggs, quartered
Fresh chopped coriander or parsley

Cook the peas in the stock with one of the onions, the bay leaf and some seasoning for 25 minutes until soft.

In a separate pan, fry the mustard seeds in the

oil for about 30 seconds until they start popping, then add the remaining onion, garlic, grated ginger and pepper. Sauté gently for about 5 minutes until softened.

Sprinkle in the spices, stir up and fry for another minute, then add the remaining ingredients with a little extra water just to moisten. Season well, then simmer gently for about 10 minutes. Spoon in the split peas, reheat, then serve hot garnished with the egg quarters and coriander or parsley.

Serves 4–6. RD

PUFFED PUMPKIN

Simple to prepare, the earthy flavour of this purée is quite delicious with plain-roasted game birds, or a joint of roast pork.

> 2 lb (1 kg) piece pumpkin
> 2 oz (50 g) butter
> Salt and pepper
> 1 level teaspoon nutmeg
> 2 eggs

Peel and chunk the pumpkin. Cook it gently in a lidded pan with very little water – it has plenty of its own.

When the pumpkin is soft (it takes about the same time to cook as does potato), drain off any excess water and purée the pulp. Return it to the pan and dry it off further. Beat in the butter. Season the pumpkin purée with salt, pepper and nutmeg, and set it aside to cool for a moment.

Separate the eggs and stir the yolks into the purée. Whisk the whites and fold them in thoroughly. Butter a soufflé dish. Pour in the mixture to within two fingers' width of the top.

Bake at 350°F (180°C, gas mark 4) for 20 minutes, until the purée is puffed and golden. It will keep quite happily in a warm oven until you are ready to serve.

Serves 4–6. EL

MARINATED VEGETABLE KEBABS

Best in summertime, cooked over charcoal on a barbecue, these could at a pinch go under the grill.

> 1 lb (500 g) small, new potatoes
> 1 lb (500 g) aubergines
> Salt
> 1 large onion
> 1 large red pepper
> 1 large yellow pepper
> 8 oz (250 g) firm button mushrooms
> Freshly ground black pepper
> 2 cloves garlic, finely chopped
> 6 tablespoons finely chopped fresh herbs
> 4 fl oz (125 ml) olive oil

Boil or steam the new potatoes in their skins until they are just cooked. Drain them and transfer to a large mixing bowl.

Cut the unpeeled aubergines into 1″ (2.5 cm) cubes. Put the cubes in a colander, salt generously, and leave to drain for half an hour. Rinse, dry and add the cubes to the potatoes.

Peel and quarter the onion and separate outside layers. If onion is very large, cut each piece in two.

Cut the red and yellow peppers into pieces about the same size as the onion segments, discarding the stalks and seeds. Add the onion and peppers to the bowl, together with the mushrooms, their stalks trimmed level with the caps.

Add salt, plenty of coarse black pepper, the garlic and herbs. Pour over all the oil and use your hands to mix thoroughly so that each vegetable piece is filmed with oil. Leave to marinate for at least two hours, but not much more than half a day.

Immediately before cooking the vegetables, thread each variety onto one or more flat-bladed skewers – mixing the onion and pepper segments if you like, as these do cook evenly together. Cook the kebabs on a charcoal grill, basting them once or twice with the marinade.

Sliding the vegetables off their skewers in straight lines onto a serving dish makes an attractive presentation.

Serves 4–6. SCP

93

MUSHROOM SUPPER DISH WITH A LIGHT CREAMY CRUST

It is possible to bake fromage frais, quark or crème fraîche as a light, tangy topping but the mixture should be stabilized first with butter and beaten eggs to keep it from separating. This topping is ideal for a moussaka, or with this all-vegetable casserole.

> 1 lb (500 g) mushrooms, sliced – a mixture of cultivated and wild would be nice
> 2 clove garlic, crushed
> 2 tablespoons walnut oil or extra virgin olive oil
> 1 oz (25 g) butter
> 3 courgettes, sliced thickly
> 2 medium leeks, sliced thickly
> ½ pint (300 ml) vegetable stock
> 1–2 tablespoons flour, optional
> 1 tablespoon fresh chopped thyme or 1 teaspoon dried
> 2 tablespoons fromage frais or quark or crème fraîche
>
> TOPPING
> 1 lb (500 g) fromage frais
> 1 oz (25 g) butter, melted
> 3 eggs, beaten
> Freshly grated nutmeg
> 2 tablespoons freshly grated Parmesan
> Salt and ground black pepper

Put the mushrooms, garlic, oil and butter into a heavy-based saucepan, cover and cook for about 10 minutes, shaking the pan occasionally, until mushrooms are just cooked.

Blanch the courgettes and leeks in the vegetable or chicken stock until only just cooked – about 3–5 minutes. Strain off liquor and reserve.

Sprinkle the flour into the mushrooms (if you want a slightly thickened sauce), stir, then gradually add the reserved stock. Bring to the boil, stirring, then add the courgettes and leeks. Season and add the thyme. Cook for 2 minutes, mix in the fromage frais, quark or crème fraîche and spoon the mixture into a heatproof casserole.

Beat the topping ingredients together, except for the Parmesan, and pour over the vegetables. Sprinkle over the Parmesan, then bake at 375°F (190°C, gas mark 5) for about 30 minutes until light-golden and cooked on top.

Serves 4.   RD

YELLOW PEPPER LASAGNE

This vegetable version of a classic pasta dish is unusual and good.

Alternate layers of wholewheat and green lasagne are filled with a sweet yellow pepper sauce and topped with three cheeses.

> 1 lb (500 g) fromage blanc
> 1 egg and 1 yolk
> Salt and black pepper
> Cayenne pepper
> 4 oz (125 g) wholewheat lasagne
> 2 oz (50 g) green lasagne
> Butter
> 2 large sweet yellow peppers
> 2 large onions, peeled
> 3 large cloves garlic, peeled
> 2 large carrots, peeled
> 7 oz (200 g) mozzarella cheese
> Grated Parmesan cheese

Set fromage blanc to drain of its whey in a plastic sieve lined with muslin. After 2–3 hours, whisk the drained cheese with the egg and extra yolk and season to taste with salt, pepper, and cayenne.

Boil the wholewheat lasagne for 15 minutes in plenty of salted water; boil the green lasagne for 10 minutes. Drain pieces of pasta side by side on kitchen paper.

Butter a 9 × 2″ (23 × 5 cm) circular Pyrex dish.

Slice seeded peppers into thin strips, very thinly slice the onions, chop the garlic, and grate the carrots. Sweat all of these vegetables in butter, in a wide sauté pan, until the peppers and onions have softened; they will greatly reduce in volume. Season well.

Grate the mozzarella cheese.

Yellow pepper lasagne (right), with an inspired salad

Line the bottom and side of the Pyrex dish with a layer of wholewheat lasagne. Spread on ⅓ of the vegetables, and top with ⅓ of the fromage blanc mixture (spread this with a wet spoon). Strew with ⅓ of the mozzarella and some grated Parmesan. Cover with the green lasagne, then half each of the remaining vegetables, fromage blanc, mozzarella, and some more Parmesan. Top with wholewheat lasagne and the rest of the vegetables, fromage blanc and two cheeses.

Trim the edges with a knife and bake at 375°F (190°C, gas mark 5) for about 40 minutes, until the top bubbles and browns attractively.

Serves 4–6.   AWS

STEAMED SEA-KALE

Sea-kale, a delicate and delicious vegetable, is best steamed, since boiling dissolves the valuable salts, and lessens the flavour. In the past, sea-kale was widely cultivated for its blanched shoots, which were considered a delicacy. It has now become a rare vegetable, and in order to have a supply, the best solution is to grow it.

Allowing 4 oz (125 g) sea-kale per person, trim and wash the vegetable, then steam for about 40–45 minutes. Test occasionally with a sharp knife. When tender, serve with melted butter or hollandaise sauce.   BGM

VEGETABLE PAELLA

La Mazorca – The Corncob – is a 'natural foods' restaurant in Alicante whose chef, Pepa Ruiz, improvises paellas from the wide range of excellent local vegetables. This is an adaptation of Pepa's recipe, using less oil than she would.

> 1 small sweet red pepper
> 2 slim, dried mild chilli peppers; in Alicante, cooks use round dried peppers called ñoras, unavailable here – buy an alternative at Lina Stores in London W1, or use mild chillis you've dried yourself
> ½ large head garlic, peeled
> Olive oil
> Salt
> 4 oz (125 g) carrots, peeled weight
> 4 oz (125 g) courgettes
> ½ large onion, peeled
> 5 oz (150 g) tomatoes, peeled and seeded weight
> 4 oz (125 g) mushrooms
> 3 oz (75 g) slim green beans
> 3 oz (75 g) young, tender peas
> 10 oz (300 g) Spanish paella rice or Italian risotto rice
> Pinch of saffron threads
> Fresh rosemary and thyme
> Vegetable broth and water

De-seed the sweet pepper and slice into thin strips, cut up the chillis and garlic, and sauté all with oil, using a paella pan or a large, deep frying pan, until the pepper is soft. Set the strips aside and purée the garlic, chilli, oil and some salt in a food processor. Reserve.

Roughly chop the carrots, courgettes, onion, tomatoes and mushrooms. In a little oil, sauté first the carrots, then the courgettes, until each is three-quarters cooked; set aside. Sauté the onion in oil until half done, add the tomatoes and mushrooms, and simmer until most of their liquid has gone. Reserve.

Slice the beans into short lengths, then boil these, followed by the peas, in boiling, salted water until nearly done. Reserve.

Clean the frying pan, pour in ¼" (5 mm) depth

Clockwise from right: Steamed fresh scallops with garlic (recipe on page 39); cold tomato and sweetcorn soup (recipe on page 29); vegetable paella

of oil, add the rice and stir over a low heat for 4–5 minutes until the grains become opaque. Stir in the saffron and herbs; add everything but the beans, peas, and pepper strips, and cover with about double the ingredients' volume of broth (adding water if needed to make this up). Add salt. Bring liquid to simmer, cover and cook – without stirring – for 20 minutes (introducing beans and peas for the last 10), or until the rice has absorbed the broth and is tender, the grains still separate. Remove the lid for the last 5 minutes. Correct seasoning and serve the paella, adorned with red pepper strips.

Enough for 4.   AWS

SWISS CHARD EN PAPILLOTE WITH TAHINI CREAM

Chard leaves are ideal for enclosing fillings as they have neither the strong flavour of spinach nor the chewy texture of cabbage. Basmati rice is used for the filling because of its lovely aroma, but patna is also suitable.

12 large Swiss chard leaves

FILLING
1 onion, chopped
1 clove garlic, crushed
1″ (2 cm) cube fresh root ginger, grated
1 oz (25 g) butter
2 tablespoons olive oil
4 oz (125 g) basmati rice, uncooked
1 teaspoon each ground turmeric, cumin,
    fenugreek and coriander
¾ pint (450 ml) water or vegetable stock
Salt and ground black pepper
2 oz (50 g) shelled unsalted pistachio nuts
3–5 tablespoons natural yoghurt, preferably
    ewes' milk

SAUCE
6 tablespoons tahini (sesame paste)
1 clove garlic, crushed
Juice of ½ lemon
Water, to mix

Trim and chop the chard stems. Blanch the leaves until just limp and bright green. Drain and cool.

Sweat the onion, garlic, ginger and chard stems in the butter and oil for about 5 minutes. Add the rice and stir-fry until opaque, then add the spices. Fry for a further minute.

Pour in the water or stock, season well, bring to the boil, then cover and simmer gently for 15 minutes. Stir in the nuts and yoghurt.

Spread the chard leaves out and spoon the filling into the centre of each. Fold up like parcels and arrange, join sides down, on a platter. Cover and keep warm.

Blend the tahini with the garlic, lemon juice, salt and enough water to make a consistency of pouring cream. Serve the sauce separately.

Serves 6.   RD

WATERCRESS FLAN

Bacon, while adding a pleasant saltiness to the filling, could be left out when catering for vegetarians. Add an extra ounce (25 g) of walnuts and additional Parmesan to the filling instead.

8 oz (250 g) shortcrust pastry
1 oz (25 g) grated Cheddar cheese
8 oz (250 g) back bacon rashers
1 oz (25 g) butter
2 bunches watercress
4 oz (125 g) button mushrooms
6 oz (175 g) cottage cheese
2 eggs
1 oz (25 g) chopped walnuts
Salt and pepper
1 oz (25 g) grated Parmesan cheese

Work the Cheddar cheese into the pastry and line an 8″ (20 cm) flan ring. Prick lightly with a fork and line with foil, and bake at 400°F (200°C, gas mark 6) for 15 minutes. Remove foil and continue baking pastry for 5 minutes. Meanwhile, chop the bacon and cook in the butter until just cooked but not coloured. Poach the watercress in a little water for 5 minutes, drain and chop. Mix the bacon and watercress and place on the base of the pastry case. Chop the mushrooms and mix with the cheese, eggs, walnuts, salt and pepper. Pour into the flan case and sprinkle with Parmesan cheese. Bake at 350°F (180°C, gas mark 4) for 35 minutes. Serve freshly baked and warm.

Serves 4–6.   MN

SPICED PARSNIP AND COCONUT FALAFELS

Little patties, traditionally made with chick peas in the Middle East.

1 lb (500 g) parsnips, peeled
1 tablespoon toasted desiccated coconut
1 tablespoon cream or yoghurt
1 oz (25 g) butter
1 egg, beaten
4 oz (125 g) fresh breadcrumbs, white or brown
1½ teaspoons mild curry powder
Salt
Ground black pepper
Sesame seeds, for coating, optional
Vegetable oil, for frying

Boil the parsnips until just tender. Cut out any tough fibres and mash the flesh. Mix with all of the remaining ingredients except seeds and oil. Taste to ensure the mixture is well seasoned. Chill until firm.

With wet hands, shape the mixture into small patties and coat in the sesame seeds.

Heat enough oil to come ½" (1 cm) up the sides of a frying pan, and fry the patties until golden brown, about 2–3 minutes on each side. Serve hot or cold.

Makes about 12.   RD

COURGETTE AND GOATS' CHEESE SOUFFLES

The creamy sweetness of courgettes combined with tangy goats' cheese is a successful liaison.

4 medium courgettes
1 shallot, finely chopped
1 clove garlic, crushed
1 oz (25 g) butter
1½ oz (40 g) flour
2 oz (50 g) creamy goats' cheese, without rind
4 tablespoons cream
2 eggs, separated
2 tablespoons fresh grated Parmesan
Salt and ground black pepper
Flaked almonds, to sprinkle

Cut the top quarter lengthwise off each courgette. They are not needed for this recipe but can be used elsewhere. Preheat the oven to 375°F (190°C, gas mark 5).

With a melon baller or teaspoon, scoop out the flesh, leaving the shells intact. Chop the flesh very finely and mix with the shallot and garlic. Season the shells.

Steam the shells for 3 minutes, or simmer in the minimum of water. Drain well, upside down.

Meanwhile, sweat the courgette mixture in the butter for 5 minutes until quite pulpy. Stir in the flour, cook for a further minute. Cut the cheese up and stir in until melted then add the cream, egg yolks, Parmesan and plenty of seasoning.

Whisk the egg whites until stiff and carefully fold in, then pile into the courgette shells.

Sprinkle with the almonds and bake for 25 minutes until risen and golden. Serve immediately.

Serves 4.   RD

POTATO AND PARSNIP AMANDINE

The flesh of baked potatoes is mixed with parsnip purée and topped with almonds (see page 91).

4 baking potatoes, about 6 oz (175 g) each
A little oil, for brushing
8 oz (250 g) parsnips, peeled and diced
1 oz (25 g) butter
2–3 tablespoons milk or cream
1 teaspoon mild curry powder
1 small onion, chopped finely
3 oz (75 g) mature Cheddar or Gruyère, grated
Salt and ground black pepper
2 egg yolks
About 1 oz (25 g) slivered almonds

Score around the middle of the potatoes with a sharp knife, then rub with a little oil. This helps keep the skins tender. Place on a baking sheet and bake at 400°F (200°C, gas mark 6) for about 1 hour, when the flesh inside should be fluffy and cooked.

Meanwhile, boil the parsnips in lightly salted water until tender. Drain and mash or purée in a food processor.

Cut the potatoes in half and carefully scoop out the flesh. Mash it well, making sure there are no lumps. (This is best done by hand, as machines can make the potato rather sticky.) Add the butter and milk or cream, then the parsnip and rest of the ingredients except the almonds. Season well.

Spoon back into the potato shells, and press on the almonds. The potatoes can be chilled at this stage (but not frozen) to be reheated later.

Return to the oven for a further 15 to 20 minutes until golden brown and piping hot.

Serves 4–8.   RD

VEGETABLE GRATIN

This gratin is a seasonal favourite, begun as a way of employing leftovers, but now made, each summer and autumn, as a succulent end in itself.

Potatoes, pumpkin and courgettes are first cooked separately, to retain individual character. The secret ingredient here is watercress, with its peppery flavour.

> *7 oz (200 g) farmhouse Cheddar*
> *3 oz (75 g) stale bread of good character,*
>   *crusts on*
> *2 medium potatoes, peeled*
> *6 oz (175 g) pumpkin flesh*
> *Salt*
> *1 lb 2 oz (550 g) courgettes*
> *Olive oil*
> *1½ bunches watercress*
> *4 large cloves garlic, peeled*
> *1 egg*
> *Freshly ground black pepper*

Cut cheese and bread into cubes – the former about ¼″ (5 mm) across, the latter somewhat larger – and put them into a roomy bowl.

Cube potatoes and pumpkin to a size roughly between those of the cubes above, and boil each, in turn, in salted water, until just cooked. Drain, cool, and add to the bowl.

Top and tail courgettes and slice them across into thin rounds; salt these, and use a wide, low-sided pan dribbled with olive oil to sauté courgettes, over high heat, until cooked and starting to colour. Cool, and add to the bowl.

Oil a 10″ (25 cm) porcelain gratin dish with a 1¼″ (3 cm) upright side.

Chop watercress leaves and mince the garlic; mix well, with the egg and plenty of seasoning, into the bowlful of ingredients.

Pile the vegetable mixture across the gratin dish, mounding it in the centre; dribble on a little olive oil, and bake the gratin at 400°F (200°C, gas mark 6) for 30 minutes until cheese has melted and the bread is deeply-coloured.

Serves 4, with a green salad (for 6–8 people, make 2 gratins). AWS

Vegetable gratin (in foreground); carrot, celery, potato and lovage soup (recipe on page 34); sole and red pepper jellies with red pepper sauce (see page 20); avocado and tongue salad (see page 105)

BEETROOT ROULADE WITH HORSERADISH

Root vegetables make particularly good roulades as there is no need for a white sauce base, which makes for greater simplicity and better flavour.

> *8 oz (250 g) raw unpeeled beetroot*
> *½ teaspoon ground cumin*
> *1 oz (25 g) butter*
> *2 teaspoons grated onion*
> *Salt and ground black pepper*
> *4 eggs, separated*

> FILLING
> *¼ pint (150 ml) double cream, lightly whipped*
> *2 teaspoons white wine vinegar*
> *½ teaspoon English mustard*
> *1 teaspoon sugar*
> *3 tablespoons fresh chopped parsley*
> *3 tablespoons horseradish relish*

99

Cook the beetroot by steaming or boiling until just tender. Peel, then purée in a food processor or blender. Beat in the cumin, butter, onion and plenty of seasoning.

Line and grease a Swiss roll tin. Preheat the oven to 375°F (190°C, gas mark 5).

Beat the yolks into the beet mixture, then whisk the egg whites until stiff and carefully fold in. Spoon into the tin.

Bake for about 15 minutes until firm and springy to the touch. Turn out onto a sheet of greaseproof paper on top of a cooling rack. Carefully peel off the paper in strips and then cover with a clean tea towel until cold.

Combine all the filling ingredients and spread on the base of the roulade. Roll on the roulade up from the narrow end. (Don't fret if it cracks slightly – that shows it's nice and light.) Chill until required. It looks pretty served in slices garnished with finely-chopped beetroot, celery and flat parsley leaves.

Serves 6.   RD

Broccoli with orange cream sauce

ORANGE CREAM SAUCE
Chop up the butter and heat gently to melt. Add the cream, orange rind and juice, the lemon and seasoning and heat through, shaking the pan, until it boils and thickens (can be prepared and reheated briefly). Pour over the broccoli and serve.

Serves 4–6.   NC

BROCCOLI WITH ORANGE CREAM SAUCE

Bright green, lightly-cooked broccoli, served with a trickle of orange cream sauce.

1½–2 lb (750 g–1 kg) broccoli spears

ORANGE CREAM SAUCE
1½ oz (40 g) butter
3 fl oz (75 g) double cream
A little grated orange rind
2 tablespoons orange juice
Squeeze lemon juice
Salt and pepper

Prepare the broccoli, stripping the stems if necessary. Plunge into plenty of boiling, salted water (or steam) until cooked but still crisp. Drain and refresh with about a teacup of cold water to set the colour and arrest the cooking but not to cool too much. Drain and set in a serving dish.

BROAD BEANS A LA RONDENA

Cheap and delicious, this Spanish dish, whose name comes from the Andalusian town of Ronda, makes a perfect summer lunch.

Coarse country bread of good character is essential to mop up the juices.

2 lb (1 kg) young broad beans in their pods (or
*   1½ lbs (750 g) mature beans, podded)*
3–4 oz (75–125 g) salt-dried ham (prosciutto)
*   or bacon*
3 cloves garlic
1 large onion
6 tablespoons olive oil
Large glass of water
Small glass dry sherry or white wine
Salt and pepper

TO FINISH
1 tablespoon fresh breadcrumbs
1 tablespoon chopped parsley
2 hard-boiled eggs, shelled and sliced

Top and tail the beans, and chop them into short lengths – following the swell of each bean. Do not do this in advance, as the beans go an odd navy blue colour at the edges. Cube the ham or bacon finely. Peel and chop the onion and garlic.

Warm the oil in a casserole. Put in the onion and garlic and fry for a moment without allowing it to take colour. Add the chopped ham or bacon. Fry for a moment longer. Add the beans, sherry or wine, the water, salt and freshly-milled pepper, and bring all to the boil. Cover and stew gently for 1½ hours – this can be done in a gentle oven at 325°F (170°C, gas mark 3). Check intermittently and add water if necessary. When the beans are tender, bubble up the stew uncovered for a moment to evaporate any excess liquid.

Stir in the breadcrumbs and the parsley. Reheat, taste and add more salt and pepper if necessary. Decorate with slices of hard-boiled egg.

Serve the bean stew in soup-plates, with plenty of bread to mop up the rich juices.

Serves 4.   EL

MATUFFI

The attraction of this *polenta*, illustrated on page 53, is in the layering of the cooked maize meal – finished to a softer consistency than is usual – with the wine-laced meat sauce; when sufficiently well-seasoned, *matuffi* is a dream of a country dish.

1½ oz (40 g) dried ceps (in Italian, porcini)
1 large onion, 1 medium carrot, peeled
1 stick celery
2 large cloves garlic, peeled
3 tablespoons olive oil
1 oz (25 g) butter
10 oz (300 g) minced lean beef
8 oz (250 g) minced lean pork

Large glass of good Chianti, plus more at the end
½ pint (300 ml) home-made beef stock
1½ lb (750 g) tinned Italian plum tomatoes, weighed without their juice
Bouquet of sage, basil, bay leaf
Salt and freshly-ground black pepper
10 oz (300 g) coarse or medium-ground yellow maize meal
2½ pints (1.5 litres) cold water, plus additional boiling water
Grated Parmesan cheese

To make the sauce, rehydrate mushrooms by soaking them in hot water for 20 minutes; drain well and chop.

Chop onion, carrot, celery, and garlic; using a wide, heavy casserole, sweat these in oil and butter till vegetables have softened and onion is turning golden. Add meats and stir until the flesh has coloured. Mix in mushrooms, Chianti, stock, tomatoes (breaking these up with a wooden spoon), herbs and some salt. Bring liquid to the boil and briskly simmer the sauce, over low heat and without a lid, for 40 minutes. Taste for seasoning, adding salt and pepper and a very modest amount of Chianti. Cool the sauce and refrigerate for several days to allow its flavours to mature.

When preparing to serve the matuffi, bring salted cold water to the boil and very slowly pour in the maize meal, beating with a wooden spoon to prevent the formation of lumps. Let polenta cook over low heat for 25 minutes, stirring constantly, and periodically adding enough boiling water to keep the mixture smooth and loose but cohesive. Meanwhile, heat the meat sauce separately.

When polenta is ready, season it well and line up 4 low soup dishes. Using a very large implement, spoon into each a layer of polenta, followed by spoonfuls of sauce, followed by more porridge and another layer of sauce, until all the polenta is used. Strew well with Parmesan and eat immediately, followed by a green salad.

Serves 4.   AWS

101

SALADS FOR ALL SEASONS

From a simple composition of fresh leaves – lettuce, endive, chicory, corn salad and rocket – to substantial combinations of crisp winter vegetables, these salads are for year-round eating

A SALAD FROM THE GOLDEN STATE

In Berkeley, across the Bay from San Francisco, Bill Fujimoto's Monterey Market is a neon-lit mad-house of superb produce – much of it organically grown – sold at rock-bottom prices.

The ebullient and knowledgeable Bill (California-born, of Japanese descent) is one of the great characters of a city not noted for the inarticulate. His discourse on the Market's three kinds of 'organic salad mix' – of which they sell 40–50 cartons a day – deftly encompasses the foggy northern coastal climate suited to growing lettuce, the criteria for a good 'mix' (based on a *mesclun* assortment of curly endive, rocket, and various small, *whole* leaves) and the characteristic local addition of Oriental or Central American greenery like *mizuna*, *shiso* or amaranthus, introduced to the state by immigrant farmers.

To make a salad, here, which is redolent of California's diversity, proceed as follows: infuse some cold-pressed, extra-virgin olive oil with chunks of peeled and bruised fresh ginger, refrigerating for two days. When ready to use, bring oil to room temperature and drain.

For each person, use some *un*-infused oil to sauté separately, till just cooked, a few peeled baby carrots; a quarter of red onion, peeled and sliced; a quarter of seeded sweet yellow pepper, unpeeled and sliced. When cooled, turn each vegetable in snipped fennel leaves and a little of the ginger oil.

Coat a mixture of small leaves – oak leaf, red chicory, curly endive, *mâche* – plus rocket and purple basil, in the gingery oil. Arrange these across plates with a tangle of vegetables, a pansy or two – and some tiny chillies just for looks; grind on black pepper and serve.   AWS

FIRE-DRIED WALNUTS AND PECANS

Barbara Tropp is a native of New Jersey, author of an exhaustive volume called *The Modern Art of Chinese Cooking* (published by William Morrow), and chef-proprietor of a San Francisco restaurant named the China Moon Café, where sparkling things happen with Chinese home cooking. Unexpected ingredients like sun-dried tomatoes or baby squash meet pot-browned noodles, and these unusual crisp nuts are one of Barbara Tropp's array of Hunanese 'little dishes' that begin a meal. The recipe is adapted from Miss Tropp's book.

>*8 oz (250 g) plump, perfect walnut and pecan*
> *halves*
>*2 teaspoons corn or peanut oil*
>*¼–½ teaspoon Maldon sea salt*
>*1½–2 tablespoons caster sugar*

Right *A salad from the Golden State, with (at left) fire-dried walnuts and pecans*

Mesclun salad with warm bacon, roquefort and raspberry dressing

MESCLUN SALAD WITH WARM BACON, ROQUEFORT AND RASPBERRY DRESSING

Bacon fat imparts the most delicious flavour to salad dressing – even better if it is accompanied by small crisp strips of lean streaky bacon and a sweet fruit vinegar like raspberry.

A mesclun is a mixed leaf salad of whatever delicious leaves are available. Gardeners can grow great quantities of rocket, purslane, spinach, sorrel and nasturtium with the greatest of ease and add these leaves to a prepared mixture of sliced endive, radicchio, crisp lettuce or whatever else happens to be in season. The sheer variety of leaves is a great talking point when entertaining – even better if you scatter the top with a selection of nasturtium, violet or hyssop flowers.

About 2 lbs (1 kg) total weight mixed prepared
salad leaves
4 oz (125 g) Roquefort or other crumbly blue-
veined cheese
8 oz (250 g) crustless white bread, diced
Vegetable oil, for frying
4 tablespoons walnut or virgin olive oil
8 oz (250 g) lean rinded streaky bacon, diced
2 tablespoons raspberry, cider or other fruit
vinegar
1 tablespoon brandy
Ground black pepper

Cover nuts with boiling water; soak for 30 minutes. Drain, pat dry, and spread evenly on a large, heavy baking sheet lined with a triple thickness of kitchen paper.

Dry for 30 minutes in centre of a 300°F (150°C, gas mark 2) oven. Turn sheet, reduce heat to 250°F (130°C, gas mark ½), and check at 10-minute intervals. Remove nuts from oven when almost dry, with a little moisture left at the core.

Warm a wok or heavy sauté pan over moderate heat till hot. Swirl in oil, add nuts, stir with a wooden spoon till glossed with oil and warm to the touch; do not scorch.

Mix in ¼ teaspoon salt, and slowly add sugar, ½ tablespoon at a time, until you reach an agreeable sweetness. The taste should be lively and sweet, with a hint of salt; add more of this if necessary. Stir constantly while seasoning; the process takes 3–4 minutes. Salt and sugar will melt and adhere to nuts, creating a shiny crunch.

Serve hot or cold as an hors d'œuvre for 10–15 people.   AWS

Mix the leaves well together. Crumble the cheese and mix this in too.

Fry the diced bread in about ¼" (6 mm) of hot vegetable oil until crisp and golden. Drain and cool. Discard the oil and wipe the pan clean.

Heat the walnut or olive oil in the pan, then fry the diced bacon over a moderate heat until crisp but not burnt.

Stir in the vinegar and brandy, season with pepper to taste then bubble up for half a minute, scraping the pan well. Keep the dressing warm until ready to use, then pour it over the leaves and toss well with the croûtons. Eat immediately.

Serves 8.   RD

SEA-KALE AND CHICKEN SALAD

Raw sea-kale makes an excellent salad with cooked chicken and mayonnaise.

1 breakfast-cup diced cooked chicken breast
½ cup chopped raw sea-kale
½ cup mayonnaise
White pepper and salt
Sprigs of watercress to garnish

Mix together the chicken, sea-kale and mayonnaise. Season to taste, and garnish with watercress.
Serves 4 as a starter.   BGM

CREOLE COLESLAW

This is a lighter and spicier version of a traditional American (and British) favourite.

¼ each red and white cabbage, finely shredded
¼ Spanish onion, sliced thinly
4 tablespoons good olive oil
½ bouillon cube dissolved in 3 tablespoons
    boiling water
3 tablespoons wine vinegar
2 tablespoons fresh chopped parsley
1 tablespoon fresh chopped basil
1 teaspoon fresh chopped thyme
Few drops hot pepper sauce (optional)
Salt
Freshly ground black pepper
1 medium carrot, grated
1 tablespoon caraway seeds, to sprinkle

Toss the cabbage and onion in the oil and leave for an hour.

Mix the strong stock with the vinegar, herbs, pepper sauce (if using) and seasoning. Mix into the cabbage and let stand for another hour or two, to allow the flavours to blend.

Spoon into a serving bowl and sprinkle over the grated carrot and the caraway seeds.
Serves 4–6.   RD

AVOCADO AND TONGUE SALAD

The blandness of avocado is an excellent foil for pickled ox tongue.

1¼ lb (625 g) meat from a boiled, pickled ox
    tongue, well-chilled – preferably one prepared
    at home according to a standard recipe
6 oz (175 g) chopped walnuts
9 oz (275 g) raw, tender spinach
6 oz (175 g) batavia, oak-leaf or other
    interesting lettuce leaves
3 ripe avocados weighing 10 oz (300 g) each
Juice of one lemon
2 tablespoons red wine vinegar
4 fl oz (125 ml) olive oil
Salt
Black pepper
3 spring onions
3 hard-boiled eggs

Cut tongue into lardon-like pieces and place these in a large salad bowl.

Lightly toast walnuts for 10–15 minutes in a 300°F (150°C, gas mark 2) oven, cool nuts and add them to the bowl.

Stem spinach, wash with the lettuce and dry well. Use a large, sharp knife to shred both sorts of leaf across into thin strips. Add these to the bowl and toss the contents with your hands.

Halve avocados, discard stones and skins and slice flesh lengthwise into slim sections; to prevent discoloration, set aside in a bowl of water acidulated with lemon juice.

Make a vinaigrette with vinegar, olive oil, and seasoning; mince the white part of the spring onions and add to the dressing. Chop eggs and stir in two-thirds of these.

When ready to serve the salad, drain the avocado and add to the bowl. Pour on vinaigrette and carefully but thoroughly toss the contents, using your hands for best results. Strew the remaining chopped egg across the top, and present, with salad servers.

Enough for 6 as a light main course, eaten with good bread.   AWS

WINTER SALADS

Good winter salads are really no more difficult than summer ones. There are not many herbs about, it is true, so for potato salad, substitute spring onion to decorate and flavour the dish. This has the advantage that onion–haters can easily pick them out. To make spring onion curls, cut the onions into short lengths, slit each one several times, leaving ½″ (1 cm) or so whole at the bottom, and put them in iced water for an hour or two, or overnight.

Beetroot salad is flavoured with toasted coriander, only a hint of vinegar and good olive oil. Buy freshly-boiled beetroot that have not been ruined with acetic acid, or boil your own. Then ball, dice or grate the beets and toss them in a dressing of eight parts mild olive oil, to one part balsamic or wine vinegar, seasoned with ground toasted coriander seeds (heat them in a small pan then grind them in a pepper grinder), salt and freshly-ground black pepper.

For a green salad with radicchio the dressing is another vinaigrette which is light on vinegar. This time the formula is eight or more parts of sunflower oil to two of walnut oil and one of wine vinegar, seasoned to taste with salt, pepper and some light French mustard.   SCP

HOME-SPROUTED BEANS

Sprouting your own beans and seeds is very satisfying and provides a constant fresh supply of tasty and highly nutritious food, which is an excellent sandwich filling or salad ingredient.

Old beans will not sprout easily, so buy in a new supply if those you have are more than a year old. Generally speaking, beans take about 2–5 days to sprout. If yours haven't sprouted within 48 hours, they are probably too old, so discard them and start again.

Suitable beans are green or brown lentils, chick peas, mung beans, aduki beans, soya beans, haricot beans and flageolet beans. It is a good idea to sprout two or three types of beans at the same time for variety.

METHOD
First, rinse 2–3 tablespoons of beans and place in a large jar with water to cover. Cover this with cheesecloth, muslin or a clean J-Cloth, secured with an elastic band.

Leave overnight, then drain through the cloth top, refill with water through the cloth, shake gently and drain immediately. Lay the jar on its side in a shaded, fairly warm place.

Rinse and drain twice a day until the beans have sprouts at least twice their length (don't let them get too long). If you can't use them at once, then bag in polythene and store in the fridge, but use within a few days.

Use fresh sprouts for all sorts of dishes, or simply sprinkle over hot meals in the same way as grated cheese. They are excellent in salads, over pilaffs or casseroles, in stuffings and croquettes. They also make a pretty garnish.   RD

A winter salad

TOFU AND LENTIL SPROUT SALAD

Here is a healthy salad using home-sprouted lentils tossed in a delicious honey soy dressing. It makes an excellent starter.

Tofu is made from coagulated soya milk, in a process similar to the making of cottage cheese. It is extremely nutritious, but rather bland in flavour. Smoked tofu has more character, and is now widely available from health food shops and delicatessens. Here, it is grilled before being cubed and mixed with the dressing.

> 8 oz (250 g) smoked tofu bean curd
> Leaves of frisée or other frilly lettuce
> 4 oz (125 g) oyster mushrooms, sliced if large
> 1 carrot, sliced thinly lengthwise with a
>   vegetable peeler
> 2 spring onions, chopped
> 4 oz (125 g) whole green beans, topped, halved
>   and blanched
> About 2–3 handfuls of freshly sprouted lentils,
>   mung or aduki beans

DRESSING
> 2 tablespoons vegetable oil
> 1 tablespoon sesame oil
> 1 clove garlic, crushed
> 1 tablespoon fresh chopped ginger
> 2 oz (50 g) walnut pieces
> 2 tablespoons light soy sauce
> 1 tablespoon dry sherry (optional)
> 1 teaspoon clear honey
> 1 tablespoon wine vinegar
> Salt and ground black pepper

Grill the smoked tofu until browned, then cut into bite-size cubes.

Line four salad plates with the frilly lettuce, mixing different coloured leaves if available.

Shake all the dressing ingredients together in a screw-topped jar.

Mix the salad foods together, then toss in the dressing. Pile portions onto the lettuce leaves, and serve at once.

Serves 4.   RD

Tofu and lentil sprout salad

SUMMER COLESLAW

Light summer coleslaw includes fine shreds of Chinese leaves, or any other salad greens, grated mooli (the long white radish), bean sprouts, mange-tout, watercress and grated carrot. The addition of chickpea sprouts lends an interesting texture and taste to this salad.

> 4 oz (125 g) small head Chinese leaves,
>   shredded
> 8 oz (250 g) mooli, grated
> 4 oz (125 g) carrot, grated
> 4 oz (125 g) bean sprouts
> 4 oz (125 g) mangetout peas, cooked 3 minutes
>   and drained
> 2 oz (50 g) chickpea sprouts
> 4 spring onions, finely shredded
> 1 bunch watercress

DRESSING
> 2 tablespoons herb vinegar
> ½ teaspoon salt
> Freshly ground black pepper
> 2 cloves garlic, peeled and crushed
> ½ carton (225 g) Greek yoghurt
> 6 tablespoons sunflower oil

Toss all the salad ingredients together in a large bowl, reserving some of the watercress. Cover with clingfilm and chill for up to 2 hours.

Just before serving, blend vinegar, seasoning, crushed garlic and yoghurt together. Whisk in oil and pour over the salad ingredients. Toss well and spoon onto plates garnished with reserved sprigs of watercress.

Serves 4–6.   SM

CALIFORNIA SHREDDED CHICKEN SALAD

The peanut butter gives the dressing a delicious Oriental flavour.

6 boneless chicken breasts, skinned
½ cucumber
2 sticks celery
3 spring onions
4 oz (125 g) mangetout, blanched
2 oz (50 g) fresh thin ribbon pasta
Sunflower oil, for frying

DRESSING
1 clove garlic, crushed
2 teaspoons grated fresh ginger
1 tablespoon smooth peanut butter
2 tablespoons fresh chopped coriander
Pinch each sugar and dry mustard powder
4 tablespoons light soy sauce
4 tablespoons rice wine vinegar
2 tablespoons sunflower oil
2 tablespoons sesame oil
Few drops Chinese hot chilli oil

Poach the chicken in light stock for 15 minutes or until cooked. Cool in the stock for an hour or two, then refrigerate. When needed, tear the chicken into chunky bite-size strips.

Slice the cucumber, not too thinly, then cut the slices into shreds. Slice the celery and onions diagonally and halve the mangetout.

Put all the dressing ingredients into a screw-top jar and shake to blend. Mix everything together

in a large bowl and chill for 2 hours.

Just before serving, snip the pasta into manageable lengths and fry in hot oil until golden and crispy. Drain well and cool. Serve the salad accompanied by the crispy noodles.

Serves 6.   RD

BROWN BASMATI, OLIVE AND GREEK CHEESE SALAD

Although not quite as fragrant as the refined white variety, wholegrain basmati rice still seems to have an elegance, and is delightful for a light summer salad. The fresh lemon and olive oil dressing should be added while the rice is still hot so that the flavour has time to develop.

8 oz (250 g) basmati rice, rinsed
2 tablespoons extra virgin olive oil
Juice 1 small lemon
A quarter of cucumber, halved
1 stick celery
4–6 oz (125–175 g) good black olives
6 oz (175 g) firm white Greek cheese, e.g. feta,
*   haloumi or kefalotiri*
2 tablespoons fresh chopped parsley or mint
*   (optional)*
Chicory and watercress or rocket leaves
Salt
Ground black pepper

Cook the basmati rice according to instructions on the packet. Drain and toss in the oil and lemon juice. Season lightly, especially with the salt to allow for the strong flavour of the olives and the salty Greek cheese.

Cut the cucumber and celery into slanting slices. Stone the olives and cube the cheese. Toss them into the rice when it has cooled. Mix in the herbs. Chill.

Serve on a large platter for a buffet dish, or individual plates for a starter, garnished with the chicory and cress.

Serves 4–6.   RD

A salad of mixed leaves

CARROT AND TURNIP SALAD WITH CORIANDER DRESSING

Lightly blanched tender root vegetables, left to cool in a flavoursome coriander dressing, make a delicious salad accompaniment for cold meats.

12 oz (350 g) carrots, peeled and thinly sliced
8 oz (250 g) young turnips, unpeeled and thinly sliced
8 spring onions, sliced

DRESSING
3 tablespoons walnut, hazelnut or olive oil
2 tablespoons sunflower oil
2 tablespoons wine vinegar
Pinch mustard powder

2 teaspoons clear honey
3 tablespoons fresh chopped coriander
Salt and ground black pepper

Blanch or steam the vegetables for just 2 to 3 minutes, until still quite crisp. Drain and mix with the spring onions. Mix up the dressing in a screw top jar and toss into the vegetables while they are cooling. Chill lightly until ready to serve.

Serves 4. RD

BYESSAR (MOROCCAN BROAD BEAN SALAD)

A salad-purée much like the Middle Eastern hummus, a dish of *byessar* brings tears of home-sickness to the eyes of emigrant Moroccans.

1 lb (500 g) shelled broad beans
2 cloves garlic, peeled and roughly chopped
1 teaspoon chopped marjoram
1 teaspoon powdered cumin
Salt and freshly milled pepper
¼ pint (150 ml) good olive oil

TO FINISH
2–3 spring onions
1 teaspoon paprika
½ teaspoon chilli powder
½ teaspoon powdered cumin
1 tablespoon olive oil

Put beans in a saucepan with enough salted water to cover, and simmer for 15 minutes, until tender. Place in the blender with ½ cup of their cooking liquid, garlic, marjoram, cumin, pepper and a level teaspoon of salt. Pour in enough cold water to cover beans. Add olive oil and process the mixture to a purée. Taste and adjust the seasoning.

Trim and finely chop the spring onions and stir them in. Transfer the purée to a bowl.

Mix the paprika and cumin with the olive oil, and dribble a scarlet swirl over the pale green purée.

Serve warm, with pitta bread for scooping.

Serves 4–6 as a first course. EL

109

SALMON AND ASPARAGUS PINWHEEL SALAD

Although similar to a roulade, this takes a fraction of the time and looks equally attractive. Each omelette is topped with thin slices of smoked salmon and asparagus spears before it is rolled up. Cool before slicing.

> *16 spears asparagus*
> *2 beaten eggs*
> *2 tablespoons cold water*
> *Salt*
> *Fresh-milled black pepper*
> *4 thin slices smoked salmon*

> GRAVLAX DRESSING
> *2 tablespoons Dijon mustard*
> *½ teaspoon English mustard*
> *2 teaspoons caster sugar*
> *1–2 tablespoons herb vinegar*
> *6–8 tablespoons sunflower oil*
> *Salt*
> *Freshly-milled black pepper*
> *8 stems fresh dill; keep a few sprigs for garnish*
> *and chop remainder*

Trim the ends from the asparagus spears and cook in boiling water for 4–5 minutes or until just tender. Drain well and reserve.

For the omelettes, add water and seasoning to eggs. Cook half the mixture in a lightly oiled 8″ (20 cm) frying pan on one side only, until set and golden. Cool slightly in the pan, top with salmon and four asparagus spears placed in pairs along the length of the omelette. Roll up and lift out of pan. Make second omelette in the same way.

Make the dressing by blending mustard, sugar and vinegar together, then whisking in the oil to make a creamy sauce. Add the seasoning and some chopped dill.

Allow half an omelette per person. Slice, and garnish with remaining asparagus spears, dill sprigs and sauce.

Serves 4.   SM

Beet and apple salad with two cheeses and walnuts

BEET AND APPLE SALAD WITH TWO CHEESES AND WALNUTS

There are a number of delicious beetroot salads – this one, with fresh horseradish and apple, is ideal for a light lunch.

> *About 1 lb (500 g) raw, unpeeled beetroot*
> *3 tablespoons fresh grated horseradish*
> *½ red apple, preferably Washington Red, grated*

> DRESSING
> *2 tablespoons fresh chopped chives*
> *4 tablespoons mayonnaise*
> *1 tablespoon wine vinegar*
> *1 dessertspoon whole-grain mustard*
> *Good pinch sugar*
> *Salt*
> *Fresh ground black pepper*

> TO SERVE
> *4 oz (125 g) mould-ripened goats' cheese*
> *4 oz (125 g) blue cheese, e.g. Roquefort, Stilton*
> *or, for colour, Blue Cheshire*
> *12–16 large fresh walnuts*
> *4 fresh celery sticks*

Scrub the beetroot: do not peel or cut the skin. Boil whole in salted water until tender – about 20 minutes depending on the size. Cool in the water, then peel and grate. Stir in the horseradish and apple.

Mix the dressing ingredients together and stir into the salad. Check the seasoning. Chill.

Serve in small mounds on plates accompanied by thin slices of cheese, the walnuts and celery.

Serves 4–6.   RD

CAJUN COLD RICE

Cajun cooking is supposed to be hotter and more rustic Louisiana cooking than Creole, the food of the town folk. But the following dish is not really a simple rice salad, suggesting that the distinctions have become blurred.

8 oz (250 g) American long grain rice
1 pint (600 ml) chicken stock
3 tablespoons good olive oil
1 tablespoon wine vinegar
1 teaspoon dry mustard powder
1 clove garlic, crushed
Yolk of 1 hard-boiled egg, mashed
Pinch cayenne
¼ pint (150 ml) mayonnaise
4 tablespoons chopped green olives
2 sticks celery, sliced thinly
2 tablespoons diced dill pickle cucumber
1 small red pepper, chopped
Salt and freshly ground black pepper

TO SERVE
4–6 whole Webbs lettuce leaves
1 hard-boiled egg plus white from dressing yolk
Small tomato wedges
Fresh chopped parsley

Simmer the rice in the chicken stock in a covered saucepan for about 15 minutes, until all the stock has been absorbed.

Mix together the oil, vinegar, mustard, garlic, mashed egg yolk and cayenne, with a little seasoning, then toss into the rice as it cools. Chill in the

refrigerator until needed.

Mix in the mayonnaise, chopped olives, celery, pickles and red pepper. Check the seasoning.

Serve spooned into the lettuce leaves and garnish with the chopped egg, tomato and parsley.

Serves 4–6.   RD

HOT BACON AND RAW SPINACH SALAD

Raw spinach leaves, tossed in hot dressing, with crisp bacon and croûtons, illustrated on page 87.

1 lb (500 g) washed and trimmed tender spinach
6 oz (175 g) diced streaky bacon
1 clove garlic, crushed
White wine vinegar
Pepper, salt if needed
Croûtons of fried bread

Tear spinach leaves into small pieces. Fry bacon and garlic gently until fat runs and bacon is crisp. Remove bacon, add a little vinegar to the pan, and mix with the fat. Toss the spinach in the pan, mix in with the bacon, and allow to heat but not cook. Serve with crisp croûtons.

Serves 4.   BGM

SALAD OF PUMPKIN AND MARIGOLD

The cubed, just-cooked flesh of the pumpkin or another of the firm, orange-fleshed winter squashes like Hubbard or Queensland blue, is very agreeable linked to the crunch of lettuce, Mediterranean rocket, and freshly-fried breadcrumbs. The slightly bitter petals of pot marigold complement the spice and zest of rocket, and their colour, with the squash, is wonderful.

For each person, cover a dinner plate with lettuce leaves – batavia and oak-leaf, for instance – and a moderate amount of Mediterranean rocket (its impact is strong) tossed in seasoned hazelnut or walnut oil. Then plunge 5 oz (150 g) per person of pumpkin or the flesh of one other of the winter squashes – cut in ½″ (1 cm) cubes – into boiling, salted water; the squash will cook within 30–60 seconds.

Drain cubes thoroughly, place in a sauté pan coated with a heated film of the same oil as used for the lettuce, and toss pumpkin in this, on a high flame, for some 30 seconds. Add salt and a small handful of dried, home-made crumbs of whole-meal bread; toss for 30 seconds longer, and distribute squash with crumbs over lettuce. Strew pumpkin and leaves with the petals of pot marigold, grind on pepper, and serve.   AWS

PERIGORD SALAD

In the same way that the products of Normandy, like apples, cider and cream, team up so well together, so do those of the Périgord, like goats' cheese, walnuts and walnut oil. There is no doubt that walnut oil is a luxury, but the flavour it adds to certain salads, especially when it is a main course like this one, certainly justifies the expense. Once the bottle or tin has been opened, store it in the fridge, or it may go off.

Périgord salad

FOR THE SALAD
8 oz (250 g) curly endive
8 oz (250 g) radicchio
1 small head of celery
8 oz (250 g) cauliflower florets
5 oz (150 g) good quality French salami, sliced
6 oz (175 g) goats' cheese
4 oz (125 g) walnuts, roughly chopped

FOR THE DRESSING
6 tablespoons walnut oil
3 tablespoons wine vinegar
3 teaspoons Meaux mustard
A pinch of brown sugar
Salt and freshly milled black pepper

Wash and thoroughly dry the endive and radicchio. Tear roughly into pieces and place in the base of a large salad bowl. Chop the celery and break the cauliflower florets into small pieces and scatter over the endive and radicchio. Cut the salami into quarters and arrange on the top, then crumble over the goats' cheese and sprinkle with the walnuts. Cover with clingwrap and place in the fridge until the salad is required.

Blend all the ingredients for the dressing together in a screw-topped jar and shake well until thoroughly blended.

Pour over the salad just before serving and toss lightly together.

Serves 6.   JR

AMERICAN SALAD DRESSINGS

For simple green salads, American variations on a basic vinaigrette might include fresh citrus juices, chilli sauce, crushed pineapple, melted bacon fat, ground pecan nuts, often with extra quality virgin olive oil and balsamic vinegar, or Japanese rice wine vinegar.

Thicker dressings, such as those included here are based on homemade mayonnaise, with the addition of anchovies and fresh herbs, or sweet red pepper and chilli sauce.

GREEN GODDESS

A dressing inspired in the mid-1920s by William Archer's play, *The Green Goddess*, and created at San Francisco's Palace Hotel. It should be made with fresh herbs only, which rather restricts the season to the summertime.

½ pint (300 ml) good homemade mayonnaise
4 anchovy fillets, finely chopped
1 large spring onion, chopped
2 tablespoons tarragon vinegar
2 tablespoons fresh chopped parsley
2 tablespoons fresh chopped tarragon
3 tablespoons fresh chopped chives
Freshly ground black pepper

Blend everything together and serve on the day of making.

ROASTED PIMIENTO

An adaptation of Thousand Island Dressing which is in turn based on Russian Dressing.

1 medium red pepper
½ pint (300 ml) homemade mayonnaise
3–4 tablespoons sweet chilli sauce
3–4 tablespoons chopped dill pickles
1 chopped green pepper
2 chopped hard-boiled eggs
A little thin cream (optional)

Grill the red pepper under a high heat, turning it frequently, until it blisters and chars. Peel, rinse and de-seed, then chop finely or pulverize.

Mix the pepper with the other ingredients, adding cream if it seems a little thick. Serve on the same day as making.   RD

SALADE GRIBICHE

The strong flavours and contrasting textures of this salad make it interesting enough to serve as a starter. Accompany with good bread.

Salade gribiche

¼ cucumber, diced
½ lettuce, shredded coarsely
4 oz (125 g) mangetout
1 stick celery, diced
8 cherry tomatoes
1 hard-boiled egg
2 oz (50 g) Emmenthal cheese, cubed
A stick of broccoli

SAUCE GRIBICHE
1 teaspoon mustard
2 fl oz (50 g) wine vinegar
5 fl oz (150 g) olive oil
1 shallot, chopped
1 teaspoon each capers and chopped gherkin
Salt and pepper

Blanch broccoli for one minute in boiling salted water. Blanch mangetout in the same way.

Pound the yolk of the hard-boiled egg to a paste, and mix with mustard and a drop of vinegar. Slowly add oil, whisking well so it emulsifies, then add vinegar and seasoning to taste. Add shallot, capers and gherkins. Pour sauce onto serving plates and arrange salad and cheese on top. Decorate with chopped egg white.

Serves 4.   CB

PICKLES AND PRESERVES

A store-cupboard stocked with home-made chutneys, syrups, jams and jellies preserves the summer fruits and flowers and adds a distinctive flavour to year-round cooking

SPICED VINEGAR

This recipe is suitable for pickling most vegetables, such as onions, red cabbage, beetroot and so on. You may add more spices, like chillies, if you like your pickles fiery hot, but the recipe here is for average British palates.

It is much cheaper to buy your own individual spices loose, than to use the supermarket jars of ready-mixed spices.

Wine vinegars make a milder pickle, and are ideal for using with the delicate flavours of mushrooms or red peppers. Experiment with the flavoured kinds, like tarragon, garlic or cider, or add a dash of raspberry vinegar for special flavour.

Malt vinegar, which, strictly speaking, is not vinegar at all, as it is not made from wine, is better for more robust and traditionally British pickles like onions and red cabbage – the clear distilled sort has the same strength as the dark brown malt variety, but shows off the dark hues of colourful vegetables like beetroot.

For every 4 pints (2.25 litres) of vinegar you need ½ oz (15 g) black peppercorns; ¼ oz (7 g) coriander seeds; a few crushed bay leaves; 2 whole chillies (dried or fresh); 1″ (2.5 cm) fresh ginger, chopped; 3 cloves garlic, halved; ½ oz (15 g) cloves; ½ oz (15 g) celery seed; ½ oz (15 g) mace flakes; ½ oz (15 g) mustard seed.

Simmer the spices with the vinegar for 15 minutes (open the window as the acrid fumes will make your eyes water), then strain, cool and use as directed.   AW

RASPBERRY VINEGAR

Fill a jar with fresh ripe raspberries, mash them lightly and cover with white wine vinegar and seal. After one month, strain off the liquid and put it into a clean bottle with a few fresh berries. It is delicious added to salad dressings and can also be used to make a refreshing summer cordial – dilute one part vinegar to five parts cold water, add a teaspoon of sugar per glass and serve with ice cubes.   JH

HERB AND SPICE VINEGAR

1¾ pints (1 litre) red or white wine vinegar
Large handful each tarragon, basil, parsley,
*   summer savory*
4 red chilli peppers
4 cloves
20 black or white peppercorns

Mix all the ingredients together, cover and leave to stand for four weeks. Strain, label and bottle. Another highly fragrant and spicy vinegar, which may be varied according to the fresh herbs which are available; the above selection gives a good balance of flavouring.   MN

Right *Three spicy vinegars (background), with jars of pickled eggs, piccalilli and green tomato chutney*

CITRON VINEGAR

This is a particularly delicious vinegar for mayonnaise or an oil-and-vinegar dressing.

1¾ pints (1 litre) white wine vinegar
2 lemons
2 limes
½ orange
Pinch salt
Pinch paprika

Put the vinegar into a pan. Thinly slice one of the lemons, with its peel on, and add to the pan. Grate the rinds of the other lemon, limes and orange into the pan. Add the juice from one lime, with the salt and paprika. Bring to the boil and cool completely. Put into a screw-top jar or bottle, and leave in a warm, sunny place for two weeks, before straining, bottling and labelling.　　　　　MN

SUMMER GARDEN VINEGAR

This is a highly aromatic vinegar, easily made by the keen gardener.

5 pints (2.75 litres) red or white wine vinegar
Large handful each tarragon, scented rose petals,
*　　fennel, nasturtium flowers*
2 garlic cloves, peeled
10 button or pickling onions, peeled
1 oz (25 g) dried elderflowers
1 large sprig thyme
3 bay leaves
3 cloves
1 oz (25 g) salt

Put all the ingredients into a large bowl. Cover with a cloth and leave to stand for four weeks. Strain, bottle and label.　　　　　MN

FLOWER VINEGAR

1¾ pints (1 litre) white wine vinegar
2 oz (50 g) edible flowers

A selection of flowers may be used, including old-fashioned scented roses, elderflowers, thyme and marjoram flowers, violets, pinks, and the flowers of basil and garlic. Spread these on a piece of clean paper, and dry in a sunny place for two days. Put into a bottle with the vinegar and seal tightly. Leave in a warm sunny place for two weeks before straining, bottling and labelling. This vinegar has a delicate flavour which is best used with a lightly flavoured oil for salads.　　　　　MN

STRONG GARLIC VINEGAR

1¾ pints (1 litre) red or white wine vinegar
4 large garlic cloves
2 small onions
2 bay leaves
2 sprigs tarragon
4 cloves
Large pinch each ground nutmeg and salt

Put the vinegar into a jar and add the crushed garlic and chopped onions. Add the other ingredients and seal tightly. Leave in a warm sunny place for three weeks before straining, bottling and labelling.

For 'country vinegar', omit the bay leaves, but include two elderflower heads and two large sprigs of mint.　　　　　MN

STERILISING AND POTTING

To prevent chutneys going mouldy, it is important to sterilize the jars. Wash them thoroughly, then stand them without lids on a baking sheet in a low oven for about ½ hour.

Spoon hot mixture into them, allowing about ½″ (1 cm) of headspace. Top with a waxed paper disc then seal with clear plastic covers. If you have vacuum seal jars (but not traditional screw tops), then omit the plastic film and cover with the original lids just after potting.

Chutneys and pickles with vinegar are best sealed with plastic if they are to be stored for some time as the acid eats into metal tops.   RD

Aubergine, okra and fresh coriander relish; and creole chow chow

AUBERGINE, OKRA AND FRESH CORIANDER RELISH

The perfect accompaniment to an Indian meal, and good with bread and cheese.

>   *1 lb (500 g) aubergines, cut in thick chunks*
>   *4 teaspoons salt*
>   *8 oz (250 g) okra, sliced*
>   *4 celery sticks, chopped*
>   *1 large onion, chopped*
>   *2 cloves garlic, crushed*
>   *2 pints (1.2 litres) white malt vinegar*
>   *1–2 tablespoons curry powder*
>   *1 dessertspoon ground allspice*
>   *2 tablespoons tomato purée*
>   *4 oz (125 g) soft brown sugar*
>   *2 tablespoons chopped fresh coriander leaves or 2*
>   *teaspoons ground coriander*
>   *1 teaspoon ground ginger*

Sprinkle the aubergines with salt and leave to drain in a colander overnight. Do not rinse, but pat dry with kitchen paper. Cook in a preserving pan with everything else, simmering for about 30 minutes. Pot in clean sterilized jars.

Makes about 2½ lb (1.25 kg).   RD

TOMATO AND SWEET PEPPER RELISH

Sweet red peppers are ideal for relishes, marrying well with the combinations of sweet, sour and spicy. This relish makes a delicious change to the usual drab-coloured autumn chutneys.

>   *3 lb (1.5 kg) red firm tomatoes, quartered*
>   *1 lb (500 g) onions, chopped*
>   *3 large red peppers, seeded and chopped*
>   *2 celery stalks, chopped*
>   *½ lb (250 g) raisins*
>   *1 lb (500 g) cooking apples, cored and chopped*
>   *1 lb (500 g) granulated sugar*
>   *2 oz (50 g) fresh root ginger, peeled and finely*
>   *grated*
>   *1½ pints (900 ml) cider or white malt vinegar*
>   *2 tablespoons ground cumin*
>   *1 tablespoon mustard seeds, 6 cloves, 6 allspice*
>   *berries (tied together in a small muslin bag)*

Put everything into a large preserving pan and bring to the boil. Simmer for about 1 hour until slightly pulpy and reduced, stirring occasionally.

Remove and discard bag of spices, pot in clean sterilized jars and seal.

Makes about 6 lb (2.75 kg).   RD

GREEN TOMATO CHUTNEY

This recipe is a perfect way to clear your windowsills of the rows of green tomatoes that have failed to ripen at the end of the season. It makes a soft, dark brown chutney, which will keep for a year or more.

4 lb (1.75 kg) green tomatoes
1 lb (500 g) onions
2 cooking apples
1 tablespoon ground allspice or 1 teaspoon each
  ground cinnamon, cayenne, paprika and
  ginger
2 teaspoons salt
2 teaspoons mustard powder
½ pint (300 ml) malt vinegar

Chop the onions and soften them by simmering in a few tablespoons of the vinegar while you slice the tomatoes (saving any juice), and peel, core and roughly chop the apples. When the onions are nearly soft, add all the other ingredients except the remaining vinegar. Simmer until the mixture is soft, stirring occasionally. Add the rest of the vinegar, and boil until the chutney reaches a jam-like consistency. Pour into jars and seal in the usual way before storing in a cool dry place. AW

GOOSEBERRY CHUTNEY

Delicious with English cheese or cold meats.

4 lb (1.75 kg) gooseberries
1 lb (500 g) dark soft brown sugar
2 pints (1.2 litres) vinegar
1 lb (500 g) onions
1½ lb (750 g) seedless raisins
4 oz (125 g) mustard seeds
2 oz (50 g) ground allspice
2 teaspoons salt

Wash the berries and cut off tops and tails. Put the sugar and half the vinegar into a pan, then boil together until a thin syrup forms. Peel and chop the onions finely and add to the pan with the raisins, bruised mustard seeds, allspice and salt. Simmer for 10 minutes.

Put the remaining vinegar into a pan with the gooseberries and boil until tender. Put the two mixtures together and simmer for 1 hour until golden brown and thick, stirring occasionally. Put into hot jars and cover with vinegar-proof lids. Keep for a month before using. MN

BREAD AND BUTTER PICKLE

A pretty pickle and simple to make. Serve with cheese, ham or sliced cold beef and, of course, bread and butter.

2 cucumbers, washed and sliced thinly
12 oz (350 g) small or button onions
1 large green, red or yellow pepper, seeded and
  sliced
3–4 tablespoons coarse salt

Piccalilli with bread and cheese

SPICED VINEGAR
1 pint (600 ml) cider vinegar
½ lb (250 g) granulated sugar
1 tablespoon mustard seeds, 1 teaspoon dill seeds,
    6 cloves (tied together in a muslin bag)

Place the vegetables in a colander, sprinkle with the salt and toss to incorporate. Leave to drain overnight then pat dry.

Meanwhile, boil the vinegar solution ingredients for 5 minutes. Arrange the vegetables in clean sterilized jars and pour over the vinegar. Press the vegetables down well, topping up with extra vinegar to cover by about ¼″ (6 mm). Seal and store for up to 2 weeks before using.

Makes about 3 lb (1.5 kg).   RD

PICCALILLI

If you want to serve this as a crisp pickle on the side of the plate, stick to the ingredients below. If you prefer a softer chutney to spread on sandwiches, add extra vinegar and cook the vegetables for longer. The piccalilli will keep for up to a year.

2–3 cauliflowers
1 lb (500 g) French beans
1 lb (500 g) pickling onions
Salt
5 chillies
1 oz (25 g) fresh ginger
2 pints (1.2 litres) white wine vinegar or more
2 tablespoons flour
1 tablespoon turmeric
4 tablespoons celery seeds
4–5 tablespoons mustard powder
4 oz (125 g) light muscovado sugar (optional)

Chop the cauliflowers into small pieces, trim and slice the beans, peel and halve the pickling onions. Put all these vegetables into a large china or glass bowl and leave for 24 hours, sprinkled with salt.

The next day, rinse the vegetables, drain them well and transfer to a large pan. Split the chillies, remove the seeds and chop the flesh. Peel and finely

chop the ginger. Put the chilli and ginger in the pan, add the vinegar and bring to the boil. Simmer for 5–10 minutes. Strain the vegetables, reserving the vinegar. Mix the spices with the flour in a saucepan, adding the sugar if you are using it, and gradually whisk in the hot vinegar. Simmer for 10–15 minutes until it has thickened, while you pack the vegetables into warm jars. Pour in the thickened vinegar until the vegetables are completely covered, then seal.   AW

CREOLE CHOW CHOW

Chinese migrant railroad workers in mid-nineteenth-century America are thought to be responsible for introducing their hot pickled vegetables, or chow, into American cuisine. This is a recipe from an old Creole book which has been adapted, scaled down and generally made more manageable. It's not unlike our own Indian-inspired piccalilli.

1 small cauliflower, broken in small florets
½ lb (250 g) white cabbage, shredded
1 lb (500 g) cucumber, diced
½ lb (250 g) button onions, peeled
1 green pepper, seeded and diced
2 red peppers, seeded and diced
1 lb (500 g) whole French beans
1½ lb (750 g) green tomatoes, chopped
5 tablespoons coarse salt

PICKLE
2 oz (50 g) fresh horseradish, grated
8 cloves garlic, crushed
4 oz (125 g) French mustard
¼ pint (150 ml) salad oil
4 pints (2.25 litres) cider vinegar
2 tablespoons mustard seed
6 oz (175 g) light soft brown sugar
½ oz (15 g) turmeric

Put all the vegetables into a large colander, sprinkle over the salt, stir well to mix then leave to drain for 12 hours. Stir occasionally to make sure the salt is

119

evenly distributed.

Put all the pickle ingredients into a large pre-serving pan. Bring to the boil then simmer for 5 minutes. Add the drained vegetables (there is no need to rinse them). Stir well and bring to the boil. Simmer for 15 to 20 minutes. The vegetables should be still a little crisp.

Pot straight away in sterilized jars and seal. Store for about 2 weeks before opening.

Makes about 8 lb (4 kg). RD

MUSHROOM KETCHUP

Before the days of commercially-bottled sauces, and powdered stocks and flavourings, this was a common concoction kept to add zest to soups and stews. If you come across a batch of dark-gilled field mushrooms, perhaps slightly battered and being offered for sale cheaply at some market stall, this is a simple way to make use of them.

> 2 lb (1 kg) dark field mushrooms
> 2½ oz (65 g) salt
> Up to ¼ pint (150 ml) wine vinegar
> 1–2½ tablespoons brandy
> 1" (2.5 cm) piece fresh ginger
> A few blades of mace
> A few black peppercorns

Wipe the mushrooms clean and put them in a glass or china dish, sprinkling them with salt. Cover and leave in a cool place for 3 days, turning occasionally and pressing the mushrooms against the side of the dish with a spoon to extract the juice. After 3 days a fair amount of liquid will have been drawn out of the mushrooms.

Place the dish in the oven at 325°F (170°C, gas mark 3) for 60 minutes, then strain the contents through a sieve, pressing hard with a spoon to extract all the juices. Throw away the mushrooms. Measure the liquid and add ¼ pint (150 ml) of vinegar and 2 tablespoons of brandy to every pint (600 ml). Pour into jars or bottles made of tough glass, and seal while still hot. Stand the jars or bottles in a pan of water and bring to a slow

Picked onions

simmer, removing them after 15 minutes. This process will stop the ketchup from fermenting.

Use sparingly in soups, casseroles, or pâtés, but remember that the ketchup contains quite a bit of salt, so don't overseason your dish. AW

PICKLED ONIONS

These taste completely different from commercial pickled onions, being much less sharp and slightly softer. Peeling the onions is time-consuming, so try to enlist some help!

If your eyes water horribly, it may help to hold a piece of bread between your teeth.

Peel the onions, using a stainless-steel knife, trying not to nick the flesh as this will discolour later. Trim off the roots and put the whole onions into a china or glass bowl. Cover with a wet brine of 2 oz (50 g) of kitchen salt to 1 pint (600 ml) water. Leave in the brine for 36–48 hours, then drain, rinse very well and pack into jars.

Cover with the cold spiced vinegar, seal and leave for 2–4 weeks. The onions lose their texture after about 9 months. AW

PICKLED EGGS

Once a common sight on pub counters, these traditional British pickles have now largely been superseded by packets of crisps. However, home-made pickled eggs go extremely well with cold meats or with the customary glass of bitter, and are the perfect accompaniment to winter picnics.

Take a dozen eggs and hard-boil them for 10 minutes. For easy peeling, transfer them to the sink and remove the shells under water. Meanwhile, boil up 1½–2 pints (750 ml–1.2 litres) of malt vinegar together with 1″ (2.5 cm) piece of root ginger, ¼ oz (7 g) coriander seeds and ½ oz (15 g) white peppercorns. Pack the eggs into a wide-mouthed jar, cover with the hot vinegar and add two whole chillies, then seal. The eggs are best left a couple of weeks before eating so the white is tinted brown by the vinegar.   AW

MAKING JELLIES

Jellies are similar to jams, but they are made with the juice of the simmered fruit only, and the fruit itself is discarded. The juice is left to drip through a jelly bag to ensure clarity.

Choose firm, just-ripened fruit. Cut out any blemishes. Cook with the measured water in a preserving pan until soft and pulpy. Stir occasionally. Spoon into a flannel jelly bag and allow to drip through naturally until no more drips form. Do not push through as this will result in a cloudy finish. Measure the juice and allow 1 lb (500 g) of granulated sugar to each pint (600 ml) of juice.

Wash out the preserving pan and dissolve the sugar in the juice stirring occasionally until it dissolves. Bring to the boil then simmer until setting point is reached. To test for this, spoon a little onto chilled saucers. Wait for a few minutes then run your fingers over the top. If a skin forms and wrinkles, the jelly is ready.

Allow the jelly to stand for a few moments, then skim off any scum with a slotted spoon.

Pour into small hot sterilized jars, seal and label.   RD

HERB JELLIES

Take advantage of an autumn glut of fresh garden herbs and surplus cooking apples, storing flavourful jellies to accompany winter roasts. Windfall apples can be used but cut out any bruises.

BASIC JELLY
5 lb (2.25 kg) cooking apples or crab apples
4 pints (2.25 litres) water
About 2¼ (1.35 kg) sugar
Suggested herbs – fresh basil, rosemary, thyme, rose geranium, lemon verbena and spearmint

Wash the apples, but do not peel or core, and cut into chunks if large. Stew gently with the water in a large preserving pan until soft and pulpy.

Strain through a jelly bag for at least 4 hours until it completely stops dripping. Complete as for 'Making Jellies' above.

ADDING THE HERBS
For clear jellies either tie up in a muslin bag and boil with the sugar, or chop and stir in after skimming.

Allow 6 to 8 tablespoons of mint or basil, or thyme and verbena – about 4 to 6 of rosemary.

Clear rosemary or thyme jellies look attractive potted with sprigs in the jars but leafy mint or basil go limp.   RD

Herb jelly

SPICED ROWANBERRY JELLY

Berries from the Rowan tree (or Mountain Ash) make a delicious sweet-tart jelly with a delicate, palate-clearing back-bite – perfect with rich game such as venison, hare or mallard. It has a stunningly pretty colour.

> *2 lb (1 kg) rowanberries, stripped from the stalks*
> *1 lb (500 g) cooking apples*
> *1 pint (600 ml) water*
> *About 1½ lb (750 g) granulated sugar*
> *Strips of peel from 1 lemon*
> *1 teaspoon cloves*

Simmer the berries and apples in the water until pulpy, about 15–20 minutes. Then proceed as for 'Making Jellies' on previous page, tying the lemon strips and cloves in a muslin bag. Remove the muslin bag before potting.
    Makes about 3 lb (1.5 kg).   RD

GOOSEBERRY AND ELDERFLOWER JELLY

Elderflowers have a wonderful muscatel fragrance and a particular affinity with gooseberries. Happily, they are in season at the same time – around the end of May or early June.
    Like gooseberry jam, this turns a delicate pink when cooked.

> *5 lb (2.25 kg) gooseberries, topped and tailed*
> *2 pints (1.2 litres) water*
> *About 2¼ lb (1.10 kg) granulated sugar*
> *4–5 large heads elderflowers*

Stew the gooseberries gently in the water until they are quite soft and pulpy, for about 15 minutes, stirring occasionally.
    Complete as for 'Making Jellies' on previous page, tying the elderflowers in a muslin bag. Remove the bag then pot in small jars and seal.
    Makes about 4 lb (1.75 kg).   RD

ELDERBERRY JELLY

Delicious with duck as well as a sweet jam.

> *2½ lb (1.25 kg) elderberries*
> *2 lb (1 kg) cooking or windfall apples, quartered*
> *1½ pint (900 ml) water*
> *About 2 lb (1 kg) sugar*
> *Peel strips from 1 orange*
> *1 stick cinnamon*

Strip the elderberries from the stalks with a fork, then simmer with the apples in the water for about 20 minutes until pulpy. Proceed as for 'Making Jellies' on page 121, tying orange peel and cinnamon in a muslin bag. Remove bag before potting.
    Makes about 3 lb (1.5 kg).   RD

RASPBERRY JAM

This does not take long to make, it sets easily and has a lovely fresh flavour. Using 1 lb (500 g) sugar to every 1 lb (500 g) raspberries, gently mash fruit and heat until juice flows. Add warmed sugar, dissolve and bring to boil. After three minutes, test mixture; it should have reached setting point. Remove from heat, and jar immediately. Cover the jars when cold.   JH

WHOLE STRAWBERRY JAM

An unusual French recipe. By spreading the cooking process over three days, the boiling time is kept to a minimum.

> *4 lb (1.75 kg) small just-ripe strawberries*
> *4 lb (1.75 kg) sugar, preferably sugar with pectin*
> *Juice of 1 lemon*

Right *Raspberry jam with Scotch pancakes*

Left to right: Raspberry vinegar; confiture de vieux garçons; strawberry and raspberry syrup

Hull and wash the strawberries. Drain well and put them in a large bowl with layers of sugar between. Leave overnight.

The next day, put strawberries, lemon juice and sugar in a heavy pan, bring to the boil slowly and boil gently for 3 minutes. Remove from the heat and leave overnight.

The next day, boil for 6 minutes; leave overnight again. The third day boil for 7 minutes, stirring lightly to distribute the fruit. Remove scum if necessary. Pot and cover.

This method for making jam keeps the full flavour, and the strawberries remain whole.

Makes 6–7 lb (3.3–3.50 kg).   BGM

LA CONFITURE DE VIEUX GARCONS (BACHELORS' JAM)

Not all bachelors are master chefs, so this delightful conserve is made without any cooking, though not without expense. It consists of just-ripe soft fruits – strawberries, raspberries or other fruits – preserved in alcohol as they ripen to perfection.

The result, after being left to mature for a month or so, is a liqueur and intoxicated fruit which may be served with ice-cream, added to fruit salads, used to flavour many luscious desserts or eaten in a small glass after a meal.

Strawberries, raspberries, other fruit in season
Alcohol, this can be eau-de-vie, brandy, rum,
*   even whisky*
1 lb (500 g) granulated sugar to each 1 lb
*   (500 g) fruit*

Choose just-ripe strawberries. Hull and clean them and place whole in a crock or wide-mouthed glass jar. Add the same amount of sugar. Cover with alcohol. When raspberries come into season, add them with more sugar, ensuring that they are always covered with alcohol. Add any other fruit as it comes into season; stoned cherries, apricots, or peaches. Always use the same kind of alcohol and seal very firmly between additions. Leave to mature for at least 1 month.   BGM

REDCURRANT BAR-LE-DUC

This French jam is quite delicious. Patience is needed, however, in the pricking of each currant to allow the sugar to penetrate the fruit. This prevents shrivelling and keeps the currants plump.

2 lb (1 kg) redcurrants
3 lb (1.5 kg) sugar

Remove stalks from the currants, wash and drain. Prick each one gently and put them in a preserving pan with the sugar. Leave overnight, The next day, stir and bring slowly to the boil. Boil for 3 minutes. Leave standing until a skin begins to form, stir gently to distribute the fruit, then pot in tiny jars and cover.
Fills 8–10 small jars.   BGM

ELDERBERRY SYRUP

The Swedes produce a range of fruit syrups throughout the year from a wide range of flavourful wild berries such as *lingon* or *hjortron*; elderberry syrup is equally popular, as is elderflower champagne. The syrups are mixed with *brännvin* (vodka), with sparkling wine, or with mineral water according to taste.

2–2½ lb (1 kg) elderberry clusters
1 pint (600 ml) water
12 oz (375 g) sugar per pint (600 ml) strained
*   juice*

Wash berries quickly and strip from the stalks with a fork. Tip into a large saucepan or preserving pan with the water, bring to the boil and simmer for about 10 minutes. Strain through a double thickness of dampened muslin draped over a bowl or through a steel sieve for about 30 minutes, pressing down a little on the pulp to help extract juices. Discard the pulp and return the strained juice to a clean saucepan. Add the sugar and heat the syrup gently until the sugar has dissolved completely. If using immediately, bring to the boil and cool before use. Otherwise, ladle the syrup into clean, warm bottles, leaving 1″ (2.5 cm) headspace before sealing by tying down corks with string, or closing clamp tops.
    Place bottles in a hot water bath and process for 20 minutes at 190°F (88°C). Remove and cool. Corks may be coated with melted wax to seal and preserve syrup.
    Makes about 1¾ pints (1 litre).
NOTE This method applies to all fruit/berry syrups, though quantities of sugar may vary.   SD

STRAWBERRY AND RASPBERRY SYRUP

Equal quantities of strawberries or raspberries
and caster sugar

Hull and pick over the berries. Put them in a basin, cover with sugar and leave overnight. The next day, mash the berries, rub them through a nylon sieve or liquidize and strain. Simmer juice for 10–15 minutes over a very low heat. Cool. Add the syrup to fruit salads and fruit cups, or pour over ice-cream.   BGM

125

BAKING BREADS AND CAKES

Here are variations on the theme of bread, with appetising additions of cheese, olives, herbs and nuts to the basic dough, as well as breakfast muffins and teatime cakes

PUMPKIN BREAD

Pumpkin has a delicate flavour that works just as well with savoury foods as with sweet ones. Used in this recipe, it makes a loaf that stays moist and does not stale too quickly.

> *1 lb (500 g) pumpkin, cooked and puréed*
> *1 lb (500 g) strong wholemeal flour*
> *2 teaspoons instant dried yeast*
> *½ teaspoon salt*
> *½ pint (300 ml) milk*
> *Beaten egg, to glaze*
> *2 tablespoons dried pumpkin seeds, roughly*
>   *chopped*

Stir the flour, yeast and salt together, then mix in the pumpkin purée and milk. Beat in the mixer or processor to make a firm dough which comes cleanly away from the sides of the bowl. If making by hand, knead well until smooth, firm and elastic. Cover with oiled clingfilm and leave to rise until doubled in volume.

Turn the dough onto a lightly floured surface, knead briefly, and break into 6 even pieces. Form each piece into a smooth ball, and place in a row in a buttered 2 lb (1 kg) loaf tin. Cover and leave until risen. Brush the top of the loaf with beaten egg and sprinkle with pumpkin seeds. Bake in a preheated oven at 400°F (200°C, gas mark 6) for about 50 minutes until the loaf sounds hollow when tapped underneath (cover the top if necessary). Turn out and leave to cool in a wire rack.   HW

PARSLEY BAPS

These have a soft crust, and being light and delicate in flavour, are particularly versatile.

> *14 oz (400 g) strong plain flour*
> *2 oz (50 g) oat bran*
> *½ teaspoon salt*
> *2 teaspoons instant dried yeast*
> *4 tablespoons chopped parsley*
> *2 oz (50 g) unsalted butter, melted*
> *½ pint (300 ml) milk*

Stir the flour, bran, salt, yeast and parsley together, then add the butter and sufficient milk to make a soft dough. Beat in a food mixer until the dough comes cleanly away from the sides of the bowl, or knead by hand to make a smooth, firm dough. Cover with oiled clingfilm and leave to rise until doubled in volume. Turn out onto a lightly floured surface, knead briefly and roll out to ¾″ (2 cm) thick. Stamp out 8 circles using a plain 3″ (7.5 cm) cutter. Place the circles on a floured baking sheet, cover with oiled clingfilm and leave to rise. Bake in a preheated oven at 400°F (200°C, gas mark 6) for about 15 minutes until well risen and golden. Dust lightly with flour mixed with oat bran.

Makes 8 baps.   HW

Right *(clockwise, from top right) parsley baps; pumpkin bread; herb spiral, page 129; potato and chive bread, page 128; neo-Georgian cheese bread, page 128*

(Clockwise, from top right) pumpkin bread, page 126; neo-Georgian cheese bread; potato and chive bread; parsley baps, page 126; herb spiral

NEO-GEORGIAN CHEESE BREAD

This recipe is based on a traditional Russian Georgian bread, which was made in individual portions resembling cheese flans and sold by street hawkers. The quality of the cheese is important – use a genuine Greek ewe's milk feta and a mature Lancashire. (If the Lancashire is still young when bought, leave in a cool place for a while to improve.) The bread is irresistible when still warm from the oven, but it is also delicious when cold and ideal for casual meals and picnics, especially accompanied by a crisp salad.

> *12 oz (350 g) granary flour*
> *1½ teaspoons instant dried yeast*
> *5–6 fl oz (150–175 ml) milk*
> *1½ oz (40 g) unsalted butter, softened*
> *8 oz (250 g) feta cheese, crumbled*
> *1 lb (500 g) Lancashire cheese, crumbled*
> *2 eggs, 1 beaten for glazing*
> *Freshly-ground black pepper*
> *2 tablespoons chopped parsley*

Stir the flour and yeast together. Add the milk and butter, and beat together in food mixer to form a soft, pliable dough that comes cleanly away from the sides of the bowl. If making by hand, bring ingredients together and knead until soft, pliable and elastic. Cover with oiled clingfilm and leave to rise until doubled in volume. Mix the two cheeses together with a fork, then work in the egg and black pepper, followed by the parsley. Turn the dough onto a lightly floured surface, knead briefly and roll out to a circle 21–22″ (53–55 cm) in diameter. Fold the dough back over the rolling-pin, lift it carefully and place centrally over a buttered 8″ (20 cm) cake tin lined with foil, allowing the excess dough to drape over the sides. Add the cheese mixture, making sure it fills the tin completely. Lift the excess dough over the filling, allowing it to fall into pleats, and twist the edges together in the centre to form a knob. Cover loosely with oiled clingfilm and leave to rise. Brush with beaten egg and bake in a preheated oven at 400°F (200°C, gas mark 6) for about 40 minutes until risen and golden. Remove loaf from tin and cool on a wire rack.   HW

POTATO AND CHIVE BREAD

This recipe produces a moist loaf: steam rather than boil the potatoes to prevent the purée, and therefore the dough, from being too wet.

> *1 lb (500 g) strong plain flour*
> *1 teaspoon instant dried yeast*
> *½ pint (300 ml) milk*
> *½ teaspoon salt*
> *6 oz (175 g) potatoes, peeled and cut into small*
> *   pieces*
> *2 oz (50 g) soft cheese or unsalted butter*
> *3 tablespoons chopped chives*
> *Melted unsalted butter for glazing*

Steam the potatoes over boiling salted water until tender. Drain well, mash until smooth and beat in cheese or butter. Mix the flour, salt and yeast together, then add to potato mixture with sufficient milk to make a firm dough. Add the chives towards the end of mixing. Beat in a food mixer until the dough comes cleanly away from the sides of the bowl, or knead by hand to make a firm, smooth dough. Cover with oiled clingfilm and leave to rise until doubled in volume. Knead briefly, then shape to fit a buttered 2 lb (1 kg) loaf tin. Brush the top with melted unsalted butter, cover with oiled clingfilm and leave until the dough fills the tin. Bake in a preheated oven at 425°F (220°C, gas mark 7) for 40–45 minutes until golden brown. Turn out to cool on a wire rack.   HW

then roll out to a rectangle, about 8½″ × 6″ (21.5 × 15 cm). Brush the dough with melted butter, leaving a ½″ (1.25 cm) border clear on one of the long sides. Spread spinach over, keeping the border clear. Sprinkle with herbs and black pepper. Dampen the clear border, roll up like a Swiss roll and seal dough well. Brush all over with melted butter, cover with oiled clingfilm and leave until well risen. Brush the top with egg and milk glaze, sprinkle with a little Parmesan cheese, then bake in a preheated oven at 425°F (220°C, gas mark 7) for about 35–40 minutes until risen and brown. Transfer to a wire rack to cool.   HW

HERB SPIRAL

With its appetising green spiral of fresh herbs and spinach, encased in garlic-flavoured dough, this loaf is attractive when sliced and extremely moreish when eaten.

11 oz (325 g) strong plain flour
½ teaspoon salt
1½ teaspoons instant dried yeast
1 oz (25 g) unsalted butter, melted
2 garlic cloves, peeled and finely crushed
4–5 fl oz (125–150 ml) milk

FILLING
1½–2 oz (40–50 g) unsalted butter, melted
6 oz (175 g) spinach purée, cooked and well drained
2 tablespoons each finely chopped parsley, tarragon, basil, thyme, rosemary
Freshly-ground black pepper
1 egg beaten with a little milk, for glazing
Freshly-grated Parmesan cheese

Stir the flour, salt and yeast together, then add the butter, garlic and sufficient milk to form a soft, pliable dough. Beat in a food mixer until dough comes cleanly away from the sides of the bowl or knead by hand until elastic. Cover with oiled clingfilm and leave to rise until doubled in volume. Turn onto a lightly floured surface, knead briefly,

OLIVE BREAD

Most recipes for olive bread seem to be Greek and call for chopped, pitted olives. But this has strong-tasting, whole black olives, using stones and all. This bread is better cooked under a grill than baked in the oven. It goes particularly well with thinly sliced salami, or tomato salad.

4 fl oz (125 ml) milk
1 teaspoon sugar
1½ teaspoons dried yeast
1 egg, beaten
2 tablespoons olive oil
4 fl oz (125 ml) natural yoghurt
1 lb (500 g) unbleached plain white flour
½ teaspoon salt
4 oz (125 g) small black olives

Heat the milk to lukewarm, about 110°F (43°C), and mix with the sugar and yeast. Whisk the mixture and set it aside in a warm place for about 10 minutes, or until the yeast has dissolved and frothed up. Stir in the egg, oil and yoghurt.

Sift the flour and salt into a bowl, make a well in the middle and pour in the yeast mixture. Stir, gradually drawing in the flour around the well, to make a soft dough.

Turn the dough onto a floured surface and knead for about 10 minutes or until it is smooth and elastic. Form the dough into a ball and roll it in a lightly oiled bowl. Cover the bowl with a damp cloth and leave in a warm place until the dough has doubled in size.

Turn the dough onto a floured surface, punch it down and lightly knead in the olives. Divide the dough into 6 pieces and shape each into a flat circle, stretching it to a diameter of about 6″ (15 cm).

Arrange the shaped dough on lightly oiled baking sheets, cover with damp cloths and leave to rise for about 20 minutes. Just before cooking, brush the tops with milk. Place the sheets, one at a time, under a very hot preheated grill. The bread should be about 3″ (7.5 cm) from the heat. Grill the olive bread for 2 to 3 minutes on each side, or until cooked through and lightly browned. Serve either hot or warm.

Makes 6.   SCP

CORNMEAL HERB BREAD

Flecked with herbs, and flavoured with Parmesan, this bread is guaranteed to disappear as soon as it comes out of the oven.

3 tablespoons dried yeast
Warm water
3 fl oz (90 ml) extra virgin olive oil
1½ lb (750 g) strong flour
½ lb (250 g) cornmeal
½ oz (15 oz) salt
2 oz (50 g) freshly grated Parmesan cheese
2 tablespoons fresh rosemary
2 tablespoons fresh sage

Dissolve yeast in 1¾ pints (1 litre) warm water, in the mixing bowl of an electric mixer or food processor with bread-making attachment. Leave for 10 minutes, so that the yeast can dissolve properly, then add olive oil, flour, cornmeal and salt. Mix on medium to low speed, until the dough wipes clean the sides of the bowl. Add cheese and chopped herbs and mix again until they are thoroughly incorporated.

Set aside and cover with a cloth or plastic film. Leave in a warm place until about doubled in size.

Take out of bowl and shape into 2 round loaves, then place them on a greased and cornmeal-dusted baking sheet. Brush with olive oil, score surface with a sharp knife and leave to rise again until doubled in size. Bake in a preheated oven at 375°F (190°C, gas mark 5) for 45–50 minutes.

Makes 2 loaves.   JD

PROSCIUTTO AND HAZELNUT BREAD

Parma ham, or *prosciutto*, packs a great deal of flavour into very little bulk; a little goes a long way. Here, used together with hazelnuts, prosciutto flavours an interesting bread to serve with plain first courses like artichokes and asparagus, or with cream cheeses.

8 oz (250 g) wholewheat flour
8 oz (250 g) strong white flour
2 teaspoons sea salt
2 oz (50 g) prosciutto, very finely chopped
2 oz (50 g) shelled hazelnuts, coarsely chopped
½ oz (15 g) fresh yeast or 1 teaspoon dried
About ½ pint (300 ml) warm water
2 tablespoons hazelnut or olive oil

Put the flours into a large bowl. Add the salt, prosciutto and nuts and mix them lightly together.

Combine the yeast with a little of the warm water and stir. Set aside in a warm place for about 10 minutes until the yeast has dissolved and begins to froth. Combine the remaining warm water with the oil.

Add the liquids to the flour all at once and stir to form a soft dough. Turn the dough onto a floured surface and knead it lightly.

Rinse, dry and oil the bowl. Form the dough into a ball, turn it in the oiled bowl and cover with a damp cloth or plastic bag. Leave it to rise in a warm place until the dough has doubled its original bulk.

Knock the air out of the dough and knead it again lightly. Set it in a well-oiled loaf tin measuring about 10″ × 3½″ × 3″ (25 cm × 9 cm × 7.5 cm). Cover and leave to rise again until the dough has doubled in volume.

Bake in a hot oven preheated to 450°F (230°C, gas mark 8) for 15 minutes, then reduce the heat to 400°F (200°C, gas mark 6) for 15 minutes. Turn the loaf out of its tin and return it to the oven until it sounds hollow when tapped. Cool the loaf on a wire rack.

Makes 1 loaf.   SCP

COURGETTE AND ONION BREAD

This is an Italian-style savoury bread which is excellent on a picnic with cheese or salami. The leftovers are also good toasted the next day and spread with a soft cheese such a Bel Paese, Pipo Crem or even Philadelphia cream cheese.

12 oz (350 g) courgettes, grated
Salt, to sprinkle
1¼ lb (625 g) strong (bread) flour
1 teaspoon salt
1 sachet easy yeast
3 oz (75 g) onion, finely chopped
2 oz (50 g) stoned black olives, chopped
½–¾ pint (300–450 ml) tepid water
Olive oil, to glaze

Layer the grated courgettes in a colander, sprinkling fairly lightly in between with salt. Leave to drain for half an hour, then rinse and pat dry with kitchen towel.

Mix the flour, teaspoon of salt and yeast in a large bowl then add the courgettes, onion and olives. Mix to a firm but still pliable dough with the water added gradually. You may not need it all.

Knead well on a floured surface for about 10 minutes. This mixture is best made by hand or kneaded by a mixer, rather than processor, otherwise the vegetable texture will be lost.

Divide the dough into 2 and either shape into ovals on a lightly greased baking sheet or place in two 1 lb (500 g) loaf tins. Glaze the tops with olive oil and leave to prove until doubled in size.

Bake at 425°F (220°C, gas mark 7) for about

Poppy seed knots

35–40 minutes, checking the tops don't burn before the bases are cooked. The bases should sound hollow when turned out and tapped. If not, return them to cook further. Turn out to cool on a wire rack to avoid the bases turning soggy.

Makes two 1 lb (500 g) loaves.   RD

POPPY SEED KNOTS

To demonstrate just how simple breadmaking can be using the new easy blend yeasts, a recipe for homemade dinner rolls that can be quickly mixed and served, freshly baked, just before a meal, whether a simple supper or special dinner.

1 oz (25 g) butter
1½ lb (750 g) strong (bread) plain flour or a
*   mixture of half wholemeal and half strong*
*   white flour*
1 teaspoon salt
1 sachet easy yeast
¾ pint (450 ml) tepid milk
Beaten egg, to glaze
Black poppy seeds or sesame seeds, to sprinkle
*   over the rolls*

Rub the butter into the flour and salt. Mix in the yeast. Beat in the milk and knead well for at least 10 minutes by hand or 5 minutes in a food processor or electric mixer.

Divide into 12 pieces and roll each out to a long sausage, pulling if necessary, on a lightly floured board. Tie into a knot.

Place on a lightly greased baking sheet, glaze well with egg and sprinkle with seeds. Cover loosely with lightly oiled cling film or foil and leave in a warm place until about doubled in size.

Bake at 400°F (200°C, gas mark 6) for about 15 minutes. Allow rolls to cool slightly before serving freshly baked.

Makes 12.   RD

SOURDOUGH BREAD

The technique of using sourdough dates back in America to the days of the Gold Rush, when yeast was not readily available. This recipe cheats slightly, by using yeast as a failsafe, but the flavour and texture are the same.

SOURDOUGH STARTER
1 lb (500 g) grapes, off the stem
Warm water
12 oz (350 g) plain white flour

BREAD
5 tablespoons warm water
2 sachets active dry yeast
½ pint (300 ml) starter (see above)
10 tablespoons warm water
1 lb 1 oz (525 g) strong white flour, unbleached
1 tablespoon salt
1 egg white

To make the starter, mash the grapes thoroughly to release the juice. Place in a covered container at room temperature for 48 hours.

Strain the fermented juice from the pulp. Add enough warm water to make 1 pint (600 ml), stir in flour and replace cover. Leave at room temperature overnight. The starter is then ready to use, or it can

Sourdough bread

be kept for longer if required. Add 1 pint (600 ml) warm water and then 12 oz (350 g) flour daily if starter is to be kept at room temperature. If it is to be refrigerated, add the water and flour twice weekly.

When starter is ready, make the bread. Pour 5 tablespoons warm water into a bowl. Sprinkle the dried yeast onto the water and set aside.

Pour ½ pint (300 ml) sourdough starter into a mixing bowl, then add 10 tablespoons warm water. Add 6 oz (175 g) of bread flour and mix, either in a food processor with a bread-making attachment, or by hand, until the dough foams (about 2 minutes), then add the yeast mixture. Mix thoroughly until blended, add remaining flour and salt and mix again.

Take the dough out of the bowl and knead on a lightly floured work surface until dough becomes smooth and elastic. This takes about 10 minutes. Place dough in a lightly greased bowl and cover with a damp cloth. Put bowl in a warm place, and leave until doubled in size.

Place dough back on the lightly floured surface and form into a round loaf. Place loaf on a baking sheet greased and dusted with maize meal. Allow to rise in a warm place covered with a damp cloth until doubled in size.

Heat the oven to 450°F (230°C, gas mark 8).

Bring about 2 pints (1.2 litres) water to the boil. Brush risen loaf with beaten egg white and score it across the top with a sharp knife. Place loaf in hot oven, with a baking tin of boiling water placed on the shelf below for 10 minutes or until the loaf begins to take colour. Then remove the water, turn the oven down to 375°F (190°C, gas mark 5) and bake loaf for another 35–45 minutes, or until it is well browned.

Makes 1 loaf. JD

GREEK EASTER BREADS

These traditional Easter sweet dough breads are ideal for breakfast or mid-morning breaks. By preparing the rolls the night before, and leaving them to prove for the second time overnight in the refrigerator, they can be ready to bake first thing in the morning.

They look pretty (and very Greek) with coloured or hand-painted eggs nestling in the centre, and are best eaten the same day they are baked.

1 lb (500 g) strong (bread) flour
1 teaspoon ground cinnamon
2 oz (50 g) caster sugar
1 sachet easy yeast
2 oz (50 g) butter, melted
2 tablespoons clear honey
2 teaspoons almond essence
4 fl oz (125 m) tepid milk
2 eggs, beaten
Extra beaten egg, to glaze
2 oz (50 g) flaked or nibbed almonds, to sprinkle
Extra warmed honey, to glaze

Sift the flour and cinnamon into a bowl or food processor. Mix in the sugar and yeast.

Mix together the butter, honey, essence, milk and eggs, then beat into the dry ingredients. Knead for about 10 minutes by hand or 5 minutes by machine until you have a smooth, pliable but firm dough. Cover with lightly greased cling film and leave to rise until doubled in size. This may take longer than usual with the extra fat and sugar.

Knock back and divide into about 12 portions. Make two long rolls with each portion, pulling and rolling as necessary on a lightly floured board.

Twist the two rolls together then curl into a circle, sealing the ends with some beaten egg. Stand on a lightly greased baking sheet. Glaze all over with beaten egg and sprinkle over the nuts. Repeat with the remaining dough until you have 12 circlets. Cover the dough lightly with greased cling film and leave to prove and rise again.

Bake at 400°F (200°C, gas mark 6) for about 15 minutes, until cooked. Remove and cool. While the breads are cooling, brush or trickle over some extra honey.

Makes about 12. RD

Greek Easter breads

BRIOCHE LOAVES

Home-made brioche baked in long narrow loaves is an excellent freezer standby if you like brioche toasted – for breakfast, or with potted shrimps, or with *foie gras*. The recipe makes two loaves.

> 2 tablespoons water
> 2 teaspoons sugar
> ½ oz (15 g) fresh yeast or 1 scant teaspoon
>   granulated dried yeast
> 1 lb (500 g) strong white bread flour
> 1 teaspoon salt
> 6 large eggs, lightly beaten
> 8 oz (250 g) lightly salted butter, softened
> 1 egg yolk beaten with 2 tablespoons water to
>   glaze

Heat the water to lukewarm (about 43°C, 110°F) and add a pinch of sugar and the yeast. Whisk and set aside in a warm place for about five minutes, or until the yeast has dissolved and frothed up.

Sift the flour, salt and remaining sugar into a warm bowl. Make a well in the centre and add the beaten eggs and the yeast mixture. Using your hand or a wooden spoon, incorporate the flour into the liquid to make a well-blended dough. Add the butter and work it in thoroughly with your hands. At this stage the dough is so soft it appears completely unworkable but it will calm down a bit during its two rising periods.

Cover the bowl with a damp cloth or plastic wrap and leave it to rise for at least two hours, probably longer, until it is light and airy.

Knock the air out of the dough and transfer it to a clean bowl. Cover it again and chill overnight. The dough will rise again very slowly and it is this slow rising which gives the brioche its distinctive fine texture.

Brush two loaf-tins generously with melted butter and set them on a baking sheet. Turn the dough on to a lightly-floured surface and knead it briefly with well-floured hands. Don't worry if it is still too soft to knead properly. Divide the dough into two pieces and shape them to fit the tins. Drop the dough into the tins, cover them and leave the loaves to rise until they have at least doubled in

volume – by the time the brioche is baked it will probably have tripled its size, so pick tins which are on the big side.

Brush the tops of the loaves with egg glaze and bake them in a preheated moderately hot oven (400°F, 200°C, gas mark 6) for 30 to 35 minutes. Rest the loaves in their tins for five minutes before turning on to a wire rack to cool.   SCP

OLIVE OIL BREADSTICKS

Delicious to nibble with drinks, or as an accompaniment for soups, these are best served as soon as they have cooled.

> 1 oz (25 g) dried yeast
> Warm water
> 3 fl oz (90 ml) extra virgin olive oil
> 1½ lb (750 g) strong bread flour
> ¾ oz (20 g) salt
> Sesame or poppy seeds

Dissolve yeast in 14 fl oz (400 ml) warm water in the mixing bowl of the food processor. Leave to stand for 10 minutes. Add oil, flour and salt, and mix on medium speed with bread-making attachment until dough has elasticity and leaves the sides of the mixing bowl cleanly.

Leave the dough to rest in a warm place for 20 minutes. Divide the dough in half, and shape into oblong loaves 12″ (30 cm) long. Oil the underside of 2 baking sheets and place the loaves on these. Brush with olive oil and cover with plastic film. Leave to prove for about 1 hour. Remove the plastic wrap and brush with more olive oil. Cover the loaves generously with sesame or poppy seeds.

Starting at the end of each loaf, cut slices of dough approximately 1″ (2.5 cm) wide and gently stretch them to double their length. This is most easily done on a greased baking sheet. Place sticks about 1″ (2.5 cm) apart on a greased baking sheet. Do not prove again, but bake immediately in a moderately hot oven (400°F, 200°C, gas mark 6) for approximately 10–12 minutes or until brown.

Makes about 40 sticks.   JD

BLUEBERRY MUFFINS

The classic American breakfast muffin.

5 oz (150 g) unsalted butter
4 oz (125 g) sugar
2 fl oz (60 ml) milk
12 oz (350 g) plain flour
1 tablespoon baking powder
1 teaspoon salt
4 large eggs
1 lb (500 g) blueberries (blackcurrant can be substituted)

Pre-heat oven to 400°F (200°C, gas mark 6). Line a bun tin with paper baking-cups.

Combine the butter and sugar in the food processor and blend until light and creamy. Add the milk slowly to the creamed butter, mixing at medium-low speed.

Sift together the flour, baking powder and salt. With mixer at low speed, stir in one egg, then a quarter of the flour mixture. Stop the mixer and scrape down the sides of the bowl. Repeat three or more times until all the eggs and flour have been incorporated into the batter. Mix at medium-low speed until the mixture is completely smooth.

Pour 2 tablespoons of batter in each paper cup and top with 1 tablespoon of blueberries, or blackcurrants if using. Turn the oven down to 375°F (190°C, gas mark 5) and bake muffins until the tops are golden brown and the centres spring back when lightly touched.

NOTE Frozen blueberries or blackcurrants can be used if fresh ones are unobtainable. Do not defrost them before use.

Makes 24 muffins. JD

Blueberry muffins

PUMPKIN AND PECAN MUFFINS

Ingredients can be prepared at night, the dry and the wet ready for mixing in the morning.

8 oz (250 g) plain flour
½ teaspoon salt
2 teaspoons baking powder
2 teaspoons mixed spice
Grated rind 1 small orange
2 oz (50 g) light soft brown sugar
3 oz (75 g) pecan nuts, chopped
2 eggs
1–2 oz (25–50 g) butter, melted
4 fl oz (125 ml) milk
6 oz (175 g) fresh or canned pumpkin purée

Sift the dry ingredients into a large bowl. Lightly grease a 12-section deep muffin or bun tin. Mix the eggs, butter, milk and pumpkin together.

Lightly and quickly blend the two lots of ingredients together with a fork. It doesn't matter if a few small lumps of flour remain. Don't overmix or the muffins will be tough.

Spoon immediately into the tins, filling to about two thirds. Bake at 400°F (200°C, gas mark 6), for about 25 minutes. Allow to stand for a minute or two before turning out.

Makes 10–12. RD

BANANA CAKE

This rich American cake serves as a sumptuous dessert, with ice-cream on the side.

4 oz (125 g) butter
12 oz (350 g) sugar
2 eggs, beaten
10 oz (300 g) plain flour
½ teaspoon baking powder
1 teaspoon bicarbonate of soda
½ teaspoon salt
5 tablespoons buttermilk
1 teaspoon vanilla essence
3 large ripe bananas, puréed
4 oz (125 g) chopped pecan nuts

BUTTERCREAM ICING
8 oz (250 g) salted butter
12 oz (350 g) icing sugar
1 tablespoon vanilla essence
1 egg white

Cream butter and sugar together thoroughly, then add beaten eggs. Sift dry ingredients, and add alternately with buttermilk, vanilla and banana purée to the butter, sugar and eggs, beating vigorously for 3 minutes after all ingredients have been incorporated, until mixture is light and fluffy. Stir in the pecans, and pour into a 10″ (25 cm) cake tin, which has been greased and floured. Bake for 30–40 minutes at 350°F (180°C, gas mark 4).

To make icing, cream butter and sugar together, add vanilla and egg white, and beat until fluffy. When cake is cool, cover with icing.

Makes one 10″ (25 cm) cake.   RD

PORTUGUESE CHRISTMAS CAKE

Bôlo rei, meaning king's cake, is a traditional Christmas recipe from Portugal combining a plain, nutty bread with a sweet, rich topping of glazed dried and glacé fruits.

1 oz (25 g) fresh yeast
3 oz (75 g) caster sugar
2 fl oz (60 ml) milk
12 oz (350 g) plain flour
2 oz (50 g) chopped hazelnuts
1 oz (25 g) sultanas
Grated zest of 1 orange
3 egg whites
2 egg yolks
2 fl oz (60 ml) port
1 tablespoon melted butter

TOPPING
Icing sugar
6 tablespoons warm apricot jam
A selection of dried and glacé fruits, e.g. cherries, angelica, dried peaches, apricots, pears
1 oz (25 g) whole hazelnuts

Prepare a leaven by mixing the yeast, one teaspoon of caster sugar and three tablespoons of the milk together in a bowl. Set it aside in a warm place to become frothy. This will take about half an hour.

Mix together the flour, caster sugar, chopped hazelnuts, sultanas and orange zest in a large bowl. Make a well in the centre of this dry mixture and set it aside.

When the leaven has risen, whisk together the egg whites and yolks till they are light and fluffy. Add the port, the remainder of the milk and the melted butter to the eggs. Pour the egg mixture into the well in the flour mixture and add the raised leaven. Mix well with the hands to form a firm dough. Knead and then place the dough evenly in a greased and floured 9″ (23 cm) ring mould. Set this aside to rise in a warm place for about 1½ hours.

When the dough has risen, dust the top with icing sugar and bake at 400°F (200°C, gas mark 6) for about 35 minutes. The cake is cooked when a skewer inserted into the middle comes out clean.

Cool the cake thoroughly on a wire rack and then brush the whole surface of the cake with 2 tablespoons of warm apricot jam. Decorate the top heavily with the dried and glacé fruits and the whole hazelnuts and then glaze the fruit with the remainder of the apricot jam. Store in an airtight container as it dries out rather quickly.   MJ

Clockwise, from top: kerstkrans, page 138; Portuguese Christmas cake; love cake

LOVE CAKE

An interesting recipe from Sri Lanka, spiced cashew nut cake or love cake probably dates back to the Dutch colonisation of the island in the seventeenth century. Readily available ingredients such as cashew nuts and spices are used to create an adaptation of a traditional European cake. Today love cake is still made in Sri Lanka by the descendants of those early Dutch settlers, but the origins of its name remain a mystery.

7 eggs, separated
1 lb (500 g) caster sugar

14 oz (400 g) raw cashew nuts, finely chopped
8 oz (250 g) semolina
½ teaspoon ground cinnamon
½ teaspoon ground nutmeg
½ teaspoon ground cardamom
¼ teaspoon ground cloves
2 tablespoons clear honey
1 tablespoon sweet sherry
Grated zest of 1 lemon

DECORATION
Toasted cashew nuts
Glacé cherries
Clear honey

137

Line an 11″ (28 cm) round cake tin with a double thickness of greaseproof paper. Brush the inside with melted butter.

Whisk egg yolks and caster sugar together until light and fluffy. Fold in the cashew nuts, semolina, spices, honey, rose water, sherry and lemon zest.

Whisk the egg whites until they form stiff peaks and fold these into the mixture. Pour into the baking tin and bake at 350°F (180°C, gas mark 4) for approximately 1 hour and 10 minutes. When cooked, the cake should be nicely browned and a skewer inserted into the middle should come out slightly moist.

Cool the cake thoroughly in the tin, then turn out and remove greaseproof paper. Decorate the top of the cake with toasted cashew nuts and glacé cherries. Dribble some honey over the nuts to create a glaze.   MJ

KERSTKRANS

As a complete departure from fruit cake, try this Dutch Christmas pastry, *kerstkrans* (or Christmas crown, illustrated on page 137), which is a delicious and easily prepared combination of almond paste, ground hazelnuts and glacé cherries.

> *4 oz (125 g) hazelnuts*
> *8 oz (250 g) glacé cherries*
> *12 oz (350 g) almond paste*
> *2 eggs*
> *1 teaspoon lemon juice*
> *1 lb (500 g) puff pastry*
> *1 teaspoon milk*

DECORATION
Glacé icing made with 6 oz (175 g) icing sugar,
> *one tablespoon cold water and ¼ teaspoon*
> *lemon juice*
Flaked, browned almonds
Halved glacé cherries
Angelica leaves

Prepare the almond filling by placing the hazelnuts and glacé cherries in a food processor and blending till the mixture is fairly fine. Add the almond paste cut into small pieces and process again until the ingredients are thoroughly mixed. Lastly, add one egg and the lemon juice and process again till a thick paste is achieved. Set aside.

Roll out the puff pastry on a floured surface to form a 34″ (86 cm) × 7″ (18 cm) strip. Trim to neaten the edges.

Place the almond filling in a narrow strip along the length of the pastry, leaving about 2″ (5 cm) at either end. Dampen the edges of the pastry with cold water, fold the two ends in on top of the almond filling, and then carefully seal the long edges over each other to form a long, narrow roll.

Place the pastry roll, seam side down, on a baking sheet lined with greaseproof paper. Dampen the two ends and bring them together to form a neat ring. Brush the pastry ring with one beaten egg and the milk. Bake in a hot oven, 425°F (220°C, gas mark 7), for 15 minutes and then reduce heat to 400°F (200°C, gas mark 6) for a further 20 minutes. At the end of this time, the pastry should be nicely brown and slightly risen.

Cool the ring on a wire rack and then decorate the top with glacé icing, cherries, angelica and browned almonds.   MJ

SIMPLE SAVARIN

Using easy blend yeast, a savarin ring is not difficult to make, and makes a splendid dessert, filled with soft fruits and served with cream.

> *6 oz (175 g) strong (bread) flour*
> *1 teaspoon salt*
> *3 oz (75 g) softened butter (plus extra for*
> * greasing)*
> *1 tablespoon caster sugar*
> *Grated rind of 1 small lemon*
> *1 sachet easy yeast*
> *3 eggs (size 3), beaten*
> *3–4 tablespoons tepid milk*

SYRUP
2 oz (50 g) caster sugar
2 tablespoons clear honey
3 fl oz (100 ml) water
2 tablespoons kirsch or white rum

FILLING
3 tablespoons warmed apricot jam
1 lb (500 g) mixed soft fruits, e.g. strawberries,
*   raspberries, cherries, grapes and kiwi*
Extra kirsch or rum, optional

Rub a 9″ (23 cm) savarin ring mould thoroughly with butter, then dust lightly with flour. It is essential that the tin is well prepared if the savarin is to turn out successfully. If you are using a new tin, make sure it is thoroughly seasoned.

Rub the butter into the flour and salt, then stir in the sugar, lemon rind and yeast. Beat the eggs with the milk and mix well into the flour, beating until it is very smooth – about 10 minutes by hand or 5 by machine. Cover and leave until doubled in size. This may take time as the mixture is rich.

Knock the dough back and knead again, then place into the ring mould, levelling with the back of a spoon. The mould may look a little uneven, but it will level out on cooking. Leave to prove again until about three quarters of the way up the sides.

Bake at 400°F (200°C, gas mark 6) for 15–20 minutes until browned on top and cooked underneath. Cool slightly, then loosen the edges and turn out. Cool completely but return the savarin to the tin for the soaking.

Simmer the sugar, honey and water together for 5 minutes. Add the kirsch or rum, then slowly pour around and into the savarin. Allow it to soak well in before turning the ring out again, onto a large plate.

Brush all over with the warm jam and fill with the fruit, which may be tossed in some more kirsch or rum beforehand. Serve chilled with whipped or pouring cream.

Makes one savarin to serve 6.

NOTE The same mixture, with 2 oz (50 g) of currants added, can be used to fill about 6 rum baba moulds. Bake for just 10–15 minutes, soak in the same syrup, and fill with cream. RD

Simple savarin and rum baba

DUCK'S EGG SPONGE WITH APPLE AND MARMALADE FILLING

Ducks' eggs make marvellous whisked sponges, as one gets the richness without the high animal fat. Because egg sizes vary, it's best not to specify exact measurements but balance up the sugar and flour to suit the egg weight. Apples and oranges are combined with cream cheese for the filling.

3 ducks' eggs
Their weight in plain flour, sifted, and the same
*   weight in caster sugar*
Grated rind of one large orange

FILLING
2 cooking apples, peeled
Juice of 1 orange
2 oz (50 g) caster sugar
4 oz (125 g) cream or curd cheese
2–3 tablespoons orange jelly marmalade

TO DECORATE
Icing sugar
A few jonquil flowers
Some strips of blanched orange rind

Grease an 8–9″ (20–22 cm) ring spring tin and line the base with greaseproof paper. Preheat the oven to 325°F (170°C, gas mark 3).

Whisk the eggs in a large, clean bowl either by an electric hand machine on a high setting (but not in a food processor), or by hand over a pan of gently simmering water, until the foam holds its shape leaving a trail when drawn back on itself.

Now, gradually sprinkle in the flour and grated orange rind, and fold in gently until incorporated. Spoon into the prepared tin and bake for 50–60 minutes, until the sponge is firm and springy to touch.

Leave to cool partially in the tin, then turn out onto plate and allow to cool completely. Peel off the paper.

Meanwhile, cook the apples with the orange juice until pulpy. Sweeten to taste, cool and mix with the cheese. Split the cake in two, spread each side with marmalade and fill with the apple cream. Sandwich together, dust with icing sugar, and decorate with the flowers and orange rind strips.

Serves 6–8.   RD

Walnut cake

Sieve the flour. Separate the egg yolks from the whites. Mix together flour, sugar, egg yolks, baking powder, melted butter and Grand Marnier. Beat egg whites until stiff, and gently fold in to the mixture. Add ground nuts. Butter a 2 lb (1 kg) loaf tin, and pour in the mixture.

Bake for about 45 minutes at 375°F (190°C, gas mark 5), until the cake is a pale golden colour and cooked through.

Makes one loaf.   MJS

WALNUT CAKE

One of the gastronomic legacies left by the Moorish occupation of Spain is the Spanish predilection for nuts. Almonds are much favoured, especially in Andalusia, and are used in both savoury and sweet dishes. This recipe for walnut cake, *bizcocho de nueces*, comes from the region of Valencia.

7 oz (200 g) walnuts, crushed lightly
7 oz (200 g) sugar
3½ oz (100 g) butter
3½ oz (100 g) plain flour
1 teaspoon baking powder
4 eggs
2 tablespoons Grand Marnier

CHOCOLATE FONDANT CAKE

For those who dislike fruit cakes, this is a wickedly rich chocolate cake, mousse-like in consistency and an ideal alternative to either Christmas cake or Christmas pudding.

It is an easy recipe, bound to please any lover of chocolate, but, once cooked, it needs to be left for three days to set in the refrigerator so must be made in advance.

8 oz (250 g) plain chocolate
8 oz (250 g) caster sugar
4 tablespoons strong black coffee

8 oz (250 g) unsalted butter, cut into small
    pieces
4 eggs, lightly beaten
1 tablespoon plain flour

CHOCOLATE MARZIPAN
3 oz (75 g) plain chocolate, melted
4 oz (125 g) marzipan

CHOCOLATE GLAZE
4 oz (125 g) plain chocolate
2 oz (50 g) unsalted butter
3 tablespoons water

DECORATION
Chocolate flakes
Chocolate leaves
Icing sugar

Melt the chocolate, sugar and coffee in a bowl over a pan of hot water. When melted, remove the mixture from the heat and allow to cool slightly. Add the small pieces of butter, stirring well to dissolve after each addition. Add the eggs and mix thoroughly. Lastly, beat in the flour. Line an 8″ (20 cm) *moule à manqué* tin with aluminium foil, allowing it to come up higher than the sides of the tin. Brush the foil with melted butter and pour in the cake mixture.

Cook in a *bain-marie* on top of the cooker for 45 minutes. Do not allow the water to boil; just simmer very gently.

Remove the cake from the *bain-marie* and finish baking it in a very cool oven, 275°F (135°C, gas mark 1), for half an hour. Cool the cake in the tin and then refrigerate the cake, still in its tin, for three days (it appears uncooked even after baking, but sets when chilled).

After three days have elapsed, the cake may be finished. Melt the plain chocolate in a bowl set over a pan of simmering water. Prepare the chocolate marzipan by mixing the marzipan with the melted chocolate in a food processor until well combined. Roll into a ball and chill in the refrigerator for about 15 minutes.

Meanwhile, carefully turn the cake out onto a serving dish and remove the aluminium foil. Roll out the chocolate marzipan on a surface lightly dusted with icing sugar, and form it into a circle the size of the top of the cake. Lay the marzipan circle on top of the cake.

Make the chocolate glaze by stirring all the ingredients in a bowl over a pan of hot water till dissolved. Cool slightly, then pour over the cake so that it is completely and evenly covered.

Just before the chocolate glaze is completely set, decorate the top of the cake with flaked chocolate (which can be made by running the blade of a sharp knife over a block of chocolate) and some chocolate leaves.

The latter can be made by dipping the underside of rose leaves in melted chocolate and then peeling them off carefully when the chocolate has set (chocolate leaves are also available, ready-made, from good supermarkets). Dust the top of the cake lightly with icing sugar.

To serve, cut the cake with a sharp knife which has been first run under hot water and then wiped dry. Store cake in the refrigerator.   MJ

Chocolate fondant cake

SNACKS AND SAVOURIES

Celeriac crisps, savoury peanut brittle and Yarmouth straws are irresistible with pre-dinner drinks, while after-dinner savouries include devils-on-horseback and anchovy tartlets

ANCHOVY TARTLETS

A hot and salty snack for late night nibbling.

½ recipe for cheese sablé dough (see page 150)
¼ pint (150 ml) double cream
1 teaspoon anchovy essence
Cayenne pepper
6 anchovy fillets

Roll out the cheese sablé dough, cut into rounds and line 12–18 small tartlet tins. Prick the bases lightly with a fork and bake at 375°F (190°C, gas mark 5) for 7 minutes. Whip the cream to stiff peaks and flavour with anchovy essence and cayenne pepper. Cut the anchovy fillets into thin strips. Spoon the cream into the pastry cases and top with a lattice of anchovy pieces. Return to the oven for 3–4 minutes. Serve very hot.

Serves 6. MN

YARMOUTH STRAWS

An after-dinner savoury which could be served at any time, these are really cheese straws with a filling of kipper fillet as an added dimension.

8 oz (250 g) shortcrust pastry
8 oz (250 g) kipper fillets
1 oz (25 g) grated Parmesan cheese
1 egg

Roll out the pastry thinly into two 3″ (7.5 cm) wide strips. Grill the kipper fillets, remove the skin and any bones, and mash the flesh. Spread the kipper on one piece of pastry and sprinkle with half the cheese. Brush a little beaten egg round the edge of the pastry and top with the second piece, pressing the edges together lightly. Brush with the remaining beaten egg and sprinkle with cheese. Cut into ¾″ (1.75 cm) strips. Place on a lightly greased baking sheet and bake at 350°F (180°C, gas mark 4) for 12 minutes. Serve hot.

Serves 6. MN

BLUE CHEESE CRISPS

These little cheese and walnut biscuits are delicious with pre-dinner drinks.

4 oz (125 g) self-raising flour
4 oz (125 g) butter
2 oz (50 g) blue cheese
2 oz (50 g) mature Cheddar cheese
Salt and pepper
2 oz (50 g) finely chopped walnuts

Right *(clockwise from top) cooked marrow bones; Camembert cheese (deep-fried, in centre); devils on horseback, page 144; Yarmouth straws; anchovy tartlets; blue cheese crisps; various cheeses*

Sieve the flour into a bowl and rub in the butter until the mixture resembles fine breadcrumbs. Crumble in the blue cheese. Grate the Cheddar cheese finely, and add to the flour with plenty of salt and pepper. Mix well to form a dough. Chill for 30 minutes.

Roll the dough into about 30 balls, and roll each ball in the chopped walnuts. Place on lightly greased baking trays, and press out lightly with a fork dipped in cold water. Bake at 400°F (200°C, gas mark 6) for 10 minutes. Leave on the baking sheets for about 5 minutes and lift carefully onto a wire rack to cool. Store in an airtight tin.

Makes about 30.   MN

Eggs stuffed with prawns and crabmeat

MILLE-FEUILLE OF BRIE

This dish is equally good as a starter, or as an after-dinner savoury, served with grapes.

> *7 oz (200 g) puff pastry*
> *5 oz (150 g) Brie cheese*
> *2 oz (50 g) butter*
> *2 oz (50 g) Greek yoghurt*
> *1 oz (25 g) hazelnuts*

Roll out the puff pastry into a rectangle about 12 × 6″ (30 × 15 cm) and bake in a hot oven at 450°F (230°C, gas mark 8) for 25 minutes until brown. Remove and leave to cool.

Place the Brie and butter in the food processor and blend to a thick paste. Add the yoghurt and process again just enough to mix. Season well.

Roast the hazelnuts. Keep some whole for decoration, and chop the rest.

Add half of the chopped nuts to the cheese mixture, and keep the rest for decoration.

When the pastry is cool, cut it into three rectangles about 4″ (10 cm) wide. Separate each piece horizontally into two layers, and use the cheese mixture to sandwich between the layers, keeping some to cover the top. Smooth the top well, and trim the edges of the mille-feuilles. Cut into portions and decorate with the rest of the nuts.

Serves 6.   CB

DEVILS ON HORSEBACK

The classic after-dinner savoury, illustrated on page 143, which can double as a hot canapé.

> *12 large plump prunes*
> *12 blanched almonds*
> *6 rashers streaky bacon*
> *3 medium slices white bread*
> *Oil for frying*

Soak the prunes until they swell (about 2 hours), then drain. Carefully remove the stones and replace with an almond. Derind the bacon rashers, cut each one in half, and smooth out thinly with a broad-bladed knife. Wrap a piece round each prune, securing with a cocktail stick. Put under a hot grill, turning once, until the bacon is crisp.

While the 'devils' are cooking, cut 4 circles of bread from each slice, using a pastry cutter. Fry the circles until crisp and golden. Put a prune on each piece of bread and serve 2 to each person as a savoury.

Serves 6.   MN

EGGS STUFFED WITH PRAWNS AND CRABMEAT

The recipe for these tiny stuffed eggs comes from Thailand, where they are known as *khai kwan*, or 'precious eggs'.

2 dozen quails' eggs, boiled for 3 minutes

STUFFING
8 oz (250 g) large uncooked prawns, shelled
4 oz (125 g) cooked crabmeat (white meat only)
1 tablespoon chopped coriander leaf
2 cloves garlic, chopped
Freshly ground black pepper
½ teaspoon salt
1 tablespoon Thai fish sauce (nam pla)
4–5 tablespoons thick coconut milk or single cream

BATTER
3 oz (75 g) plain flour
6 fl oz (175 ml) warm water
1 tablespoon vegetable oil
¼ teaspoon salt

Peel and halve the eggs. Scrape out the yolks, set aside the halves, and put the yolks in a bowl.

Chop or mince the prawns, and mix them with all the other stuffing ingredients, except the coconut milk or cream. Add this mixture to the yolks in the bowl, and mix well with a fork. Add the coconut milk or cream, incorporating a spoonful at a time, until the mixture is well blended and moist. You may find you need less than 5 tablespoons of the cream.

Divide the filling into 48 equal portions and put one portion into each half egg white, piling up the filling and shaping it so that you end up with the shape of a whole quail's egg.

To make the batter, put the flour, water, oil and salt in a bowl, and beat until smooth. Dip each of the stuffed eggs in the batter and deep-fry in hot oil (350°F, 180°C) for about 3 minutes or until golden brown, keeping the filling downwards while frying. Take them out with a slotted spoon and drain on absorbent paper.

Serve hot or cold as a starter on a bed of lettuce dressed lightly with *nam chim* (Thai sweet-and-sour chilli sauce), or use *nam chim* as a dip if the *khai kwan* are handed around as an appetizer with drinks.
Makes 48.   SO

TINY TEA EGGS

This is a novelty appetizer which you can serve at a drinks party or as the start of a home-cooked Chinese meal. Hand them round on a salver with a small dish of ground Szechuan red peppercorns mixed with sea salt for dipping into.

12 quails' eggs, hard-boiled and unpeeled
1 pint (600 ml) black tea (try smoky lapsang souchong or the stronger keemun)
1 tablespoon soy or oyster sauce
1 star anise
Good pinch salt

With a teaspoon, tap the shells all over to craze them. Put in a saucepan with the rest of the ingredients and bring to the boil. Simmer gently for 15 minutes, checking that the liquid doesn't boil dry. Remove with a slotted spoon and when cool enough to handle, peel.
Serve warm, if possible.   SO

EGGS PRINCESS

If quails' eggs are fresh – i.e. not near their sell-by date, so they don't spread out when cooked – and fried in very hot fat or oil, they make pretty, round frilly shapes.

Then they can be popped onto any flat contrasting morsel – toasted croûtes, rounds of buttered bread, baked open-cup mushrooms, small lettuce leaves and so on. The following is just one idea. Another would be to spread toasted rounds of French bread with *tapénade*, and top each with a fried quail's egg.

12 small size leaves of crisp round lettuce
12 thin slices small good salami, e.g. Italian or
    Hungarian
12 quails' eggs, broken into egg-cups (this can be
    done in batches)
1 oz (25 g) butter
1 tablespoon sunflower or olive oil
Ground black pepper

First, spread out the lettuce leaves on a platter and
top each with a slice of skinned salami.

When ready to serve, heat the butter and oil
until quite hot in a large frying pan and fry the eggs
quickly. The fat should be hot enough to make the
whites go frilly round the edge.

Scoop out onto the salami, grind over some
pepper and hand round as soon as possible. Your
guests can fold up the lettuce leaves slightly to eat
all at one go. Don't bite into the yolk or it might
dribble onto your chin.

Makes 12 bite-size servings.   RD

QUAILS' EGG AND VINEGAR BACON TARTLETS

The perfect party snack, these can be prepared
ahead and assembled quickly at the last minute.

6 oz (175 g) plain flour
Good pinch cayenne pepper
3 oz (90 g) butter or margarine
1 oz (25 g) freshly grated Parmesan cheese

FILLING
1 lb (500 g) sweetcure streaky bacon, de-rinded
    and chopped
1 teaspoon French mustard
1 tablespoon raspberry vinegar
3 tablespoons fromage frais
1 spring onion, chopped
12 quails' eggs

Make the pastry first by rubbing the flour, cayenne
and fat together then mixing in the Parmesan

cheese and combining with enough cold water to
make a firm dough.

Roll out thinly and use to line 12 tartlet cases,
re-rolling if necessary. Prick the bases lightly, and
chill for 20 minutes while you preheat the oven to
400°F (200°C, gas mark 6).

Bake the cases for 12–15 minutes until crisp,
then cool and remove. These can be stored in an
airtight tin for a few days until needed.

To make the filling, preheat a heavy-based
frying pan until quite hot. Add the chopped bacon
and stir well, then turn down to a medium heat,
stirring occasionally until the fat runs and the bacon
crisps up.

Pour off as much fat as possible. Mix the
mustard and vinegar and pour into the pan, stirring. Cook until nearly evaporated. Off the heat,
blend in the fromage frais until creamy, add the
spring onion then spoon into the tartlet cases. If
liked, the filling can be cooked ahead to this stage
and then reheated gently when required in a warm
oven just before serving.

Wipe out the pan, add 3 tablespoons sunflower
oil or a good ounce of butter and break the quails'
eggs into egg-cups in batches. Fry for about a
minute and scoop out on top of the bacon.

Alternatively, hard-boil the eggs, peel and
halve then place 2 halves on each bacon-filled tart.
Eat them as soon as possible.

Makes 12 tartlets.   RD

PROSTINNANS SILL

This delicious Swedish herring snack is known as
the Vicar's wife's favourite.

2 double fillets of Majtes or salt herring (soak
    salt herring in cold water for 2 hours)
1 small knob of butter
3 or 4 young, tender leeks, washed and trimmed
1 tablespoon or so of unsalted butter
3 freshly hard-boiled eggs, still warm (or boil
    and shell in advance, then warm in hot water
    just before incorporating)
¼ pint (150 ml) thick cream, stiffly whipped

Prostinnans sill, served with sour cream

Chop herring fillets (well drained, if appropriate) into neat, bite-sized pieces and warm gently in the knob of butter. Shred the leeks very finely and melt (do not brown) in the tablespoon of butter in a separate pan – this may take about 10 minutes. Dice the shelled eggs finely, and combine quickly with the hot herring and leek – a warm mixing bowl is desirable. Finally, fold in the whipped cream deftly, and pile the warm mixture immediately onto rounds of buttered, dark, soft rye bread, small crispbreads, or the larger-size 'Rahms' ready-made croustade shells, which may be heated and crisped in the oven.

Makes 18–24. SD

CELERIAC CRISPS

Served hot, these make the perfect partner for roasted poultry, pork or winter game. Left to cool they are good with drinks.

1 large celeriac bulb
Vegetable oil to a depth of several inches for
* deep-frying*

Peel the celeriac bulb and slice it into rounds, as thin as possible. Drop the slices into a bowl of cold water acidulated with a tablespoon or two of lemon juice or vinegar.

147

Heat the oil in a deep pan. Drain the celeriac and dry thoroughly on both sides with paper towels. When the oil is hot, drop some slices into the fat and cook for about 5 minutes, until they turn brown and crisp. Watch carefully: when they begin to colour they brown rapidly. Do not crowd them in the pot but deep-fry them in batches.

Remove the cooked slices with a slotted spoon, allowing excess oil to drip back into the pan. Drain them in one layer on paper towels and salt lightly. Serve the celeriac crisps while still hot with roasted poultry, pork or winter game.

Serves 4.   ER

BACON-FILLED PIRAGI

Rich or time-consuming yeast-raised doughs invariably have a festive air – and aroma – about them. No Latvian festivity, winter or summer, would be complete without trays full of *piragi* – savoury, bread-dough and smoked bacon rolls. Occasionally they would accompany bowls of light soup in the manner of Russian *pirozhki*, but they are most often encountered as the ideal party snack, whether served hot or cold.

Bacon-filled piragi

Other fillings exist, based on savoury fish, cabbage or soft cheese mixtures, but this is undoubtedly the most popular.

½ lb (250 g) smoked pork in the form of speck, pancetta or poitrine fumée (this could well be a piece of meat already used to flavour a casserole or sauerkraut)
½ lb (250 g) streaky bacon – could be green if pork is well smoked
1 medium onion, peeled and finely chopped
½ teaspoon freshly-grated nutmeg
Freshly-ground black pepper
Additional pinch of salt if required

YEAST DOUGH
1 tablespoon dried yeast, or 1 oz (25 g) fresh yeast
2 tablespoons warm water
1 teaspoon sugar, if using dried yeast
8 fl oz (250 ml) milk
2½ oz (65 g) unsalted butter
1 lb (500 g) strong, plain unbleached flour
1 teaspoon salt
2 tablespoons thick, soured cream
1 egg, beaten
Additional egg, beaten with 2 tablespoons water to form egg-wash

Finely dice the pork and bacon. Fry gently in an ungreased pan until the fat runs (if pork has seen casserole-use, fry bacon first). Remove the meat from the pan with a slotted spoon and gently soften the onion in the bacon-fat. Remove when soft, and add, with 1 tablespoon of the rendered fat, to the drained meat. Add nutmeg, pepper to taste, and a little salt if the meat was not very salty. Set the mixture aside to cool while preparing the dough – chilling in the refrigerator will make for easier mounding of the filling.

Cream the yeast with the water (and sugar, if using dried yeast) and set aside for 10 minutes until activated. Scald the milk and butter in a saucepan, then cool to blood temperature. Sift the flour and salt into a warm mixing bowl, and form a well in the centre. Pour milk-and-butter, soured cream and egg into the well and gradually incorporate liquids into flour with a wooden spoon, or the dough hook of a food-mixer. Once amalgamated, leave the dough to rest 10 minutes, then turn out onto a floured surface and knead vigorously for 10 minutes (or continue with the mixer dough-hook) until the dough feels elastic.

Place in a greased bowl, cover, and set aside in a warm place to prove and rise until double the original volume (about 1½ hours).

Knock back the dough, knead briefly, then roll and stretch the dough on a floured surface to form a large rectangle (about 15″ × 22″/40 × 55 cm). Facing the shorter side of the rectangle, make 8 rows of 4 or 5 small mounds of filling, starting 1″ (2.5 cm) from the edge. Fold the dough-edge nearest you over the first row and filling, and using a 2″ (5 cm) round pastry cutter or rim of a glass, cut out a semi-circle round each dough-covered mound. Ensure edges are well sealed before transferring to a greased baking sheet. Neaten the pastry rectangle edge roughly, retaining trimmings, and repeat the procedure until you have formed 40 or 48 piragi. If you have sufficient dough trimmings and fillings, re-knead and roll out the dough and make some more pastries.

Piragi may be bent round in a crescent shape before baking, if wished. Arrange piragi on greased baking trays, ensuring they are not touching, and brush lightly with egg-wash. Leave to rise a further 10 minutes while the oven is heating. Bake at a fairly hot temperature (400°F, 200°C, gas mark 6) for 10–12 minutes, until golden-brown. Serve hot, warm or cold.

Makes 40–48.

NOTE The same dough may be used to make another traditional savoury yeast pastry from Latvia – ķimeņmaizītes, or caraway rolls. Small portions of the risen dough are formed into balls the size of a large marble, and placed on greased baking sheets. Make a deep indentation into each by pushing a thumb firmly into the centre of each ball of dough. Brush with egg-wash as before, then press a small piece of unsalted butter (about ¼ teaspoon) into the indentations, and sprinkle generously with caraway seeds.

Bake for 8–10 minutes in a hot oven, and serve either hot or cold.   SD

Turkish cheese boreks

TURKISH CHEESE BOREKS

Best served while still warm, these crisp, cigar-shaped filo pastry rolls are excellent with pre-dinner drinks, as part of a *mezze*.

> *1 lb (500 g) feta cheese, crumbled*
> *1 egg yolk*
> *Freshly-chopped mint*
> *1 egg white, lightly beaten*
> *1 packet of filo pastry*

Mix the cheese with parsley to taste, and add yolk of egg to mixture.

Cut a double layer of filo pastry into rectangles about 9 × 5″ (23 × 13 cm) working quickly and keeping extra pastry under a damp teacloth to prevent it drying out. Put a sausage-shaped layer of cheese filling diagonally across the corner of each rectangle, and starting from that corner, roll the pastry up diagonally, folding the sides as you go, to make a neat parcel shaped like a cigar, and using the egg white to stick the pastry together.

Deep fry in hot oil until crisp and brown, drain on kitchen paper, and serve.

Makes about 30 boreks.   VJ

CHEESE SABLES WITH MUSTARD CREAM

These rich cheese shortbreads make good appetizers, and may be served as plain biscuits or with this mustard cream filling.

> 6 oz (175 g) plain flour
> ¼ teaspoon salt
> Pinch mustard powder
> 6 oz (175 g) butter
> 6 oz (175 g) mature Cheddar cheese
> ¼ pint (150 ml) double cream
> 3 teaspoons wholegrain mustard

Sieve the flour, salt and mustard powder into a bowl. Rub in the butter until the mixture resembles fine breadcrumbs. Grate the cheese finely into the bowl, then mix and press together to make a soft dough. Wrap in foil and chill for 1 hour.

Roll out thinly on a floured board (the dough is rather fragile) and cut into 2″ (5 cm) rounds. Place on ungreased baking sheets and bake at 375°F (190°C, gas mark 5) for 12 minutes, until golden. Leave on the baking sheets for 5 minutes and lift carefully onto a wire rack to cool. Store in an airtight tin.

To serve, whip the cream to soft peaks and fold in the mustard until evenly coloured. Sandwich pairs of biscuits with this filling.

Makes about 24.   MN

CURRIED HOT NUTS

Very quick to make, with no cooking skill required, these mixed nuts just need to be reheated for a few minutes in the oven before nibbling.

> 2 tablespoons sunflower oil
> 1 teaspoon curry paste
> 1 lb (500 g) mixed, unsalted nuts (blanched almonds, shelled hazelnuts, pecans, Brazils and unsalted cashews)
> ½ teaspoon garlic salt
> Fine sea salt or crushed rock salt, to sprinkle

Heat the oil in a saucepan and cook out the curry paste for a few seconds. Stir in the mixed nuts and garlic salt.

Fry gently until the nuts are lightly cooked but not too browned. Sprinkle over the salt and serve warm. They can be reheated.

Serves 4–6 as a savoury.   RD

POTTED CHEESE WITH WALNUTS

These make unusual gifts, covered with large cellophane jam pot covers, and secured with elastic bands which can then be disguised with pretty, thin ribbon.

> 6 oz (175 g) mature red Leicester, Cheshire or Cheddar cheese, grated
> 2 oz (50 g) freshly grated Parmesan cheese
> 2 oz (50 g) butter, softened
> 1 tablespoon chopped chives, or spring onion tops
> ½ teaspoon ground mace
> 2–3 oz (50–75 g) roughly chopped walnuts
> Capers and small sprigs of rosemary or thyme, to garnish
> Ground black pepper

Blend the cheeses and butter until smooth, then stir in the chives or onion, mace, nuts and pepper.

Divide between four ramekins, swirl the tops attractively, and garnish with the capers and herbs.

Chill until ready to give away, or serve with toast.

Makes 4.   RD

SAVOURY PEANUT BRITTLE

These Indonesian snacks, rempeyek kacang, are delicious any time, but go particularly well with drinks: pre-dinner or cocktail party.

To achieve the right crispy brittle texture, they are fried first in the frying-pan, then in the wok.

Potted cheese with walnuts (left) and curried hot nuts

4 oz (125 g) fine rice powder
8 fl oz (240 ml) cold water
2 kemiri *(candlenuts)*
1 garlic clove, peeled
1 teaspoon salt
2 teaspoons ground coriander seed
5 oz (150 g) shelled peanuts (halved if large)
Vegetable oil for frying

Sift the rice powder into a deep bowl. Liquidize the candlenuts and garlic using half of the water and pour this into the rice powder. Add the salt and ground coriander and the remaining water. Mix well, and add the halved peanuts.

Heat 8 fl oz (240 ml) of oil in a non-stick frying-pan. Take up a tablespoon of the batter with some nuts in it, and pour it quickly into the frying-pan. You can do 5–6 spoonfuls at a time; fry these for about 2 minutes. Then remove them from the pan with a slotted spoon and put them to drain on a plate lined with paper towels. Repeat this until all the batter is used up.

Pour the remaining oil from the frying-pan into a wok, adding about 2 more cupfuls, and heat this oil to 350°F/180°C. Fry the half-cooked rempeyek, perhaps 8 or 10 at a time, in the hot oil for 2 minutes until golden brown, turning them several times. Drain and leave to cool.   SO

DEVILLED MUSHROOMS

Quickly made from everyday ingredients, these are a welcome treat at any time of day.

1 lb (500 g) medium-sized flat mushrooms
4 oz (125 g) butter
½ pint (300 ml) double cream
2 teaspoons Worcestershire sauce
1 teaspoon wholegrain mustard
Fingers of dry toast

Wipe the mushrooms but do not wash them. Leave them whole and fry in butter until just tender. Drain off surplus liquid and place the mushrooms in a shallow ovenware dish. Season the cream with sauce and mustard, and pour over the mushrooms. Put under a medium grill until very hot and bubbling. Serve the mushrooms at once with fingers of hot dry toast.

Serves 4–6.   MN

DEVILLED SARDINES

A storecupboard savoury for after dinner.

12 sardines canned in oil
3 medium slices white bread
½ oz (15 g) butter
½ oz (15 g) plain flour
2 teaspoons anchovy essence
1 teaspoon Worcestershire sauce
¼ pint (150 ml) chicken stock
½ teaspoon lemon juice
2 tablespoons single cream
Watercress or parsley sprigs

Bone the sardines and re-form the fish. Toast the bread, remove crusts and cut each slice into four strips. Place in a single layer in a shallow ovenware dish. Place a sardine on each one and sprinkle with a little of the oil from the can. Heat in the oven at 350°F (180°C, gas mark 4) for 5 minutes.

Meanwhile, melt the butter in a small pan. Work in the flour and cook for 30 seconds, stirring

well. Add the anchovy essence, sauce and stock, and stir over a low heat until thick and creamy. Stir in the lemon juice and the cream. Pour over the sardines and heat in the oven for 2 minutes. Serve at once garnished with watercress and parsley.

Serves 6.   MN

GOURMANDISES
GRUYEROISES

This is based on a Valais peasant dish described in *Cooking with Pomiane* (Bruno Cassirer, 1962).

2 small tomatoes, or 1 medium
2 oz (50 g) grated Gruyère
2 rashers unsmoked streaky bacon, cut in half,
*   rind and bone removed*
2 thickish slices wholemeal bread – such as
*   Poilane's sourdough*
Dijon mustard

Gourmandises gruyeroises

Remove skin and pips from tomatoes and lightly chop the flesh. Toast one side of each slice of bread.

Spread untoasted sides generously with mustard. Pile mixture of cheese and tomato firmly on to the mustardy side of the slices, pressing gently and taking care that it comes right to the crust all of the way round.

Grill until cheese goes golden. Lay two half rashers on each slice and grill until starting to brown. Dust lightly with freshly ground pepper, and serve.

Serves 1 or 2.   HDM

DARK AND WHITE CHOCOLATE COLETTES

For those who enjoy fresh Belgian chocolates, these little chocolate cases filled with a ganache of white chocolate are an attractive alternative. They do take a little time to make, but are not difficult. You could offer them as presents, nestling on small china plates, when flowers or wine seem inappropriate. They are always well received.

*5 oz (150 g) bar dark chocolate (such as
    Sainsbury's Deluxe Chocolate for Cooking)*
A little grated dark chocolate, optional

FILLING
24 large seedless raisins
3 tablespoons white rum
7 oz (200 g) white chocolate
7–8 tablespoons double cream
3 oz (75 g) unsalted butter
2 egg yolks

Break up the dark chocolate and put into a heat-proof bowl. Melt slowly over a pan of gently simmering water. Do not allow to overheat or the chocolate will 'seize' and go lumpy. If you have a microwave oven, heat for 2–2½ minutes on full, depending on the wattage, then stir until smooth.

Using a teaspoon, line about 24 petit four paper cases with the chocolate, about half a spoon at a time and spreading it around with the tip of the

spoon. Leave to reset on a cooling tray, then very carefully peel the cases off, if you like, although they can be left on.

Put the raisins into a small saucepan with 2 tablespoons of the rum. Heat gently then leave to cool.

Meanwhile, melt the white chocolate with the cream and butter in the same way, over a gentle heat or in the microwave oven. Stir in the remaining spoon of rum and the egg yolks. Allow to cool until thickened, then beat until smooth and the consistency of thick mayonnaise. Spoon into a nylon piping bag fitted with a ½" (12 mm) star nozzle.

Put a rum-soaked raisin into each case, then pipe a whorl of the white chocolate ganache on top. Sprinkle with a little grated chocolate if liked. Leave in the fridge until ready to give away.

Makes about 24.   RD

HAZELNUT AND COFFEE CLOUDS

Although not strictly speaking sweets or savouries, these little, crisp meringues nevertheless are greatly enjoyed at the end of a meal with coffee.

They can be made in advance and stored in an airtight container.

2 egg whites
4 oz (125 g) caster sugar
1½ oz (40 g) ground roasted hazelnuts
2 teaspoons coffee essence

Whisk the egg whites until forming stiff peaks, then gradually whisk in the caster sugar until you have a stiff and glossy mixture. Fold in the ground nuts and essence.

Pipe in small stars or spoon in small mounds onto a baking sheet lined with greased greaseproof, Bakewell or rice paper.

Bake at 300°F (150°C, gas mark 2) for about 25 minutes, or until crisp. Remove with a palette knife onto a cooling tray.

Makes about 24.   RD

MOVEABLE FEASTS

Chilled soups and salads, a cold galantine, salmon
in a pastry case and home-made brioche have all
the makings of a perfect picnic. With cake and
fruit to follow, here is a sensational outdoor feast

GALANTINETTE

A boned, stuffed bird is certainly good cause for
compliments at a picnic, but the average home
cook requires much time struggling to bone the
bird neatly in the first place.

However, this simpler version should draw
equally admiring gasps of delight.

18 back rashers of bacon, derinded
1½ lb (750 g) turkey breast fillets, sliced
3 tablespoons dry sherry
1 lb (500 g) stewing pork, minced
½ lb (250 g) chicken livers, finely chopped
1 onion, chopped
2 cloves garlic, crushed
3 oz (75 g) butter, melted
3 tablespoons brandy
1 teaspoon thyme
2 oz (50 g) pistachios or 20 stuffed olives
3 oz (75 g) fresh white breadcrumbs
3 tablespoons fresh chopped parsley

Place a large sheet of foil on baking sheet and
lightly grease. Lay the bacon rashers in two lines
with the 'oyster' ends meeting in the middle. Overlap the slices very slightly.

Toss the fillets in the sherry and lay them on
top in a long line down the centre. Season well.

Mix everything else together, season well and
spoon on top of the fillets.

Draw the outer edges of the rashers up and
over the filling and press well down. Wrap over the
foil, sealing the ends well.

Bake at 350°F (180°C, gas mark 4) for about
1¼ hours. Allow to cool and chill in the foil.
Unwrap, remove any jelly or meat residue (use
these in the courgette soup, page 158, if liked) and
cut into slices. Overwrap in cling film to stop the
galantinette turning brown in the air.

Serves 8–10.   RD

SPICED CARROT SALAD

This is a good portable vegetable salad as it can be
dressed in advance without turning limp.

Serve it with small wedges of Little Gem
lettuces, as they hold their shape and can be easily
eaten with fingers.

1 lb (500 g) carrots, grated
2–3 oz (50–75 g) raisins
2 oz (50 g) flaked or slivered almonds, toasted
¼ pint (150 ml) well-flavoured vinaigrette
1 teaspoon ground cumin
Salt and pepper

Simply toss everything together and store in a well-
sealed picnic container until required. Can be made
the night before, but not frozen.

Serves 6.   RD

Right *Galantinette, with spiced carrot salad*

RARE LAMB SALAD WITH HAZELNUT DRESSING

This is a particularly good mixture of flavours, colours and textures, and needs only simple accompaniments such as the courgette and tomato salad and new potatoes, or crusty bread and fingers of crisp Little Gem lettuces.

2 lb (1 kg) lean rolled leg or shoulder of lamb
3 tablespoons hazelnut oil
4 oz (125 g) shelled hazelnuts, lightly toasted
1 medium onion, ideally red, sliced thinly
4 oz (125 g) thin green beans, tailed, halved and
* lightly cooked*
Salt and ground black pepper

Season the lamb lightly, then roast at 375°F (190°C, gas mark 5) for about 45–50 minutes. Cool, then cut into thin slices and then shreds. Mix in a bowl with the oil and nuts, and check the seasoning.

Meanwhile, soak the onion slices in cold water for about 2 hours. Mix with the lamb and nuts, and the cooked beans. Cover and chill for a further two hours then cover ready for transporting.

Serves 6–8. RD

COURGETTE AND TOMATO SHREDDED SALAD

This simple salad makes a light, refreshing accompaniment to the rare lamb salad with hazelnut dressing described above.

1 lb (500 g) courgettes
8 oz (250 g) firm tomatoes
Juice of 1 small lemon
Salt and ground black pepper

Trim the courgettes (don't peel them), then grate coarsely into a large bowl. Dip the tomatoes briefly into a bowl of boiling water, then peel and skin. Cut into quarters, remove the seeds then slice the flesh. Mix this into the courgettes with the lemon

juice and seasoning to taste. Chill the salad thoroughly before packing into a rigid picnic container for easy transportation.

Serves 6. RD

FRESH BITTER LEMON CRUSH

A light and refreshing drink.

Chop 3 lemons and a small orange into chunks, then blend in a food processor or liquidizer until pulpy. Add icing sugar to taste and either some sprigs of lemon balm or mint, or a few shakes of Angostura Bitters. Strain through a sieve, rubbing well with a ladle. When you've squeezed as much juice as possible from the pulp, discard it. Transport the juice concentrated, ready to dilute with sparkling mineral water. RD

SALMON NELSON

This is the fish equivalent of Beef Wellington. Ask your fishmonger to fillet and skin a large tail piece of salmon. Serve with home-made *rémoulade* sauce.

2 lb (1 kg) tail piece salmon, skinned and filleted
2 tablespoons fresh chopped chives
Few sprigs fresh sorrel or parsley or dill, chopped
Juice 1 small lemon
2 × 12 oz (375 g) packs frozen puff pastry,
* thawed*
2 tablespoons semolina
1 egg, beaten
Salt and ground black pepper

SAUCE
2 egg yolks
¼ pint (150 ml) extra virgin olive oil
¼ pint (150 ml) sunflower oil
2 tablespoons white wine vinegar
1 teaspoon Dijon mustard
2 tablespoons capers, chopped
1 tablespoon gherkins, chopped

Courgette and tomato shredded salad, with salmon Nelson, and rare lamb salad with hazelnut dressing

Season the salmon fillets and flavour with the herbs and lemon juice. Lay them on top of each other.

Roll out one pastry piece to a shape about 1½″ (4 cm) larger all round than the fish. Prick it well and place on a baking sheet. Bake at 400°F (200°C, gas mark 6) for 15 minutes until golden brown. If it has risen, then press down. Sprinkle over the semolina, and brush the edges with beaten egg. Lay the fish on top. Roll out the remaining pastry so that it is large enough to overlap completely. Fit over the top and press well to seal. Trim the edges and crimp.

Re-roll any trimmings and cut out long thin strips if you want to decorate the pie. Brush all over with more egg, then make a lattice pattern on top with the strips. Press firmly onto the pastry top and glaze again. Return to the oven and bake for 15 minutes then reduce the heat to 350°F (180°C, gas mark 4) for a further 40 minutes, checking to see the pastry doesn't burn.

Cool, then loosen the base with a thin palette knife and transfer the pie onto a thin board.

Make the sauce as you would a mayonnaise, in a food processor or by hand, beating the oil gradually into the seasoned egg yolks. When thick and creamy add the remaining ingredients. Slice pie thinly, and hand sauce separately.

Serves 6–8.   RD

157

Courgette and fresh tomato soup, and potted trout

COURGETTE AND FRESH TOMATO SOUP

This soup tastes equally good hot or cold so it can be adapted right at the last minute to our unpredictable climate.

>*1 lb (500 g) courgettes, chopped*
>*1 onion, chopped*
>*1 oz (25 g) butter*
>*2 tablespoons olive oil*
>*1 lb (500 g) tomatoes, peeled and chopped*
>*1½ pints (900 ml) light stock*
>*½ pint (300 ml) dry white wine or cider*
>*5 large leaves fresh basil, chopped*
>*1 orange, grated rind and juice*

Sweat the courgettes and onion in the butter and oil for about 10 minutes in a large covered saucepan.

Add the rest of the ingredients, bring to the boil, then simmer for 20 minutes.

Blend until smooth and serve hot from a Thermos or cold. Garnish with some thin slices of tomato and fresh sprigs of basil.

Serves 6.   RD

POTTED TROUT

Very quickly made and ideal for your guests to nibble while you unpack the rest of the hamper.

>*8 oz (250 g) filleted smoked trout, skinned*
>*2 oz (50 g) curd or cream cheese, softened, or*
>   *2 fl oz (65 ml) cream*
>*2 oz (50 g) butter, softened*
>*1 tablespoon fresh chopped chives or spring*
>   *onions*
>*¼ teaspoon ground ginger*
>*Ground black pepper*
>*Cayenne and chopped parsley, to garnish*

Mash the trout with a fork then blend with the cheese or cream, butter, chives or onions, ginger and pepper. Do not put through a blender. The mixture should have some texture.

Spoon into small ramekins, garnish and cover with cling film until required. Serve with bread sticks, or brioche rolls.

Serves 3–4.   RD

PARSNIP AND APRICOT SOUP

An adaptable first course, which can be served hot or cold. The combination of root vegetables, root ginger and the fruity sharpness of apricots is particularly pleasing.

>*1 small onion, chopped*
>*1" (2.5 cm) cube fresh root ginger, peeled and*
>   *grated*
>*2 tablespoons sunflower oil*
>*12 oz (375 g) parsnips, peeled and diced*

12 oz (375 g) carrots, peeled and diced
3 pints (1½ litres) light stock
4 oz (125 g) dried apricots, chopped
Salt and ground black pepper
Small tub fromage frais, if serving hot
½ pint (300 ml) buttermilk, if serving chilled
Some chopped chives or flaked almonds, to serve
(optional)

Gently fry the onion and ginger with the oil in a large saucepan for 5 minutes. Add the parsnips and carrots, stir, cover and sweat on a low heat for 10 minutes. Add the stock, apricots and seasoning. Bring to the boil, then cover and simmer for 30 minutes until softened. Blend in a liquidizer or food processor until smooth.

If serving hot, add swirls of fromage frais; to serve cold, chill then mix in the buttermilk. Check the seasoning if served chilled as it may need more. Garnish with chives or almonds if liked.

Serves 4–6. RD

Parsnip and apricot soup

CURRIED APPLE SOUP

Here's an unusual soup that is an excellent way of using cooking apples.

It takes minutes to prepare and can be served hot or, if you have time, chilled, when it is equally good, if not better.

2 lb (1 kg) cooking apples
1 medium onion
½ oz (15 g) butter
1 level tablespoon mild curry powder
1¾ pints (1 litre) chicken stock
Bay leaf
1 level tablespoon sugar
Seasoning
½ small carton single cream

Peel, quarter, core and slice the apples. Slice the onion and sauté it in the butter in a saucepan for about 5 minutes, then stir in the curry powder and cook for a further minute or two. Add the apples, bay leaf and stock, and bring to the boil. Season, lower the heat and simmer, covered, for 10 minutes until the apples are really soft.

Remove the bay leaf and liquidize the soup. Taste it and add the sugar (it should need very little) and a little more curry powder if you like – remember that this takes about 10 minutes to develop its full flavour, so don't go overboard! Adjust the seasoning, stir in the cream and either heat through and serve with Melba toast, or chill well.

Serves 6. AW

RIFREDDO SUSANNA

Layers of veal, mortadella and prosciutto baked with beaten egg and Parmesan, to form a succulent terrine-like loaf, which is perfect for picnics or cold buffets.

1 lb 2 oz (550 g) thin slices of veal
5 oz (150 g) thinly sliced mortadella
5 oz (150 g) thinly sliced prosciutto
4 oz (125 g) grated Parmesan
4 eggs

Sausage in brioche, and rolls of brioche dough

Beat eggs with a fork and add the Parmesan.

Butter a deep cake tin or something similar in shape, and put in first a layer of mortadella, then a slice of veal dipped in beaten egg, then a slice of prosciutto. Continue this procedure until all of the ingredients are used up. Dot the top with butter and cover the dish with foil. Cook in a bain-marie in the oven for 2 hours, at 350°F (180°C, gas mark 4). When it is cooked, tip the terrine out of the tin and weigh it down while it cools.

Serve cold, thinly sliced, preferably the day after it is made. (This dish does not require salt, as the ingredients are quite salty.)

Serves 6. PF

PICNIC BRIOCHE

Instead of bread or rolls, why not make a fuss of picnic guests with home-made brioches. The use of easy-blend sachets of yeast (not to be confused with the dried granular type) takes much of the guess-work out of yeast cookery.

The baby brioches below are delicious hol-lowed out and filled with cold salmon or chicken mixed with a good home-made mayonnaise.

2 oz (50 g) butter
9 oz (275 g) strong plain flour
¼ teaspoon salt

1 sachet easy blend yeast
2 eggs
3 tablespoons warm milk
Extra beaten egg, to glaze

Rub the butter into the flour and salt until it resembles fine breadcrumbs. Stir in the yeast. (Note – easy-blend types of yeast must not be mixed with liquid first.)

Beat the eggs and milk and then mix into the flour and knead until smooth. Cover with lightly greased cling film and leave in a warm place until doubled in size. In summer this shouldn't take more than about an hour.

Knock back the dough, divide into six pieces and knead lightly. Tear off about a quarter of each piece and shape both into round balls.

Drop the larger of each ball into six well-greased 4″ (10 cm) brioche tins, press a slight hollow on the top, glaze with some beaten egg and top with the smaller balls. If you haven't any brioche tins, then divide the dough into eight and use deep patty tins.

Glaze the tops well, cover with greased cling film and leave to rise again to about double the size. Bake at 425°F (220°C, gas mark 7) for about 15 minutes until golden brown. Turn out and cool.

To serve – use like rolls or remove the tops, hollow out and fill with creamy fish or meat salad.

Makes 6.   RD

SAUSAGE IN BRIOCHE DOUGH

Use the same brioche dough recipe as above.

Mix some chopped fresh sage, parsley and marjoram into one pound of best quality sausage meat. Then roll to a neat shape about 8″ (20 cm) long. Roast on a greased baking tray at 350°F (180°C, gas mark 4) for about 40 minutes. Cool and roll in flour to cover the surface.

Make up the brioche dough to the first proving. Knock back and roll out on a lightly-floured board to a rectangle large enough to wrap up the whole sausage.

Enclose the sausage completely in the dough, sealing with beaten egg. Glaze well, cover with greased cling film and leave to prove until doubled in size.

Bake at 425°F (220°C, gas mark 7) for about 20 to 25 minutes until golden brown. Cool on a wire tray, slice when quite cold.

Serves 4–6.

NOTE: like all home-made yeast dishes, brioches are best eaten fresh but can be made about 24 hours in advance. If you want to freeze them, do so as soon as they have cooled.   RD

A TERRINE OF PIGEON AND PORK

This is a rather neat little meat roll which is easy to carve. The quails' eggs are optional.

12 oz (375 g) smoked streaky bacon, derinded
4 wood pigeon breasts, skinned and diced
1 lb (500g) lean pork, diced
1 onion, chopped
1 clove garlic, crushed
1 tablespoon oil
3 tablespoons fresh chopped parsley
1 teaspoon dried thyme or 2 sprigs fresh, chopped
3 tablespoons dry sherry
8 quails' eggs, hard-boiled and peeled (optional)
Salt and ground black pepper

Chop about a quarter of the bacon and lay the rest out in overlapping slices on a large sheet of lightly oiled foil on a flat baking sheet. Mix chopped bacon with the meats, onion, garlic, oil, herbs, sherry and seasoning. Arrange mixture down the middle of the bacon slices in a thick line. If using quails' eggs, press these into the mixture, also in a line.

Draw the bacon slices up over the meat enclosing it in a roll, and then overwrap firmly but not too tightly in the foil. Bake at 350°F (180°C, gas mark 4) for about 1½ hours. Cool, pour away any fat, then chill without unwrapping. Unwrap when quite cold and firm. Serve cut in fairly thick slices.

Serves 6–8.   RD

161

American picnic cake

Beat the oil, eggs, rind and orange juice together, then beat into the flour and sugar, mixing well. Stir in the carrots, walnuts and raisins, spoon into a greased and lined 2-lb (1 kg) loaf tin. Bake at 325°F (170°C, gas mark 3) for 1 to 1¼ hours. Cool in the tin upside down, then demould and split in half.

For the icing, simply cream everything together. Sandwich the two cake halves together and swirl the rest on top. Decorate with some broken walnuts and thin strips of fresh orange rind.   RD

VINEGAR CAKE WITH SOFT FRUITS

In this old-fashioned fruitcake, the wine derivative *vin aigre* is used, in combination with bicarbonate of soda, as the principal leavening agent (acid + alkali = carbon dioxide bubbles), reinforced by the belt-and-braces measure of a little baking powder. Be reassured – the cake does not taste vinegary.

Serve this with fresh raspberries and blueberries, sprinkled with demerara sugar and anointed at the last minute with a few drops of raspberry vinegar.

> Butter for cake tin
> 14 oz (400 g) plain flour
> ½ teaspoon baking powder
> 6 oz (175 g) cold, unsalted butter
> 6 oz (175 g) soft, light brown sugar
> 5 oz (150 g) dried currants
> 4 oz (125 g) raisins
> 1 beaten egg
> 4 fl oz (125 ml) milk, plus more for the end of
>   the process
> Scant 3 tablespoons white wine vinegar
> 1 teaspoon bicarbonate of soda
> Fresh blueberries and raspberries
> Petit Suisse cheese
> Demerara sugar
> Raspberry vinegar

AMERICAN PICNIC CAKE

An excellent cut-and-come-again cake with a delicious creamy icing.

> 8 oz (250 g) self-raising flour
> 1 teaspoon baking powder
> Pinch of salt
> ½ teaspoon cinnamon
> 4 oz (125 g) dark soft brown sugar
> 2 fl oz (65 ml) sunflower oil
> 2 eggs
> Rind and juice of 1 orange
> 6 oz (175 g) carrot, grated
> 4 oz (125 g) walnuts, chopped
> 3 oz (75 g) raisins
>
> ICING
> 2 oz (50 g) unsalted butter, softened
> 4 oz (125 g) cream or curd cheese, softened
> 4 oz (125 g) icing sugar, sifted
> ½ teaspoon vanilla essence

Sift the flour, baking powder, salt and cinnamon into a large bowl. Add the sugar.

Butter the base and side of an 8½″ (21 cm) circular cake tin with a 3″ (7.5 cm) side.

Sift flour and baking powder into a large bowl, dice butter and rub this in to the dry ingredients; stir in sugar, dried fruits and beaten egg.

Pour all but a few tablespoons of the milk into the jug and mix in the vinegar. Heat remaining milk slightly and dissolve in this the bicarbonate of soda. Add milk and soda to milk and vinegar; the blend will froth wildly and should be quickly poured over the bowl's contents and rapidly incorporated. Add further milk, if necessary, in order to bring the batter to a dropping consistency, and spoon all into the buttered tin. Smooth the mixture and make a slight dip in the centre, where the cake will otherwise rise too high.

Bake cake at 375°F (190°C, gas mark 5) for 30 minutes; lower the heat to 350°F (180°C, gas mark 4) for 45 minutes more, then to 325°F (170°C, gas mark 3) for 30–40 minutes further, until a skewer inserted in the centre emerges clean and hot.

Cool cake completely, remove from tin, and serve cut into thin slices, with the fresh fruits and some mashed Petits Suisses strewn with demerara sugar and a little raspberry vinegar.

Makes one 8½″ (21 cm) circular cake which keeps well.   AWS

Fruit tartlets with lemon cream

FRUIT TARTLETS WITH LEMON CREAM

It seems pointless to take elaborate puddings to a picnic. The journey itself would necessitate a somewhat solid and indestructible texture. Small wonder that fresh fruits and a pot of cream are normally popular. So, on a similar theme, serve a pile of light crisp tartlets flavoured with orange flower water, a bowl of prepared fruits and some tangy lemon curd cream for guests to put together on site.

PASTRY
4 oz (125 g) plain flour
2 oz (50 g) cornflour
2 tablespoons icing sugar
5 oz (150 g) unsalted butter, softened
2 egg yolks
1 tablespoon orange flower water or 1 teaspoon vanilla essence

TOPPING
5 oz (150 g) soured cream or curd cheese, softened
3 tablespoons lemon curd, preferably home-made
1 lb (500 g) fresh berry fruits – e.g. strawberries, raspberries, pitted cherries
4 oz (125 g) seedless white grapes

Sift the flours and icing sugar together, then rub in the butter until it resembles fine breadcrumbs. Beat the yolks and flower water together then mix with the flour to a firm but fairly soft dough. Knead lightly then cover and chill for half an hour.

Roll out on a lightly floured board to a thickness of a 10p piece and cut out about 24 × 2½″ (7.5 cm) rounds, re-rolling as necessary. Prick the bases and fit into shallow bun tins. Bake at 375°F (190°C, gas mark 5) for 10–12 minutes until pale golden and crisp. Cool on a wire rack, then pack into a rigid air-tight container.

Meanwhile, beat the cream (or cheese for a firmer texture) with the lemon curd, and spoon into a bowl. Chill and cover. Prepare the fruits.

To serve, let your guests spoon lemon cream into the base of each tartlet and top with fruits.
Makes 24.   RD

THE GRAND FINALE

Colourful fruit salads, compotes and sorbets provide a natural and fresh-tasting conclusion to a meal, while chocolate puddings, ice-cream, cakes and pastries strike a more indulgent note

CASTAGNACCIO

The Ristorante la Mora is a halt at Ponte a Moriano, on the road from Lucca to the Garfagnana mountains in Tuscany. Sauro Brunicardi and his family are expert restaurateurs, known for the warmth of their reception and their deft cooking of local dishes threatened with eclipse as the region – traditionally a poor one, save for the city of Lucca – grows in affluence.

Castagnaccio, a cake of chestnut flour seasoned with raisins and nuts, is a very old recipe, typically 'lucchese', though also made in other parts of Tuscany; the Ristorante la Mora incorporates walnuts and zest of orange, no sugar – chestnut flour is heavy and sweet – and the hot scent of rosemary. Its dense smokiness is not to everyone's taste, but those who like it tend to be strongly partisan.

The chestnut flour should be found, in London, from the end of October at either of the two Fratelli Camisa shops in Berwick Street and Charlotte Street, W1.

> *Olive oil*
> *14 oz (400 g) chestnut flour*
> *About 18 fl oz (500 ml) water*
> *Pinch salt*
> *1½ oz (40 g) walnuts, coarsely chopped*
> *Handful of raisins*
> *Some freshly-grated zest of orange*
> *1 oz (25 g) pine nuts*
> *Leaves stripped from 2–3 branches of fresh
>   rosemary*

Generously oil the sides and base of a 10″ × 1″ (25 × 2.5 cm) circular cake tin or fireproof dish.

Slowly stir water into chestnut flour, working it constantly with a wooden spoon, until the mixture is smooth and liquid enough to pour easily (you may not need all the water). Beat in 3 tablespoons of olive oil, the salt, walnuts, raisins and zest of orange; pour batter into the dish, spread it evenly, strew with pine nuts and rosemary, dribble with oil.

Bake the *castagnaccio* at 440°F (200°C, gas mark 6) for 40 minutes, until the surface has cracked and turned a deep, rich brown. Eat the cake about 15 minutes after removal from the oven.

Serves 6, generously.   AWS

APPLE CAKE MARYROSE

An English recipe from Maryrose Crossman of Somerset, whose summer pudding is admirable and whose apple cake, made in part with wholemeal flour, is unusual, palatable and as rapidly consumed as produced. For apples, you can substitute fresh raspberries in season, or chopped dried apricots (previously rehydrated by soaking and brief simmering in water).

Right *Castagnaccio (in foreground) and apple cake Maryrose*

1 × 14 oz (400 g) Bramley apple
5 oz (150 g) unsalted butter, plus butter for the
*   tin*
2 large eggs
8 oz (250 g) caster sugar
A few drops almond essence
4 oz (125 g) self-raising flour
Pinch salt
4 oz (125 g) wholemeal flour
Icing sugar

Peel, core, and thinly slice the apple; melt and partly cool the 5 oz (150 g) butter. Butter an 8 × 2½" (20 × 6 cm) circular springform cake tin. Beat the eggs and sugar until thick and well-aerated, whisk in melted butter and almond essence. Sift together self-raising flour and salt, stir in wholemeal flour; beat these well into egg and butter base.

Spread half the mixture over the tin, cover with apples, followed by the remaining batter. Bake the cake at 350°F (180°C, gas mark 4) for something between 1 and 1½ hours; timing varies, but the top should brown to a thick, crisp crust.

Cool cake completely and dust with icing sugar. Slice and serve for tea, or after dinner with chilled sweet muscat wine.

Serves 6.   AWS

LAVENDER AND HONEY ICE-CREAM

Once people have overcome the hesitation of tasting such a fragrant food, lavender ice-cream wins many converts. It is particularly good with fresh strawberries.

1 pint (600 ml) milk
½ pint (300 ml) double cream
8 tablespoons clear honey
2–3 tablespoons caster sugar (optional)
3–4 tablespoons dried lavender flowers
6 egg yolks
2 egg whites
Few drops violet food colouring (optional)

Scald the milk, cream, honey, sugar (if using) and lavender until on the point of boiling. Allow to stand for 30 minutes, then strain and reheat to boiling. Meanwhile, beat the egg yolks in a bowl and slowly pour on the scalded milk, whisking continuously. Pour back into the saucepan and, on the lowest heat possible, stir the custard until it is the consistency of single cream and will coat the back of the spoon. Strain and allow to cool completely. Add a few drops of food colouring if liked, stir well and freeze until nearly firm.

Remove, and beat well until slushy (this can be done in a food processor). Whisk the egg whites and carefully fold into the beaten mixture. Return to the freezer until firm. Allow to thaw for a few minutes before scooping out.

This is nice served in honey snap cups.

Serves 6–8.   RD

HONEY SNAP CUPS

It's not so much the technique that makes these tricky – more the timing. For this reason, it is better to bake them singly.

2 oz (50 g) butter
2 tablespoons clear honey
2 oz (50 g) soft brown sugar
1½ oz (40 g) plain flour
Pinch each ground ginger and salt
Squeeze fresh lemon juice

Melt the butter with the honey, and sugar. Beat in the flour, ginger, salt and lemon juice. Set aside.

Lightly grease a baking sheet, then drop dessertspoons of the mixture, singly, onto the sheet. Bake at 325°F (170°C, gas mark 3) for about 10–12 minutes until golden brown and lacy around the edges. Remove from the oven, allow to cool for a minute, until firm around the edges, then slip off the baking sheet with a palette knife and immediately press over an orange.

When firm, remove and cool completely on a wire tray. Store in an airtight tin until required. Will keep for about 24 hours like this.

Makes about 8.   RD

Pecan and maple pie

PECAN AND MAPLE PIE

A favourite party pie, this is instantly recognizable, popular and lives up to its delicious gooey promise. This version isn't crammed with nuts as some recipes direct because it detracts from the filling and can make the pie rather dry.

PASTRY
3 oz (75 g) butter or sunflower margarine
6 oz (175 g) plain flour
1 teaspoon cinnamon

FILLING
3 eggs, beaten
4 oz (125 g) dark soft brown sugar
¼ pint (150 ml) golden syrup
3 fl oz (1 ml) maple syrup
½ teaspoon vanilla essence
Pinch of salt
4 oz (125 g) shelled pecan nuts

Rub the fat into the flour and cinnamon then mix to a firm dough with a little cold water. Roll out and line into a 9″ (23 cm) flan dish, making sure the sides are quite high so they don't shrink back. Chill for about 30 minutes.

Bake blind at 400°F (200°C, gas mark 6) for 20 minutes, removing the foil and beans for the last 5 minutes of baking.

Beat the eggs, sugar, syrups, essence and salt. Sprinkle the nuts into the pastry shell and pour over the syrup mixture, coating the nuts.

Bake at 350°F (180°C, gas mark 4) for about 40 minutes until slightly risen and firm. Cool and serve with softly whipped cream mixed with a little soured cream.

Serves 6–8.   RD

A VELVETY CURD CHEESECAKE

As smooth and rich as its name suggests, this is a traditional baked cheesecake which has generally been superseded by American desserts set with gelatine. Its success depends on a relatively short baking time which stops the cheese from curdling and the cake sinking when it cools. Serve in moderate wedges with fresh soft fruits.

SPONGE BASE
3 oz (75 g) self-raising flour
2 oz (50 g) butter or margarine, softened
2 oz (50 g) icing sugar
1 egg yolk
2 tablespoons milk

TOPPING
8 oz (250 g) medium-fat curd cheese
8 oz (250 g) quark
1 teaspoon vanilla essence
1 small lemon, grated rind and juice
2 oz (50 g) butter, melted
2 oz (50 g) caster sugar
2 tablespoons cornflour
5 fl oz (150 ml) soured cream
2 eggs, separated

First make the base. Line the base and sides of an 8″ (20 cm) loose-bottomed tin with greased foil or greaseproof paper. In doing this, make sure the edge of the paper overlaps the base so the mixture doesn't leak out on cooking.

Mix all the sponge ingredients together in a blender or processor until smooth, then spoon mixture into the prepared tin. Bake at 375°F (190°C, gas mark 5) for about 25 minutes, until the sponge is firm.

Meanwhile, put all the topping ingredients except the egg whites into a bowl and beat until smooth and well blended.

Whisk the egg whites until forming soft peaks and fold into the cheesecake mixture. Spoon on top of the sponge.

Return to the oven at 350°F (180°C, gas mark 4) for 30 minutes until the cake edge feels firm. Turn off the oven without removing the tin and leave the cake to cool overnight – it continues to cook slowly as it cools. Chill before demoulding and serving dusted lightly with icing sugar.

Serves 8–10.   RD

HONEY AND CINNAMON CREAM

A simple dessert which can be used with any fruit in season – strawberries, soft red berries, cherries, lightly stewed apples and pears or grapes. Without fruit, the mixture makes a delicious alternative to cream for other puddings, especially tarts and pies.

>   *8 oz (250 g) fromage frais, low-fat or fat-free*
>   *2 tablespoons clear honey*
>   *½ teaspoon ground cinnamon*
>   *8 oz (250 g) grapes, halved and pitted*
>   *A little extra honey and cinnamon*

Mix together the fromage frais, honey and cinnamon until smooth, then stir in the grapes.

Spoon mixture into four dishes and trickle over a little extra honey. Sprinkle with cinnamon, and serve the creams chilled.

Serves 4.   RD

HONEYED PEAR AND ALMOND PIE

This is a particularly nice tart for a Sunday lunch or afternoon tea. Serve slightly warm with lightly whipped cream.

>   *12 oz (350 g) shortcrust pastry, bought or home-made*
>   *3 large dessert pears, not too ripe*
>   *½ pint (300 ml) water*
>   *4 tablespoons clear or set honey*
>   *2 strips lemon peel*
>
>   FILLING
>   *2 oz (50 g) soft margarine*
>   *2 oz (50 g) caster sugar*
>   *2 eggs, separated*
>   *4 oz (125 g) ground almonds*
>   *4 oz (125 g) stale cake crumbs (e.g. Madeira or ginger cake)*
>   *1 teaspoon grated lemon peel*
>   *Pinch ground cinnamon*
>   *Icing sugar, to dust*

Roll out the pastry into a 9″ (23 cm) flan tin with a loose base. Trim, and allow to rest while you make the filling. Core the pears and peel thinly. Cut in half then poach in the water with 2 tablespoons of honey and the lemon peel strips for about 15 minutes until just tender. Allow to cool in the syrup if you have the time. Drain, and discard the pear syrup (this can be used up elsewhere as a drink or in a fruit jelly).

Cream the margarine, sugar and remaining 2 tablespoons of honey. Beat in the egg yolks then stir in the ground almonds, cake crumbs, lemon peel and cinnamon.

Whisk the egg whites until stiff, then carefully fold into the cake mixture. Spread this over the base of the flan cases and press down the six pear halves on top.

Bake at 375°F (190°C, gas mark 5) for about 30 to 35 minutes until risen, firm and light brown. Cool until lukewarm and serve dusted with a little icing sugar.

Serves 6–8.   RD

Honeyed pear and almond pie (left) and summer red fruits compôte, decorated with borage flowers

SUMMER RED FRUITS COMPOTE

Raspberries, redcurrants and figs are all fruits that have an affinity with honey. Here they are steeped for several hours in a warm honey syrup, before being chilled and served decorated with the pretty blue flowers of the bee plant – borage. Accompany with thick Greek yoghurt and shortbread, home-made if possible.

1 lb (500 g) redcurrants, de-stalked
3 tablespoons clear or set honey
3 tablespoons water
1 lb (500 g) fresh raspberries, hulled
3 ripe figs, quartered or sliced
Grated rind 1 orange, optional
Borage flowers, to serve

Poach the redcurrants with the honey and water over a gentle heat for about 5 minutes until just cooked and the juice is starting to run.

Place the raspberries and figs in a large bowl and sprinkle with the orange rind. Pour over the redcurrants and juice and leave to steep for 2–3 hours. Chill before serving decorated with the borage flowers.

Serves 4–6.   RD

Gascony apple and Armagnac tart

GASCONY APPLE AND ARMAGNAC TART

Made with filo pastry, this is easier to make than Normandy apple flan and just as much of a treat to the eyes.

> *6 sheets filo pastry*
> *3 oz (75 g) butter, melted*
> *2 Bramley or 3 Granny Smith apples, peeled and thinly sliced*
> *Icing sugar, to taste*
> *Ground cinnamon or freshly grated nutmeg (optional)*
> *Armagnac (or Cognac), to sprinkle*

Brush the base of a 10″ (25 cm) flan tin liberally with butter. Lay and press in three sheets of filo, brushing well in between with butter.

Trim the edges with kitchen scissors, leaving them slightly ragged. Save the scraps of filo and allow to dry slightly so that they curl a bit.

Scatter half the apple slices on top, brushing with more butter and sprinkling with icing sugar

and spices, if using. The amount of sugar you use depends on the tartness of the apples.

Top with the remaining filo sheets, brushing with butter and trimming as before. Scatter the remaining apple on top, sweetening to taste. Casually arrange the pastry scraps on top to cover, and brush or trickle over the last of the butter.

Stand the flan dish on a flat baking sheet and bake at 375°F (190°C, gas mark 5) for about 25 minutes until the pastry is crisp. Check occasionally to see that it doesn't burn. Cool the flan and remove to a serving plate. Dust with a little more icing sugar and, just before serving, sprinkle with plenty of Armagnac.

Serves 4–6. RD

CASSATA SICILIANA

A sumptuous Italian chilled dessert which is best prepared the day before serving. Easy to assemble, it takes advantage of the Italian cakes often seen hanging from the ceiling, in decorative boxes, of delicatessens.

> *1 × 250 g panettone (Italian cake, available from Italian delicatessens)*
> *12 oz (350 g) ricotta*
> *2 oz (150 g) bitter chocolate, cut in small pieces*
> *3 oz (75 g) candied peel*
> *4 oz (125 g) caster sugar*
> *5 tablespoons maraschino*

Slice the top off the panettone in one neat piece, and hollow out the cake as much as possible without piercing the sides.

Put ricotta in a basin and whisk it with sugar until smooth. Add chocolate, candied peel and 1 tablespoon of maraschino, and mix well.

Soak the cake crust with the remaining maraschino, and fill with the ricotta mixture. Replace the top of the cake, wrap in tin foil and refrigerate until ready to serve.

Remove foil and add more maraschino if you like. Sprinkle with icing sugar, and serve in slices. (This dish is best made the day before use.)

Serves 6. PF

FIG AND PLUM ICE-CREAM

For figs and plums at their late summer peak.

> 13 oz (375 g) very ripe figs
> 6 oz (175 g) very ripe yellow plums
> 3 tablespoons white wine
> ½ pint (300 ml) milk
> 4 small egg yolks
> 3 oz (75 g) soft light brown sugar
> 6 fl oz (175 ml) double cream
> Cognac or Armagnac

Stem and quarter the figs, quarter the plums and discard the stones. Put fruits with the wine into a heavy saucepan and barely simmer, covered and stirring often, for 10–15 minutes until the fruits are tender. Purée in a food processor, taking care to leave some texture.

Scald the milk, beat yolks and sugar until very thick, whisk in milk and pour the mixture back into the milk pan. Whisk over a medium heat until the custard *just* boils. Immediately sieve into a bowl, and stir in the fruit purée. Cool and chill.

When the mixture is cold, beat in chilled cream, Cognac or Armagnac as a slight accent, and freeze in your ice-cream maker. Quantities given make 1½ pints (900 ml).

Let the ice-cream soften in the refrigerator for 30 minutes before scooping to serve accompanied by brandy snaps.

Serves 4–6.   AWS

Fig and plum ice-cream

PLUMS AND PEACHES IN SLOE GIN SYRUP

Stewed fruits have never held a great attraction for many of us, but fruits macerated in a hot syrup retain texture and absorb delicious flavours.

November is the month to start assembling the ingredients for this summertime dessert. Found growing in hedgerows on chalky uplands, sloes are best gathered after the first frosts have hit them. The fruit should be pricked all over with a needle, and left immersed in gin, sweetened with a little sugar, for at least 6 weeks. Strain the gin, which by now will be a lovely burgundy colour, and discard the spent sloes.

> 1½ lb (750 g) ripe plums
> 2 large peaches
>
> SYRUP
> 6 oz (175 g) sugar
> ¾ pint (450 ml) water
> 2 strips orange peel
> 1 cinnamon stick
> 6 tablespoons sloe gin

Halve the plums and peaches and stone. Slice the peaches then put both fruits into a heatproof bowl.

Dissolve the sugar in the water over a gentle heat, stirring occasionally, then add the other syrup ingredients, except for the sloe gin. Bring to the boil, then simmer for about 5 minutes and stir in the gin. Pour the syrup over the fruit, cover and leave until cold. Chill before serving with light, crisp biscuits and lightly whipped cream mixed with natural yoghurt.

Serves 4.   RD

BALTIC FLAT-BREAD TARTS

Flat-bread based fruit tarts are particularly well-suited to a buffet table, as they can be cut and served in bite-sized pieces with none of the worries presented by crumbling pastry or oozing filling.

Yeast and cardamom aromas are a *sine qua non* of festive Baltic baking, and the wide variety of possible toppings allows a colourful display of all that is seasonal, or skilfully preserved for such an occasion.

SWEET YEAST DOUGH
1 lb (500 g) strong, plain unbleached flour
1 teaspoon salt
6–8 pods cardamom, husks removed and seeds ground
1 oz (25 g) fresh yeast
2 tablespoons warm water
1 teaspoon malt syrup
7 fl oz (200 ml) milk
3½ oz (100 g) unsalted butter
2 eggs, beaten, plus 2 yolks (these are optional, but will give a more golden dough)
3½ oz (100 g) caster sugar (preferably light, unrefined)

Sift flour, salt and cardamom into a warmed mixing bowl, and form a well in the centre. Crumble the yeast and blend with the water and malt. Set aside for 10 minutes in a warm place to activate the yeast. Scald the milk with the butter, then cool to room temperature. Beat the eggs with the sugar to partially dissolve the latter, then pour all liquids, including activated yeast, into the well in the flour. Gradually incorporate the liquid into the flour using a wooden spoon, then beat vigorously for 2 to 3 minutes until the dough is smooth and slightly elastic (it will remain slack and 'sticky'). Scrape down the sides, but leave the dough in the mixing bowl. Grease the surface of the dough lightly with unsalted butter or safflower oil. Cover and leave to prove for an hour until almost triple in bulk. Alternatively, the dough may be left to prove slowly in the refrigerator for 4 hours, then a further 4 hours at room temperature.

Fillings, as suggested in the recipes below, may be prepared while the dough is proving.

Knock back the risen dough, which will be too slack to knead on a board; knead it briefly in the mixing bowl, with one hand. Flour a pastry board generously, and tip half the dough out onto the board. With floured hands, flatten the dough a little, dredge more flour onto the surface and roll out to form two rectangles 12″ × 8″ (30 × 20 cm). Alternatively – and this makes for a softer pastry – press the dough without rolling into lightly-greased swiss-roll tins of the above dimensions, using floured knuckles.

Arrange topping over the dough and leave to prove a little more while heating the oven. Transfer the tarts to lightly-greased baking sheets (unless using swiss-roll tins) and bake in a pre-heated, moderate oven (350°F, 180°C, gas mark 4) for 30 to 40 minutes.

Cool the tarts in the tins; if not eating immediately, enclose in plastic wrap as soon as they have reached room temperature. Slice into squares shortly before serving.

Makes 36–48 pieces.

TOPPINGS
Amounts are for each trayful, i.e., half of given quantity of dough.

Wash 14 oz (400 g) young rhubarb, and cut the stems into tiny batons. Pour in a single, but generous, layer over dough. Strew with sugar and cinnamon to taste.

Wash and dry 14 oz (400 g) blueberries, lingonberries or cranberries. Arrange on dough and sprinkle with sugar as before – cranberries will need rather more sugar than blueberries. A traditional treatment of cranberries is to cook until skins are soft with apples reduced to a purée. Sweeten to taste.

Take 14 oz (400 g) flavourful eating apples or firm pears, peeled, cored and thinly sliced into crescent shapes. Arrange in 3 overlapping rows, on the rolled-out dough, and sprinkle with lemon juice, caster sugar and cinnamon to taste. Sprinkle cinnamon crumble topping between rows of apple.

Baltic flat-bread tarts: left, blueberry and cranberry; right, rhubarb, and apple with cinnamon crumble

CINNAMON CRUMBLE

4 oz (125 g) plain flour
2 teaspoons ground cinnamon
2½ oz (65 g) unsalted butter, softened
2 oz (50 g) unrefined, light sugar

Blend all ingredients with fingers until rough crumbs are formed. Use a pressing, rolling action to compact and round the crumbs slightly (unlike the light touch employed when making shortcrust pastry). Either sprinkle over the dough or coat the fruits individually, reducing the quantity of sugar according to taste.   SD

POIRE PARFAIT WITH RASPBERRY SAUCE

A frozen, creamy concoction perfumed with eau-de-vie de poire, and served with contrasting fresh raspberry sauce.

Prepare the parfait the day before, and make the raspberry sauce in advance too, if you like.

FOR THE PARFAIT
2 eggs, separated
3 tablespoons Poire liqueur
1 oz (25 g) sifted icing sugar
¼ pint (150 ml) double cream, lightly whipped

173

Left to right: Poire parfait with raspberry sauce; yoghurt with apple and raisins; tropical fruit salad

FOR THE SAUCE
8 oz (250 g) raspberries
1 tablespoon sifted icing sugar

TO GARNISH
1 ripe pear
1 tablespoon lemon juice

Whisk the egg yolks with the liqueur until the mixture is pale. Stiffly whisk the egg whites, then whisk in the sugar a teaspoon at a time. Continue whisking, and slowly pour in the egg yolk mixture. Fold in the cream, then turn into a container and freeze for 4 hours or until firm.

There is no need to remove the parfait and beat it further during the freezing process, as the addition of beaten eggs gives a mousse-like consistency. It is, however, advisable to take the parfait out of the freezer 30 minutes before serving, and to leave it in the refrigerator to soften.

Purée the raspberries with the sugar, then sieve to remove all the pips. Peel the pear, core and cut into cubes. Place on a plate, squeeze over the lemon juice and put on one side until required.

Divide the sauce between 4 small plates, then arrange scoopfuls of the ice-cream on top. Decorate each one with a few cubes of fresh pear.

Serves 4.   JR

YOGHURT WITH APPLES AND RAISINS

A simple variation of fruit yoghurt, but one that will prove to be very popular among the large number of Greek yoghurt devotees. Which yoghurt you choose, i.e. cows', goats' or sheep's is a matter of personal choice, although the sheep's yoghurt does tend to be slightly sharper, so is generally better for savoury recipes.

2 oz (50 g) seedless raisins
¼ pint (150 ml) medium-sweet cider
2 dessert apples
2 × 8½ oz (260 g) cartons Greek yoghurt

Put the raisins in a small basin, pour over the cider and leave to macerate overnight. Core the apples and cut into ¼" (5 mm) pieces. Add to the raisins and mix well.

Divide half the yoghurt between 4 glasses, then spoon a quarter of the raisins and apple mixture into each. Cover with the remaining yoghurt and chill for at least 2 hours before serving.

Serves 4.   JR

TROPICAL FRUIT SALAD

A good tropical fruit salad has a unique scent and taste, but the secret of it is to ensure that all the fruit you use is really ripe. The recipe below is a basic one which you can vary in all sorts of ways, by adding other fruit, such as star fruit, mangosteens and rambutans, or by replacing the lychees and paw paw with some of these fruits.

These fruit salads are best served lightly chilled and look most attractive served in a home-made ice bowl, which is very simple to make. Half-fill a mixing bowl with water and place on a flat surface in your freezer. Suspend a small bowl inside and weight this down to give you the thickness of ice you require.

Leave until the water is completely frozen, then pour a little water into the inner bowl to loosen it and remove this, then pour a little water over the larger bowl and remove it as well. Replace the ice bowl in the freezer until it is required.

6 large passion fruit
1 mango
1 paw paw
6 oz (175 g) lychees

Halve the passion fruit and scoop out the pulp with a teaspoon and place in a bowl. Peel the mango, cut the flesh into as neat slices as possible and add to the passion fruit. Do the same with the paw paw, cutting the flesh into cubes and discarding the seeds. Peel the lychees, cut them in half and remove the stones. Add to the fruit salad, cover and chill until just before serving.

Place the ice bowl on a serving plate and fill with fruit salad.

Serves 4.   JR

PECHE RAFRAICHIE BOURGUIGNONNE

This fruit dessert, illustrated on page 176, is especially welcome in summer months.

1½ lb (750 g) fresh raspberries
9 fl oz (275 ml) good Beaujolais
2 tablespoons icing sugar
8 large peaches
2 oz (50 g) flaked almonds, toasted

Reserve 18 raspberries for decoration, and purée the remaining raspberries through a fine sieve to remove the seeds. Add the Beaujolais and sweeten with a little icing sugar.

Toss the peaches into boiling water for 2–3 minutes to loosen their skins. Slice the peeled peaches into the sauce and leave to chill for 3–4 hours in the refrigerator.

Serve the peaches either on dessert plates or in shallow glass dishes. Decorate with raspberries and toasted flaked almonds. The peaches will keep in the sauce for up to 2 days, improving in flavour.

Serves 6.   SW

Pêche rafraîchie bourguignonne, page 175

Line an 8″ (20 cm) springform cake tin with greaseproof paper. Crush the digestive biscuits in a plastic bag, melt the butter in a saucepan, and stir in the crumbs. Spread the crumbs on to the bottom of the tin, and press firmly with a spoon.

Peel 4 oz (125 g) of the grapes and remove the pips with a clean hair-grip. Soften the gelatine in 3 tablespoons of cold water for 2–3 minutes, then dissolve over a saucepan of hot water.

Loosely whip the cream and blend in the yoghurt. Add the wine to the dissolved gelatine, and stir in the yoghurt-cream mixture.

Whisk the egg whites with the sugar until they form soft peaks, and carefully fold into the now-setting mousse. Add the peeled grapes and pour into the prepared tin. Leave to set in the refrigerator for at least 2 hours. (At this stage it may be frozen for up to 8 weeks.)

Release from the tin and remove the paper. Cut the remaining grapes in half and arrange over the surface. To prepare the sauce, liquidize the apricots in their syrup and pass through a fine sieve.

Serves 6.   SW

WINE AND YOGHURT GRAPE TORTE

Muscat grapes are available during the month of October, so this is the time to take advantage of their delicious perfume, combined here with cream and yoghurt.

BISCUIT BASE
4 oz (125 g) digestive biscuits
2 oz (50 g) unsalted butter

MOUSSE
1 lb (500 g) muscat grapes
3 teaspoons powdered gelatine
5 fl oz (150 g) double cream
5 fl oz (150 g) natural yoghurt
3 fl oz (75 g) dry white wine
2 egg whites
2 tablespoons caster sugar

SAUCE
8 bottled apricots in their syrup

VANILLA AND ROSE CONES WITH RASPBERRY SAUCE

Liqueur de framboise is superb in this dish, but an eau de vie, crème de cassis or kirsch could be substituted, as flavouring for the raspberry sauce. The biscuit cones can be prepared ahead.

VANILLA CONES
2 eggs
3 oz caster sugar
3 tablespoons plain flour (level measuring spoon)
1 tablespoon beurre noisette
½ teaspoon natural vanilla essence

FILLING
8 fl oz (250 g) whipping cream
1–2 teaspoons caster sugar
1–2 teaspoons rosewater
Tiny rose geranium leaves (optional)

RASPBERRY SAUCE
8–10 oz (250–300 g) raspberries
2–3 tablespoons redcurrant jelly
Sugar if necessary
1–2 tablespoons liqueur de framboise or eau de
vie (optional)

VANILLA CONES

Break the eggs into a bowl, whisk in the sugar until well mixed then gradually work in the flour. Heat a little butter until it is bubbling and brown and smells nutty and pour into the mixture, leaving the sediment behind. Whisk in the vanilla essence. Place about four tablespoons of the mixture, well apart, on greased baking sheets. Spread with the back of a spoon to even 3″ (8 cm) circles and bake in a hot oven (400°F, 200°C, gas mark 6) for 6–8 minutes when the circles should be pale golden and browning round the edges. Bake any leftover mixture in the same way.

Carefully lift off the baking sheet with the aid of a palette knife and form into cones round your fingers. Stand them for a while in narrow flute glasses to keep their shape but remove and cool on a rack once they have firmed into shape (if you cool them completely standing in a glass, the steam cannot escape and they don't crisp properly). Store in an airtight tin.

FILLING

Whip the cream with light sweetening and rosewater to taste, until firm enough to pipe. Turn into a piping-bag with a large rose nozzle. Keep in fridge until ready to serve.

SAUCE

Set one raspberry aside for each cone, for decoration. Process the remainder with the redcurrant jelly, sugar if necessary and the raspberry liqueur. Sieve to remove pips.

TO ASSEMBLE

Spoon a pool of sauce onto each plate. Pipe some cream into each cone, top with a raspberry and two tiny rose geranium leaves and lay two on each plate. Serve at once.

Serves 4–6.   NC

HONEY AND RAISIN OMELETTE

Accompanied by a sweet, grapey Muscat wine, this makes an elegant and unusual dessert.

3 fresh eggs
½ eggshell of water
Lightweight olive oil
Dessertspoon very thick honey
3 oz (75 g) washed raisins, soaked overnight in
a little dark rum
A good pinch of nutmeg

Mix eggs, water and a pinch of salt in a bowl. Heat enough oil in a Japanese *tamago-yaki nabe* pan (available from The Conran Shop, Fulham Road, London SW7) to cover its base. Pour off excess oil.

Pour one third egg mixture into pan, and 'muddle' using a wooden utensil, e.g. the handle of a spoon. Do not use metal. With the aid of a plastic spatula, roll the omelette to the end of the pan which is away from you.

Rolled honey and raisin omelette

177

Pour half the remaining egg into the vacant end of the pan, and muddle it. When nearly set, gently drop the raisins, honey, and nutmeg onto the surface. Using the spatula, roll omelette back to your end. Pour rest of egg into the space, muddle, and roll whole omelette away from you. Tip onto serving dish.

Serves 2.   HDM

BOMBE NOEL

It is very useful to have a homemade iced pudding to hand over Christmas, which can be removed from the freezer and served at just a few minutes' notice when a casual gathering turns into a more formal meal. Made in a pudding mould it also becomes a good alternative to The Pudding.

6 tablespoons demerara rum
4 oz (125 g) stoneless raisins
2 oz (50 g) citron peel, chopped
1 oz (25 g) angelica, chopped
1 pint (600 ml) double cream
½ pint (300 ml) rich milk
2 vanilla pods or 1 teaspoon vanilla essence
6 egg yolks
3 eggs
8 oz (250 g) caster sugar
100 g (3½ oz) bar Menier chocolate, broken

Heat 4 tablespoons of rum and mix with the fruits and angelica. Leave to stand overnight.

Scald the cream and milk with the vanilla pods and leave to steep for half an hour. Remove the pods. (If using vanilla essence, however, steeping is not necessary.)

Whisk the yolks, eggs and sugar, and pour the milk on to the mixture, whisking hard. Return to the stove and, on the lowest heat possible, stir with a wooden spoon until slightly thickened. If the custard looks as if it is starting to curdle, pour it at once into a large cold bowl. It's best to have one at the ready. Allow the custard to cool.

Melt the chocolate in a basin over water that is barely simmering. Do not allow it to overheat or it will go lumpy. Stir until smooth then gradually mix into ¾ pint (450 ml) of custard and remaining 2 tablespoons of rum. Cool, chill and freeze separately, beating occasionally while it freezes.

Mix the rum-soaked fruits into the remaining custard, then chill and freeze, beating occasionally. When firm and nearly solid, spoon the mixture into a 2 lb (1 kg) basin or bombe mould. It helps to have the basin in the freezer half an hour beforehand. Press the ice-cream up the sides to make a hollow. Return to the freezer until firm. Spoon the chocolate ice in the middle then refreeze. Cover, and label if the bombe is to be stored for some time.

Allow to thaw for half an hour in the fridge, before cutting into slices.

Serves 6.   RD

CRANBERRY AND RASPBERRY SHERBERT

A pretty ruby-red, bitter-sweet sorbet.

1 lb (500 g) fresh or frozen cranberries
1 lb (500 g) fresh or frozen raspberries
De-pithed peel and juice of 1 orange
8 oz (250 g) caster sugar
¼ pint (150 ml) ruby or tawny port
2 egg whites

Simmer the fruit with 1 pint (600 ml) of water and orange peel for 15 minutes. Rub the pulp through a sieve with a wooden spoon. Discard the pips and skins. Return juice and pulp to saucepan with sugar. Reheat, stirring until dissolved, then boil – not too fiercely – for 5 minutes.

Cool, then stir in the orange juice and port. Chill, then place in freezer and, when partially frozen, remove and beat until slushy. Whisk the egg whites to soft peaks and fold in. Return to the freezer, cover and seal. Allow to thaw slightly until soft enough to scoop out.

Serves 6.   RD

Right *Bombe noel; cranberry and raspberry sherbert*

HOT CHOCOLATE SOUFFLE

Most of the preparation, up to the point of whisking the egg whites, for this classic pudding can be done in advance. The soufflé can then be assembled and put in the oven as you serve the main course.

4 oz (125 g) plain chocolate
2 tablespoons water
½ pint (300 ml) milk
1½ oz (40 g) butter
1½ oz (40 g) plain flour
¼ teaspoon vanilla essence
4 large eggs
2 oz (50 g) caster sugar
Icing sugar

Preheat the oven to 375°F (190°C, gas mark 5) with a baking sheet placed in the centre of the oven. Thoroughly grease a 2-pint (1.2 litre) soufflé dish with butter and sprinkle with a little of the caster sugar.

Put the chocolate into a pan with the water and 2 tablespoons milk. Stir over a low heat until the chocolate has melted and add the remaining milk. Bring to the boil and remove from the heat.

Melt the butter over a low heat. Stir in the flour and cook over a low heat for 1 minute. Take off the heat and add the hot milk and chocolate. Return to the heat and bring to the boil, stirring well until thick. Add the vanilla essence and leave the mixture until cool.

Separate the eggs and beat the yolks and sugar into the chocolate sauce. (At this point, the mixture may be left for up to 8 hours before the dish is completed.)

Whisk the egg whites to stiff, but not dry, peaks. Fold into the chocolate sauce and pour into the prepared dish. Run a spoon around the edge (this makes the soufflé rise with a 'cauliflower' top). Place on the hot baking sheet and bake in the oven for 40 minutes.

Sprinkle with a little icing sugar and serve immediately with cream.

Serves 4–6.   MN

MOCHA RUM CREAM

Simple to prepare, this chocolate dessert is at once both rich and light.

½ pint (300 ml) whipping cream
½ pint (300 ml) natural yoghurt
3 oz (75 g) plain chocolate
3 tablespoons water
1 tablespoon instant coffee powder
2 tablespoons rum
2 tablespoons dark soft brown sugar

Whip the cream to soft peaks and fold in the yoghurt. Put the chocolate, water and coffee powder into a bowl over a pan of hot water. When the chocolate is melted, remove from heat and stir into the rum with the sugar. Leave until cool, then fold into the cream. Spoon into individual pots and chill before serving.

Serves 6–8.   MN

CHOCOLATE ALMOND PUDDING

There can be nothing more comforting in winter months than an old-fashioned steamed pudding.

4 oz (125 g) unsalted butter
4 oz (125 g) icing sugar
4 oz (125 g) plain chocolate, grated
4 oz (125 g) ground almonds
6 eggs, separated

Well-grease a 2-pint (1.2 litre) pudding basin with butter, and sprinkle with caster sugar. Cream together the butter and icing sugar until light and fluffy and work in the chocolate, almonds and egg yolks. Beat until very soft and light. Whisk the egg whites to stiff peaks and fold into the chocolate mixture. Spoon into the prepared basin. Cover with greased greaseproof paper and foil, and steam for 1 hour. Turn out onto a warm serving dish and serve at once with whipped cream.

Serves 6.   MN

Left to right: Mocha rum cream (in glasses); chocolate cream Sophie; chocolate almond pudding, about to be steamed

CHOCOLATE CREAM SOPHIE

This sumptuous dessert is perfect for serving to chocoholic dinner guests, as it can be prepared in advance and kept in the refrigerator until it is needed.

4 oz (125 g) fresh brown breadcrumbs
4 oz (125 g) demerara sugar
8 teaspoons cocoa
4 teaspoons coffee powder
½ pint (300 ml) double cream
¼ pint (150 ml) single cream

Stir together the breadcrumbs, sugar, cocoa and coffee powder until evenly coloured. Put the creams into a bowl and whip to soft peaks (it is most important that the cream is not whipped too stiffly or it will be impossible to assemble the pudding neatly).

Arrange in layers in a glass bowl, starting with crumbs and finishing with cream, and using three layers of each. Cover with plastic wrap and leave in the refrigerator for at least 4 hours before using. If liked, sprinkle the surface with some grated plain chocolate, or decorate with chocolate leaves, just before serving.

Serves 6.   MN

PERFECT CHOCOLATE PUDDING

An adaptable chocolate pudding which is equally good hot or cold.

3 oz (75 g) plain chocolate
2 oz (50 g) unsalted butter or block margarine
½ pint (300 ml) milk
2½ oz (65 g) caster sugar
¼ teaspoon instant coffee powder
2 eggs
5 oz (150 g) fresh white breadcrumbs

Put the chocolate and fat into a bowl over a pan of hot water. When the chocolate has melted, remove from the heat. Heat the milk to lukewarm and add gradually to the chocolate, with the sugar and coffee powder. Cool to lukewarm.

Separate the eggs and beat the yolks into the chocolate mixture, with the breadcrumbs. Whisk the egg whites to stiff but not dry peaks and fold into the mixture. Grease a 1½ pint (900 ml) pudding basin and spoon in the mixture. Cover with greased greaseproof paper and foil, and steam for 1½ hours. Leave in the bowl for 5 minutes and turn onto a serving dish. Serve hot with chocolate sauce or cold with whipped cream.

Serves 6.   MN

CHOCOLATE CHEESECAKE

A rich, baked cheesecake from California, with a crunchy chocolate-flavoured base. Make the cake the day before you wish to serve it, as it needs time to set and chill.

14 oz (400 g) semi-sweet dark chocolate
2 tablespoons unsalted butter
1 lb 4 oz (625 g) cream cheese
8 oz (250 g) caster sugar
12 fl oz (350 ml) double cream
1 teaspoon vanilla essence
3 eggs
3 tablespoons cocoa powder

TOPPING
8 fl oz (240 ml) soured cream
2 tablespoons caster sugar
Chocolate shavings

CRUST
8 oz (250 g) chocolate-flavoured-biscuit crumbs
4 oz (125 g) sugar
4 oz (125 g) butter, melted

Combine all the ingredients for the crust, press into the bottom of a greased 9″ (23 cm) springform tin and bake for 10 minutes in the oven at 400°F (200°C, gas mark 6). Allow to cool while you make the filling.

Melt the chocolate and butter in a double boiler and set aside. Cream the sugar and cream cheese together, add eggs, cream, vanilla, cocoa powder and chocolate-butter mixture and blend well. Pour into the prepared crust and bake at 325°F (170°C, gas mark 3) for 1¼ hours. Chill, still in the mould, for 8 hours or overnight.

Next day, unmould the cheesecake, spread top with soured cream blended with sugar, and sprinkle with chocolate shavings.

Serves 10.   CW

CARAMEL FRAPPE

For more than a decade, Robert Linxe has made and purveyed the best chocolates in Paris, and probably the world. At his Maison du Chocolat in the faubourg St-Honoré, and the branch at 52 rue François-I, off the Champs-Elysées, his array of chocolates and exquisite cakes can be tasted with cups of hot chocolate or perfectly-realized spoonsful of sorbet and ice-cream.

To complete the seduction, there are glasses of *caramel frappé* made from ice-cream, cream and caramel, whizzed to the ultimate milkshake. Robert Linxe makes his own *glace de caramel*, but in London Baskin-Robbins' *crème de caramel* ice-cream can be used to good effect; if there is none available near you, substitute the best coffee ice-cream you can find.

you are going to make this milkshake often, prepare a larger quantity of caramel and store it for frequent use.

To produce 2 milkshakes, put ice-cream, chilled cream, and 1½ tablespoons of the dilute caramel into the blender and whizz till all is well mixed. Pour into stemmed glasses and consume without delay, using fat straws or a spoon.

Serves 2.　　　　　　　　　　　AWS

Caramel frappé

2 oz (50 g) granulated sugar
Knob unsalted butter
4 large scoops crème de caramel or coffee ice-
　cream
Generous ¼ pint (150 ml) single cream

Make a caramel by melting sugar in a small, heavy saucepan, then letting it colour to a rich shade. Stop caramelization by adding the knob of butter, swirling pan as the mixture bubbles. Carefully add some hot water; the caramel will splutter angrily and start to solidify, but swirl the pan and set it over a low heat to liquefy the mixture. Increase the water by 1–2 fl oz (30–60 ml), and stir the caramel with a small metal spoon until it is liquid enough to remain so when cold.

Pour the result into a glass jar and refrigerate, covered; caramel will keep, thus, for a year, and if

SUMMER PANCAKES

Oven-baked pancakes filled with soft fruit.

1 lb (500 g) soft summer fruits; strawberries, raspberries, peaches, kiwi fruit, bananas, black cherries

THE PANCAKES
4 eggs (size 3) separated
2 tablespoons clear honey
2 oz (50 g) caster sugar
2 oz (50 g) wholemeal flour
1 tablespoon cornflour

FILLING
10 fl oz (300 g) natural yoghurt
5 fl oz (150 g) double cream
1 tablespoon clear honey or icing sugar

TO DECORATE
1 tablespoon icing sugar

Preheat the oven to 425°F (220°C, gas mark 7).

Put the yoghurt into a coffee filter or muslin and leave to drain for an hour. Line two baking sheets with greaseproof paper and put to one side. Separate the eggs into two mixing bowls. Using an electric mixer if you have one, whisk the egg yolks with the clear honey until it is stiff enough to form a thick ribbon across the surface. With a clean whisk, beat the egg whites, gradually adding the sugar, until stiff enough to form peaks. Carefully fold the beaten egg whites into the yolks with a metal spoon. Sieve the flour and cornflour together over the eggs, and fold in with a large metal spoon. Spoon the mixture on to prepared trays, putting 3 pancakes on each tray, spreading each one out into a 5″ (13 cm) circle. Bake near the top of the oven for 10–12 minutes. Allow the pancakes to cool on the paper. (At this stage the pancakes will keep in the refrigerator for up to 8 weeks, or can be frozen for later use.)

To make the filling, whip the cream loosely with the honey or icing sugar, and blend with the now firm yoghurt. Put a spoonful of this cream on to each pancake, arrange the soft fruits over the top, and fold in half. To finish, dust with icing sugar and caramelize with a heated skewer.

Serves 6. SW

CHOCOLATE CHESTNUT CAKE

This is a stylish union, the cake easily-made and not overly sweet. It rises well – falling naturally as it cools – handles amiably, and keeps for several days if left uncut.

Butter and flour for cake tin
4 oz (125 g) semi-sweet dark chocolate
1½ oz (40 g) unsalted butter
8 oz (250 g) tinned unsweetened chestnut purée
4 eggs and 1 extra egg white
2 oz (50 g) caster sugar
Icing sugar and double cream to serve

Butter an 8 × 2″ (20 × 5 cm) circular cake tin, flour sides and line bottom with a round of buttered, floured greaseproof paper.

Melt broken chocolate and butter in a covered pan set into a low pan of just-boiled water; beat smooth. Sieve in chestnut purée and beat again.

Separate eggs, whisk yolks with sugar until thick, and beat in the chocolate mixture. Whisk the 5 egg whites until stiff, beat ⅓ into chocolate base to lighten this, then fold base into whites and pour into tin. Smooth and rap on the work surface to settle contents. Bake at 350°F (180°C, gas mark 4) for 50 minutes or until a trussing needle thrust into

the centre tests clean and hot. Cool cake in its tin on a rack.

To serve, release cake and peel paper from base. Turn right side up and sieve icing sugar across top. Serve sliced, with whipped cream.

Enough for 6–8. AWS

COCONUT CAKE WITH STRAWBERRIES

Irresistible to children and adults alike.

5 oz (150 g) unsweetened desiccated coconut
Butter and flour for cake tins
4 oz (125 g) soft unsalted butter
6 oz (175 g) caster sugar
½ teaspoon vanilla essence
8 oz (250 g) plain flour
Pinch salt
Generous 1½ teaspoons baking powder
Generous 4 fl oz (125 ml) milk
9 egg whites
12½ oz (365 g) granulated sugar
¼ pint (150 ml) water
Almond essence
Fresh strawberries

Lightly toast coconut in a 275°F (140°C, gas mark 1) oven. Cool.

Butter two 8 × 2″ (20 × 5 cm) circular cake tins, flour the sides, and line the bottom of each with a round of buttered and floured greaseproof paper.

Cream butter in a largish bowl; gradually beat in caster sugar and vanilla. Sift flour with salt and baking powder; sift this into base alternately with milk, beating well after each addition and ending with flour. Beat in 1 oz (25 g) coconut.

In a large bowl, whisk 4 egg whites until stiff, beat ⅓ into the butter base to lighten it, then combine base with the rest of the beaten whites, trying not to knock all air from the mixture. Spoon batter into tins, smooth and spread evenly, and bake at 375°F (190°C, gas mark 5) for 30–45 minutes until risen tops are browning and cakes pull

Clockwise from top: Cherry and mint tart, page 186; chocolate chestnut cake; coconut cake with strawberries

away from sides of tins. They will not rise much. Cool cakes in their tins on a rack.

When ready to assemble, release cakes, peel paper from both bases and turn right side up. Using a serrated knife, carefully split each cake horizontally into 2 equal layers; cut away the rounded top of one to make it flat. You will then have 4 very thin layers, one of them retaining its rounded top.

To make the icing, dissolve granulated sugar in water and boil syrup until it registers 245°F (118°C) on a sugar thermometer.

Simultaneously, use a hand-held electric beater to whisk the 5 additional whites to stiff peaks. When sugar is ready, pour this slowly and steadily into whites, beating them at high speed; continue beating till icing is cold, glossy, and stands again in stiff peaks. Beat in a little almond essence and fold in most of the remaining coconut.

Place a flat layer of cake, cut side up, on a cake stand and spread generously with icing. Assemble the layers, with icing between, ending with the rounded top. Press cake lightly together and cover top and sides with remaining icing – there should be a generous amount for this – swirling the icing attractively. Strew with rest of coconut.

Eat on the day made, with plenty of sliced, fresh strawberries.

Serves 8. AWS

CHERRY AND MINT TART, CHERRY AND MINT SAUCE

The combination of this fruit and herb is deliciously unexpected.

10 oz (300 g) rich home-made shortcrust pastry
9 fl oz (generous 260 ml) milk
3 egg yolks
Caster sugar
1 oz (25 g) plain flour
Kirsch
2½ lb (1.25 kg) fresh dark cherries, not too
  sweet
Small bunch fresh mint
Lemon juice
1 × 12 oz (350 g) jar morello cherry conserve

Thinly roll pastry to line a 9″ (23 cm) flan ring placed on a heavy baking sheet. Chill.

Make a pastry-cream by bringing the milk to simmer in a small, heavy saucepan while beating yolks, until thick, with 1½ oz (40 g) of sugar. Sift and beat the flour into the yolks. Strain in milk, whisking egg base constantly. Pour all into the milk pan, and whisking continuously over a low heat, bring mixture to the first boil. Raise heat slightly and beat cream vigorously for 2 minutes; there should not be the slightest lump. Whisk in a few drops of kirsch. Scrape cream onto a plate and press cling film across the surface to prevent formation of skin.

Stem and pit cherries. When pastry-cream is cold, spread most of it in a thin layer across base of tart shell. Stew this with 3–4 shredded mint leaves, cover surface with a tightly-packed single layer of cherries and bake at 400°F (200°C, gas mark 6) for 40–45 minutes, until pastry is baked and browning. Cool.

Meanwhile, to make a *coulis* or sauce, purée the remaining cherries in a food processor with just enough mint leaves and lemon juice – and a little sugar if required – to give a well-balanced result.

Briefly simmer cherry conserve with ½ teaspoon of kirsch. Sieve conserve into a bowl (leaving debris behind), and when tart has cooled,

lightly spoon what is now warm jelly over the surface to glaze it.

Serve within a few hours of assembling, with spoonfuls of warmed sauce and sprigs of mint on each dessert plate.

Serves 6.   AWS

PORT JELLY

Port jelly is a perennial favourite and hard to beat. The reason it tastes so good is that only half the wine is heated, so it is a pretty alcoholic pudding. If you have an elaborate, old-fashioned jelly mould, this is the time to use it. Serve the jelly with fruit or cream. Any dark red or purple fruit – figs, grapes, plums – looks striking.

3 tablespoons gelatine crystals or 10 leaves
1 pint (600 ml) port
2 teaspoons lemon juice
4 oz (125 g) castor sugar
4 cloves
1 stick cinnamon

Soak the gelatine in a quarter of the port and all the lemon juice or a few minutes until it is soft. Then add another quarter of the wine and the sugar and spices and heat the mixture without allowing it to boil. Stir until the gelatine has dissolved completely then remove it from the heat and allow it to cool. Strain the cool but still liquid jelly into a clean bowl and add the rest of the port.

Pour the jelly into a wetted mould and leave it to set in cool place. Then unmould it, dip mould into hot water, and turn it out on to a plate.

Serves 6.   SCP

FRUIT SALAD WITH LIME AND GINGER SYRUP

This fruit salad will provide a good use for any jar of stem ginger you may be given over Christmas. Combined with exotic fruit and ginger ale, it makes an unusual and most refreshing dessert.

Fruit salad with ginger and lime syrup

1–2 limes, grated rind and juice
3 tablespoons stem ginger syrup
2 tablespoons clear honey
Small knob chopped stem ginger (optional)
½ pint (300 ml) flat ginger ale or boiling water
1 large mango
1 small pineapple, peeled, cored and cut in
  chunks
1 medium-size melon, scooped into balls
2 kiwis, peeled and sliced
1–2 star fruit, sliced
Strips of lime peel (optional for decoration)

Mix the lime rind, juice, syrup, honey, chopped ginger (optional) and the ginger ale or water. Cool, if necessary.

Slice the mango widthways across each side of the stone. Cut the flesh from the skin in chunks. Mix with the other prepared fruits and pour over the syrup. Allow to macerate overnight.

Decorate with strips of lime peel and serve well chilled.

Serves 6.   RD

FIGS WITH CUSTARD AND ARMAGNAC

Figs are a native of southern and southwestern France, so it seems natural to bake them in a slow oven with sugar and a dribble of Armagnac, the distinctive southwestern grape brandy.

The sugar and spirit form a syrup with the fig juice, and the fruit halves are eaten warm with a just-made pouring custard spiked with some more of the liquor.

½ pint (300 ml) milk
1 vanilla pod split down the middle
Armagnac
12 ripe figs
Demerara sugar
3 yolks of very fresh eggs
2 tablespoons caster sugar
8 fresh fig leaves, if available, washed

Scald milk with vanilla and 2 tablespoons Armagnac; remove pan from the heat, cover, and leave to infuse for 30 minutes.

Snip stem tip from each fig, slice all in half from top to base, unskinned, and place halves, cut side up, in a large, flat baking dish (or 2 of these) into which they will fit without overlapping. Sprinkle with demerara sugar and dribble all figs with a thin stream of Armagnac.

After milk has been standing for 30 minutes, place fruit in a 275°F (140°C, gas mark 1) oven. Whisk egg yolks and beat in the caster sugar until yolks are thick. Whisk in milk and sieve the mixture back into the milk pan.

Over a brisk heat, beat egg, sugar and milk until the custard thickens and is just about to boil. Immediately sieve this into a clean bowl and stir to cool slightly.

After the figs have baked for 30–40 minutes, remove from the oven, spoon over them the syrup which has formed, divide the fig leaves – if you have these – among 4 dessert plates, and serve 6 halves per person, cut side upward, with the warm custard passed separately.

Serves 4.   AWS

187

INDEX